Illustrated Rigging

FOR SALMON • STEELHEAD • TROUT

Robert H. Campbell
Illustrated by Jesse Sandberg

Illustrated Rigging

FOR SALMON ▪ STEELHEAD ▪ TROUT

ROBERT H. CAMPBELL

ILLUSTRATED BY JESSE SANDBERG

Frank Amato PORTLAND

Dedication

*For my father, Theodore Campbell, whose love
of the outdoors, if not genetically passed on,
was certainly taught and learned.*

Acknowledgements

In nearly three years of writing the column "Illustrated Rigging" for *Salmon Trout Steelheader* Magazine, I have received much help along the way. I wish to thank professional fishing guides Bob Toman, Terry Mulkey, Chris Vertopoulos, David Johnson, Pete Field, Tyler Courtney, Lee Darby, Dan Ponciano, Bob Rees, and Brian Campbell for all of your assistance and mentoring. Fishing with you and around you has made me a better angler and writer. You guys truly are the "Best of the Northwest."

Thank you to Jim Martin, retired Chief of Fisheries for the Oregon Department of Fish and Wildlife, for sharing your vast knowledge and experience with a needy writer, and for rowing me down a particularly nasty stretch of the North Santiam that I would never have attempted in my own drift boat. Thanks as well to Steve Williams, current Deputy Administrator of ODFW's Fish Division, for your contributions and enlightening back-fence evening chats, and for the seemingly endless supply of Dungeness crab.

Thank you to the following friends and associates who, in some way great or small, directly or indirectly, contributed to this body of work: Kelly Reichner, Jason Hambly, Brian Price, Seth Fisher, Dave Eng, Mike Scheehean, Dave Neels, Tim Rooney, Scott Harris, "Spinner Dave" Kaffke, Mike Perusse, Mike Laverty, Dan Grogan, Eric Linde, Buzz Ramsey and Nick Amato.

Thanks to my primary illustrator, Jesse Sandberg, for taking the time from swinging a hammer, riding bulls and chasing the ladies to provide illustrations for a writer whose drawing skills failed to develop further than the fourth grade. Appreciation to Jesse Paulson for filling in when needed.

Much gratitude to the Amato Family for affording opportunity to a struggling writer.

Thank you to my big sister, Susan, who in my youth found time to take me fishing when nobody else could.

Finally, thank you most to my lovely wife, Katherine, who in our ten-plus years together has disallowed me to venture afield but once. Without you, baby, I fear that I would be a penniless fisher of carp. Thanks for the go!

Table of Contents

Introduction

A heart-warming little native steelhead from the Sandy River.
Right: Lisa Pollack and Brian Price after a successful day at Buoy Ten.

When Nick Amato approached me with the idea of writing a column about rigging tackle, I was thrilled at the chance to help my fellow anglers catch more fish. With the varied angling opportunities of our region, the question of proper rigging is always a hot topic among anglers new and old. At the tackle store where I work, we endeavor to show our customers how to set-up for the multitude of fisheries in our area. In fact, over the course of a year filled with constantly changing fishing seasons, we string up dozens of rods and reels with the appropriate rigging in order to demonstrate to our customers what works. You see, the problem with being a sportfisher in the Pacific Northwest is that there exists so darn many angling opportunities from which to choose. You can take sturgeon, halibut, albacore tuna, large and smallmouth bass, walleye, shad, smelt, bottom fish, pan fish, surf dwellers, squawfish and carp, chuck them all out the window and that still leaves you with salmon, trout and steelhead.

I began to see where Nick was headed with his brainstorm. In my home state of Oregon, we are fortunate to have salmon, trout and steelhead angling opportunity nearly year round. The multitudes of different angling situations, water types and conditions, and techniques used can leave even a seasoned angler scratching his or her head when it comes to

rigging. When you go from fishing winter steelhead to spring chinook, on to trout fishing in lakes, then to summer steelhead, trolling for salmon in the ocean, and bobber fishing fall chinook in tidewater, the rigging changes with the species and techniques used to catch them. Therefore, "Illustrated Rigging" was launched in *STS* Magazine to show the beginner how to tie basic salmon and steelhead set-ups, and to help absent-minded anglers like myself remember how we did it last year.

This book is comprised of information gleaned from fellow anglers, fishing guides and my own experiences in over thirty years of fishing for salmon, trout and steelhead in the Pacific Northwest. Keep in mind that the rigs shown are not the answer to every fishery and angling situation, rather, a solid point to begin your Northwest sportsfishing career. Also, rigging is constantly changing as anglers develop new techniques and methods for different areas, and keeping up with new developments and tackle trends is part of the fun of angling. Remember, too, that rigging can be very site-specific and that a bait-trolling rig used on Tillamook Bay may differ greatly from one employed on Rogue River Bay. When targeting a new area, ask around and watch what the locals are using; there's nothing like local knowledge to shorten the learning curve. Good luck! I'll see you on the water.

Steelhead Rigs

Winter Steelhead Drift-Fishing Rigs

Jason Hambly drift-fished a corky and yarn combo to subdue this chrome winter steelhead.

Drift fishing has long been the most popular and effective technique for catching one of our most beloved sportfish, the venerable steelhead. Few serious steelheaders will ever forget the first steelie they brought to the beach—water churning with defiance, hands numbed to the point of uselessness, the sense of accomplishment exceeded only by the amount of adrenaline coursing through our veins. For most of us, that first fish came while employing the tactic of drift fishing. Drift fishing allows a bait or lure to be presented in a smooth, enticing fashion at or near current speed, and this is what the steelhead are looking for. Drift fishing lets an angler effectively cover all of the types of water that steelhead frequent. From expansive runs to narrow current seams, from boiling pools to that tiny pocket behind a boulder, drift fishing allows an angler to cover it all with confidence. And while other methods rise and fall in the world of steelheading, drift fishing is here to stay, and for good reason: It works! Following are some of the more popular rigs used in drift fishing today.

Diagram 1

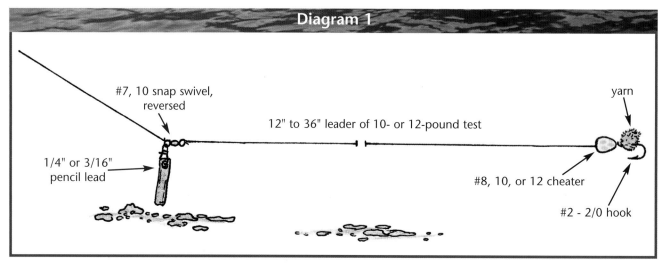

#7, 10 snap swivel, reversed

1/4" or 3/16" pencil lead

12" to 36" leader of 10- or 12-pound test

yarn

#8, 10, or 12 cheater

#2 - 2/0 hook

Diagram 1 This is a widely used rig in conventional drift fishing. Begin by running your mainline to a reversed #10 snap swivel and tying off to the eye of the barrel. By reversing the swivel, the rig will not become tangled nearly as much when casting. Using needlenose pliers with a punch, cut the appropriate size lead for the water you intend to fish, punch a hole in the top of the weight and attach to the snap. Now all that remains is to tie on your leader and you're ready to fish. I suspect that the main reason this set-up is so common comes from the ease with which it is rigged. All an angler needs to do is spend an hour or so at home tying leaders and cutting and punching various sizes of lead, and he or she is ready for hours of uninterrupted drift fishing. Which brings us to one important aspect of this technique that isn't often discussed: Preparedness.

In the long run, being prepared to fish before hitting a stream ultimately results in more fish landed. This is a simple matter of time economy. Drift fishing is a methodical, time consuming technique. Extended drifts and complete coverage of the water are required in order to increase the chances of a hook-up, and this all takes time. In order to maximize his chances, an angler should show up to the river prepared. This means that a good supply of leaders are already tied and neatly stowed in a Pip's Box or some other sort of leader wallet. Your weight system, be it pencil lead or slinkies, should be assorted by size and ready to go. Yarn, pliers, extra swivels, a hook file—these should all be neatly organized in your vest or drift boat and at the ready. I can't count the number of times that I've watched some poor soul in a crowded run spend his day tying rigs and fumbling for gear while everyone else was busy fighting fish. Don't let this happen to you. Remember that old business school expression: Failing to prepare is preparing to fail.

Diagram 2 Here is a rig which incorporates a weight system that is designed to release the lead when it becomes hopelessly snagged on the bottom. By aiming your rod tip directly at the snag and pulling straight back on it, it is possible to release the lead without breaking off your entire set-up, thus saving you valuable "wet time." Use fine wire or one of the super braid lines to tie the surgical tubing to the eye of a #8 or #10 three-way swivel. Match the surgical tubing to the size lead you intend to employ—quarter-inch tubing for quarter-inch lead, and so on. Use a section of tubing about an inch and a half long, and only insert the pencil lead about a half inch into the tubing; any more than this will create too much suction on the lead and it most likely won't release before your line breaks. Another trick is to wet both the lead and the tubing before insertion as this will allow the weight to more easily pull free.

It should be noted here that there exist endless ways in which to rig for drift fishing, and the information herein is merely a general guideline. River conditions, the type of rod and reel one uses and the size of the fish in any given river are just some of the factors which will determine how one rigs his or her terminal gear. Let's start by looking at line. Standard monofilament is hard to beat in the hostile environment of most rivers. A highly abrasion-resistant line such as Maxima or Trilene Big Game performs great when fishing around the boulders, snags and woody structure that steelhead so love. Ten- or twelve-pound mainline is standard on most rivers, and common sense dictates that your leader's breaking strength should be two pounds less than this so that it breaks before your mainline, thus saving part of your set-up and, once again, saving you valuable fishing time. Remember to match your line and leader size to the conditions at hand. When rivers drop and clear steelhead get more cautious, so

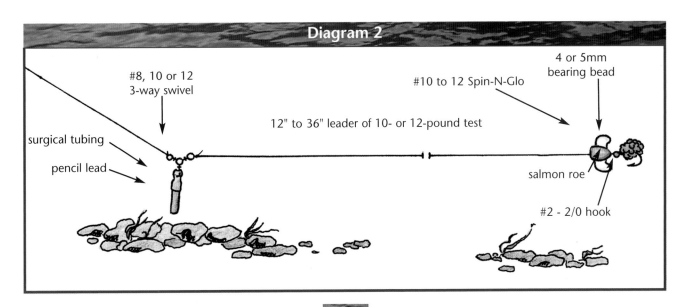

Diagram 2

#8, 10 or 12
3-way swivel

#10 to 12 Spin-N-Glo

4 or 5mm
bearing bead

12" to 36" leader of 10- or 12-pound test

surgical tubing

pencil lead

salmon roe

#2 - 2/0 hook

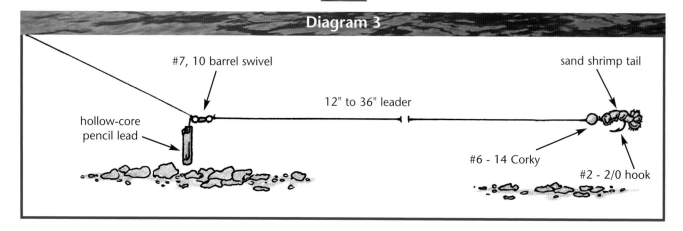

Diagram 3

#7, 10 barrel swivel

sand shrimp tail

hollow-core
pencil lead

12" to 36" leader

#6 - 14 Corky

#2 - 2/0 hook

it may be necessary to lengthen and lighten your leader. In especially "skinny" river conditions, it is advisable to use fluorocarbon leaders as this material nearly disappears in water. Conversely, when fishing for trophy steelhead in the brawling rivers of the Olympic Peninsula or Oregon Coast, increasing the weight of your mainline and leader is definitely a good call. Standard leader length varies from one to three feet depending on conditions.

Super braided lines like Berkley's Fireline or Western Filament's Tuff Line XP have drastically risen in popularity the past few seasons, especially for anglers who prefer to use spinning gear. These fine diameter lines don't have near the memory of a tough mono so they don't coil as much, allowing for smooth, friction-free casts with a spinning reel. Another advantage to the braided lines is that they have very little stretch, which some anglers claim allows for better feel and an improved hook set. Whatever line you choose, be sure to invest in a high quality brand name that is reputable. Do not pinch pennies when it comes to your line! After all, this is what connects you to, or disconnects you from the fish.

Drift bobbers come in many sizes and alluring colors, and they serve two main purposes. Because steelhead cannot see in a downward direction, it is necessary to present your bait or lure at, or slightly above eye level in order to achieve the best results. Buoyant drift bobbers such as Corkies, Oakies, Spin-N-Glos and Cheaters provide just enough floatation to achieve this. Generally, the higher and heavier the water conditions are, the larger the drift bobber you will want to use. This is because the heavier flows will push a smaller lure to the bottom out of the steelhead's field of vision—not the presentation we're looking for. Also, heavier flows usually means the water has more color to it, and a larger lure will show up better under such conditions.

The second purpose of the drift bobber is to serve as an added attractant or irritant to the fish. For some reason, steelhead love (or hate) a brightly colored lure drifting obtrusively down their stream. Once again, there are limitless colors and

ways to rig your leader, but a good rule of thumb is the lower and clearer the conditions, the smaller the bobber you should use. On the other hand, if a river is high and colored, use a larger lure in a brighter color. Fluorescent pink and orange work great under these conditions as they both gather and reflect light, and therefore, a lot of color. Don't neglect to use a small piece of yarn when rigging up for drift fishing. Yarn often gets tangled in a steelhead's teeth, allowing you an extra moment or two to set the hook after detecting a subtle take. Attach it to the egg loop with a single overhand knot. Hooks are also very important in drift fishing. There are many excellent brands available, but you will want to choose a round bend style with an upturned eye for best hook setting potential. And make certain they are SHARP! A hook file is a necessity when drift fishing.

One could write for days on the various rods and reels available to the steelheader, but I'll keep it short. Whether you choose a level wind or spinning outfit, select quality gear, for even a small steelhead will test it. Reels should be the best you can afford with a reliable drag system. Rods may range anywhere from seven to ten feet or more in length, but eight and a half to nine feet is standard. The tip should be very sensitive in order to detect the often subtle bite of a resting steelhead, and the butt section should provide some power for fighting and turning powerful fish in a heavy current.

Diagram 3 Here is another set-up that allows for the remainder of the rig to be saved when the weight becomes snagged. Begin by tying the mainline to a #7 or #10 barrel swivel, leaving an extra long tag end on which you will attach the hollow-core pencil lead. Do not cut the lead with your pliers, as most often this will close the hollow core. Instead, use the cutting edge of your pliers to score the lead, then grip the lead with the pliers and your free hand and wiggle it back and forth. The lead will break off cleanly at the score and the hollow core will be accessible. Next, insert the tag end into the core and use your pliers to crimp the lead so it stays on the line. This rig works extremely well in really grabby

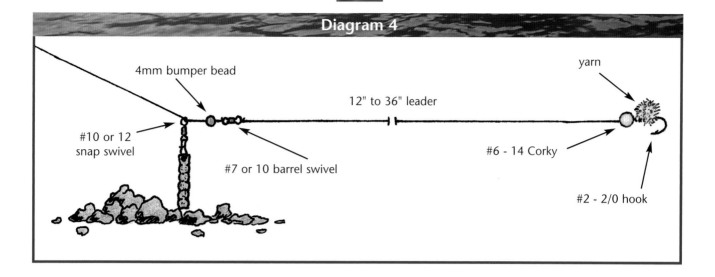

Diagram 4

4mm bumper bead

yarn

12" to 36" leader

#10 or 12 snap swivel

#7 or 10 barrel swivel

#6 - 14 Corky

#2 - 2/0 hook

water such as boulder fields and around timber, as it is very easy to pull free from the lead, preserving the rest of the rig.

Another key component to drift fishing is the presentation itself. When possible by the absence of other fishermen, an angler will position himself at the top of a promising stretch of water and methodically work his way through the run. He or she begins the presentation by casting the rig slightly upstream. How far upstream depends on the depth and speed of the current. The faster and deeper the water, the farther upstream it is necessary to cast. The goal is to have the weight reach the bottom and therefore be fishing just as it is passing downstream of the angler. As soon as the weight hits the water, it is advisable to hold your rod as high as possible to keep as much line off the water as you can. It is also advisable that while doing so, slowly reel to take in any slack that has developed in the cast, keeping just the slightest of tension between your rod tip and the rig. There are a several reasons for doing this.

First of all, our goal is to have as natural a presentation as possible, which requires the rig to be moving downriver at or slightly slower than the current speed for best results. If the slack is not immediately taken out of the cast, a downstream belly will form in the line caused by the force of the current against it. This can cause the entire rig to be dragged along at a most unnaturally quick pace, which is a definite turnoff to all but the most suicidal of steelhead. Also, by eliminating the slack and reducing the current's pull on the line, your rig will sink slightly faster thus saving—you guessed it—more time. This may seem insignificant, but multiply a few seconds times several hundred casts made in a day of drift fishing—you get the picture. Another reason to immediately take up the slack and maintain immediate contact with the rig is that you may have just put your bait right on a steelhead's nose. What if he takes it and there is slack in the line? You won't feel a thing and the fish will spit before you even knew he was there.

Diagram 4 This rig is my personal favorite for drift fishing for steelhead. This set-up incorporates the use of a slinky rather than pencil lead. A slinky is nothing more than lead shot placed inside nylon parachute chord. The shot and chord come in a variety of matching sizes so it is easy to make slinkies in weights to match any drift fishing situation. The slipperiness of the nylon makes this weight system less likely to become snagged than pencil lead, but because it is also soft, it does sacrifice feel. The TAP TAP TAP you feel using pencil lead becomes more muted with a slinky, resulting in more of a tap tap tap.

Begin tying this rig by running your mainline through the eye of a #10 or #12 snap swivel. Then run it through a 4mm bead and tie off to a #7 or #10 barrel swivel. Then, merely open the snap and fasten it through the nylon chord of the slinky. Because the weight is somewhat independent of the mainline, it is much more obvious when a steelhead grabs your offering. Instead of feeling the fish through your weight, you'll feel the fish directly through your line. One of the toughest aspects of drift fishing is learning what is and what is not an actual take. Experienced steelheaders often speak of "The Instinct." This refers to an angler's almost supernatural ability to set the hook on a fish he may have never even felt take. For some inexplicable reason, the angler set the hook and a fish was there. "The Instinct" is very strong in my own father, Ted Campbell. You could blindfold him and outfit him in a pair of welding gloves and he would still out-drift fish me ten to one. Long ago I conceded that dad quite selfishly failed to pass on this wonderful trait, and that's why I use the slider rig. I still get out-fished, just not as badly.

Suggested references on drift fishing for steelhead include *Color Guide to Steelhead Drift Fishing*, by metalhead guru Bill Herzog, and the video *Steelhead Drift Fishing* with Nick Amato and Bill Herzog. Fish on!

Trophy-Steelhead Rigs

The author holds a large steelhead hooked by Pete Field in a coastal river in mid-March.
Is it a twenty-pounder? Maybe, maybe not, but who cares?

Certainly there exists some disagreement on what exactly constitutes a trophy steelhead. It can be argued that any bright steelie that leaves its lie to smack a lure, bait or fly should be considered a trophy, and I will not contradict this kind of thinking. Every steelhead, from the chromest of winter hens to the reddest of Deschutes River bucks, is a treasure. But no matter how hard our wives or girlfriends try to convince us otherwise, the irrefutable fact remains: we live in a world where size does indeed matter. For many hard-core steelheaders the pinnacle of our sport is reached only after landing a fish of mammoth proportions. Here in the Pacific Northwest, the generally accepted definition of a trophy steelhead is a fish weighing near to, or greater than, twenty pounds. Such fish often surpass forty inches in length. But before dragging these wild beauties into the boat to weigh or measure, please remember this: Steelhead

this large are a rare animal. The genetic cargo they carry is invaluable and imperative to both future generations of twenty-pound steelhead and the anglers that will hopefully get to fish for them. Proper handling of these fish is vital for their survival. Remove these fish from the water only when it is necessary to better control them or to snap a quick photo. Do not risk injury to a steelhead by manhandling it in order to "validate" the twenty-pound or forty-inch benchmarks. If a fish makes your eyes bulge like a bullfrog's or keeps you awake at night for the following week, suffice it to say that it's a trophy. Always make certain a fish is ready to swim on its own before releasing it. If it seems overly tired or has trouble righting itself, ventilate the fish by holding it head first into the current. When the fish is ready he will let you know with a quick flip of his powerful tail and the ensuing shower you receive!

So what makes a twenty-pound steelhead and why are they so rare? These are questions best answered by an expert on fish biology. Luckily, I know a couple. Steve Williams is the assistant administrator of the fish division for the Oregon Department of Fish and Wildlife. Don't let the lofty title fool you. Steve spent over twenty years as a field biologist studying salmon, trout and steelhead in their natural environment. I asked Steve what factors contribute to making a twenty-pound steelhead. "There are basically two factors that lead to a steelhead of this size," he replied. "Genetics and food source. First of all, with genetics, you have to be careful not to generalize. Every river system has its own unique characteristics—river gradient, obstacles like falls, size of spawning gravel—and over time, the certain characteristics within the fish that lead to survival in that system are passed on genetically by the successful spawners. One of those characteristics is size. Perhaps a river system has only large spawning gravel available, and only the largest steelhead are able to move the gravel to build a redd and successfully cover the eggs. Over time, the survival trait of a large size is passed on genetically by the successful spawners, and then you have a river that is known for its big fish. Another example can be made with steelhead returning to Idaho's Clearwater River. These fish have to travel a long way to get back to their home stream, and a larger fish is going to have the advantage of successfully making that trip because it has more reserved energy. So you see, steelhead adapt over time to the conditions of a specific watershed and develop traits that allow for survival, and sometimes one of those traits is size."

"The other factor that contributes to growing a large steelhead is food source, and with steelhead this has to do with how long the fish spend in the ocean and under what conditions. For whatever reason, steelhead spend anywhere from one to four years in the ocean before returning to fresh water to spawn. Most return as one- or two-salt fish, but some spend three or four, and these are the fish that really put on the pounds. If ocean conditions happen to be good like they have been recently, there is an abundance of food and the fish grow extremely well. So the reason that some steelhead are bigger than others is for the same reasons that I am bigger than you, Robert. I eat more and am predisposed genetically to be so."

Jim Martin is a retired chief of fisheries for ODFW. He is currently the conservation director for Pure Fishing, the parent company of Berkley, Abu Garcia and Fenwick, among others. Jim is a fanatical steelhead angler as well as one smart cat. Most of what we discussed for this article has been left out, and not because it was impertinent, but because it was so far over my head that I was unable to decipher it! But Jim did touch upon why a twenty-pound steelhead is such a rare bird; here's what

Nick Amato with a 20-pound Clackamas River steelhead. This hog was missing its right mandible—probably incurred during smolt-hood.

he had to say: "You have to realize that with all populations of animals that a shorter life cycle is an advantage for survival. A shorter life cycle reduces the chances of mortality while increasing the likelihood of propagation, and successful propagation is the key to the survival of a species. That's why most steelhead return to freshwater after only a year or two in the ocean, therefore most of our steelhead weigh between five and ten pounds. There exists a homing instinct in steelhead that is triggered by hormones within the fish. Again, in most steelhead this occurs after one or two years in the salt. However, in a very small percentage of steelhead, this trigger occurs later, after three or even four years in the ocean. And this goes back to what Steve was saying about food source: The longer the animal is at the food trough, the larger it will grow.

"Then there is the issue of genetics," Jim continues. "In a river environment there exist selective pressures that over time will shape the genetic identity of a race of steelhead. Look at the Skeena River System, for example. Obviously, in that system there are conditions present that favor a bigger fish. I would also like to dispel a myth regarding large steelhead. Most anglers have been taught that a twenty-pound steelhead has already spawned once, if not several times. But what we were able to determine through scale studies is that nearly all steelhead

Diagram 1

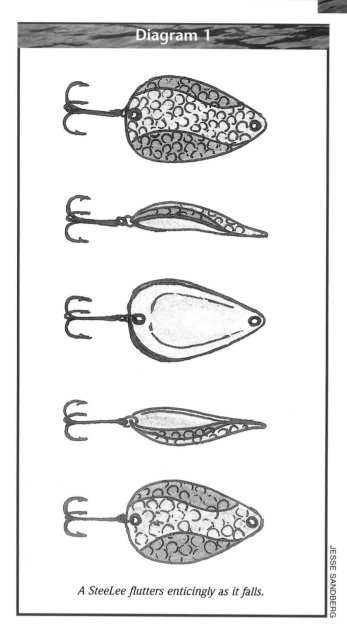

A SteeLee flutters enticingly as it falls.

JESSE SANDBERG

targeting larger fish. Seldom will a twenty-pound steelhead be found in a shallow tailout. My friend Chris Vertopoulos agrees. Chris is a successful Oregon salmon and steelhead guide who spends his winter and early spring chasing after trophy steelhead on north coast rivers. "I often fish deeper, heavier water when targeting trophy steelhead," says Chris. Big fish like to hang out around cover, so a rock garden in good current with sufficient depth is a good place to fish. You'll also find larger steelhead holding at the head of a pool or run, nosed right up to the break. In this location, the faster, choppier water near the surface provides cover while down deeper there is often a cushion of slower water that allows a fish to conserve energy. The same water that held chinook salmon in the fall will sometimes harbor a trophy steelhead in March."

Diagram 1 Trophy steelhead can be taken with any standard steelheading technique, but there are some stand-outs. Many anglers have already discovered that casting spoons is an effective method for hooking monster steelhead. Spoons like the SteeLee and Little Cleo have been in use for years, and something about the flash and thump that they emit drives big buck steelhead crazy. Spoons are an extremely versatile lure as they can be fished in several different ways. Probably the most common method is to cast straight across or slightly downstream, letting the lure sink before lifting the rod to put just enough tension on the line to make the spoon swing across a probable lie. One mistake I often see by novice hardware anglers is that they begin cranking their reel like mad the second the lure hits the water. This will sometimes catch fish, but is not the best technique. The force of the current against the lure on a taut line should impart the fluttering action of the spoon, not reeling in at hyperspeed.

Another spoon fishing technique is a little more tricky. "Fluttering" a spoon involves letting a spoon tumble with the current so that it flutters as it sinks and passes through a fish's cone of vision. The key to this method is the amount of tension kept on the line. Too much tension and the spoon will swing through the lie, not enough and it will have a short swim before settling on the bottom. This is a difficult technique to master but perhaps the deadliest way to fish a spoon. A really good spoon fisherman will instinctively know when his spoon is about to hang on the bottom and will lift his rod so that the lure will rise in the water column, then he may drop it again allowing the spoon to fall and flutter some more, thus extending his drift. This is also a deadly technique for fishing around cover, for spoons are easy to cast and allow for pinpoint accuracy. Tie on a SteeLee and pitch it in among the boulders, allow it to flutter down to where the big boy hangs, then hold on!

caught in freshwater were on their FIRST spawning cycle, including the twenty-pounders. Once again, this tiny percentage of huge fish just spent more time in the ocean and/or possessed a big-fish genetic identity. After spawning, these fish show that very little energy actually goes toward growth, as most goes toward refurbishing the fish for another spawn cycle."

It should be noted that large steelhead behave a little differently than the average fish that stack up in runs or fan out across tailouts. Most notably, trophy steelhead tend to be attracted to different types of water than average fish. Big steelhead love cover, and most steelhead rivers afford cover in a variety of ways. Boulders, overhanging trees, log jams, undercut banks and fast, choppy surface current are types of cover that will attract trophy steelhead. Depth provides another type of cover for big steelhead, so focus on water that is eight to fifteen feet deep when

Diagram 2 Backtrolling plugs is another effective technique for trophy steelhead. This diagram illustrates the many types of cover which may be available to steelhead in any river. This technique really shines because it allows a group of anglers to cover large swaths of potential holding water. It also allows a skilled oarsman to back the lures directly into the type of cover big steelhead like to hold around, providing an in-your-face presentation that steelhead often react to violently. Most plug fishermen begin by letting out forty to sixty feet of line, depending on current depth and speed, and the type of plug being used. The oarsman then holds the boat back just enough to let the current force the plugs to dig down to depth, then allows the boat to slowly slip downstream as he maneuvers it to cover the best water.

Wiggle Warts, Brad's Wigglers, Tadpollys and Kwikfish in sizes K10 and K12 are all excellent lures to use in this technique. When river conditions are optimum, that is, dropping or holding with that beautiful steelhead-green color, I like plugs in metallic green, red, pink or cerise. The blue and green pirate colors also work well. When water conditions are higher with more color, use darker plugs in black, blue, and purple because they silhouette well under such conditions. You may also want to increase the size of the plug when fishing colored water, and a K13 Kwikfish or Hot Shot S.E. are both excellent choices. The old Hot Shot Mark 2 and #20 are among my favorite high water steelhead plugs, so if you see some at a garage sale or flea market, please let me know! One common mistake made when plug fishing happens when the fish first grabs on and the rod buries.

The angler's first instinct is to rip the rod from the holder and set the hook. Resist this temptation at all cost! A steelhead needs time to turn on a plug and drive the hooks home. Most of the time a steelhead hits a plug so hard that it will hook itself if you can stand to let the drama play out without grabbing the rod. If not, a vicious hook-set on a striking steelhead usually results in the plug being pulled away from the fish, or worse—a broken rod or line. A good rule of thumb is to wait until the fish is actually pulling line from the reel before grabbing the rod.

Rods used for backtrolling plugs are most often seven and a half to eight and a half feet long. They should have a fairly light, sensitive tip in order to telegraph that the plug is constantly working properly, and so that the fish can have the plug when it strikes. I still like to use monofilament line for pulling plugs because of the inherent stretch, which I feel gives the fish a better opportunity to turn on the plug. Many anglers do successfully use super braids for plug fishing, and their smaller diameters can be an advantage when fishing deeper runs because they allow a plug to dive deeper. Be sure to use a high quality reel with a smooth drag and plenty of line capacity, for a trophy steelhead in heavy current will test even the best of gear. Abu Garcia, Daiwa, Shimano and Penn are all reputable brands.

Diagram 3 The steelhead rag was a well-kept secret for many years before its successful use was leaked. It is now in wide use by anglers who have come to realize the big fish catching abilities of this drift lure. Rags are made out of an extremely buoyant

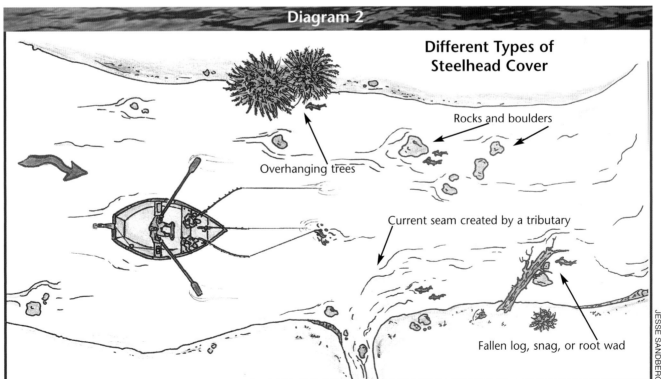

Diagram 2

Different Types of Steelhead Cover

Rocks and boulders

Overhanging trees

Current seam created by a tributary

Fallen log, snag, or root wad

JESSE SANDBERG

The author caught this large steelhead from ten feet of water with the float set only four feet from the jig.

foam cylinder and therefore float higher in the water column than other drift lures. This keeps the rig up where large steelhead can see it. In good current the rag also has the added attraction of wobbling from side to side like a tadpole, making the lure seem very lifelike. By using different colors of yarn, a rag provides good contrast which is yet another feature appealing to steelhead. The set-up shown here incorporates the use of a clever weight system shown to me by Dudley Nelson, a retired State Police Game Enforcement Lieutenant. Twist an eye on the end of a rigid piece of spinner wire, say .033" or greater, and run it through the hollow core of a piece of 1/4-inch pencil lead. The length of the lead and wire will depend on the water to be fished, so it's best to have an assortment of sizes at hand. This system acts like a walleye fisherman's bottom walker, and helps to keep the rig drifting along without snagging up when fishing grabby water, just the type of water that trophy steelhead like to hang in.

One last word of advice: Certain river systems are known to consistently put out greater numbers of trophy steelhead than others. If you really want to increase the odds of hooking up with one of these mystical creatures, do some research, pick a river, and learn its nuances by spending as much time as possible streamside. Believe me, it will be time well spent!

Try Northwest Angling Experience, operated by guide Chris Vertopoulos, for a good chance at a trophy steelhead. (503) 349-1377.

Chris Vertopoulos holds a giant winter steelhead caught in an Oregon coastal river on a rag.

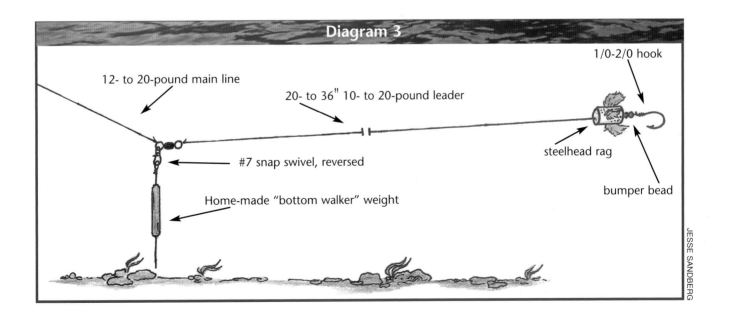

Diagram 3

1/0-2/0 hook

12- to 20-pound main line

20- to 36" 10- to 20-pound leader

steelhead rag

#7 snap swivel, reversed

bumper bead

Home-made "bottom walker" weight

Columbia River Summer-Steelhead Rigs

NICK AMATO

There are three primary techniques employed for summer steelhead on the Columbia: anchor fishing, trolling and plunking. This beautiful native was caught with trolling tackle.

In spite of the many problems facing the mighty Columbia River and its salmon and steelhead runs, it remains one of the greatest conduits for anadromous fish in the world. Each year, hundreds of thousands of salmon and steelhead swim the Columbia to reach their spawning grounds. Summer steelhead are just one of the many runs of fish present in the Columbia in season, and sometimes their numbers can be staggering. The 2003-2004 upriver summer steelhead run, for instance, was estimated at 416,000 fish, the fifth largest return since the completion of Bonneville Dam in 1938! The 2004-2005 steelhead forecast is not quite so rosy, but is still impressive: 388,100 summer fish are expected to pass Bonneville, and this number does not include Skamania stock steelhead returning to lower river tributaries below Bonneville. With numbers such as these, summer steelhead angling on the Columbia and its tributaries should once again be excellent in the coming season.

For management purposes, Columbia River summer steelhead are categorized into several different groups according to genetic origin, spawning destination and run timing. It is important for anglers to be familiar with the three primary groups because the runs differ somewhat, especially where run timing is concerned. Lower river stocks are mostly hatchery fish

derived from Washington State's famous Skamania steelhead. These hard-fighting chromers return to such rivers as the Elochoman, Cowlitz, Kalama, Lewis and Washougal rivers in Washington. In Oregon, Skamania stock steelies return to rivers in the Willamette basin and the Sandy River. These rivers are all tributaries to the Columbia, so fishermen get a shot at these fish in the big river before they turn up their home streams. The lower river component of the overall Columbia summer steelhead run tends to arrive earlier than upriver stocks, with numbers peaking some time in May, June or early July depending on location and water conditions. The leading edge of these runs sometimes begin to show in tributaries as early as late February or early March, providing a welcome surprise to anglers chasing late-winter steelhead.

"A-run" steelhead are one of two distinct groups of fish comprising the upriver summer run, that is, fish passing Bonneville after July 1st on their way to upriver tributaries. Steelhead passing Bonneville in April, May and June are considered Skamania fish returning to tributaries of the Bonneville pool and are therefore counted as lower river fish. A-run steelhead numbers traditionally peak at Bonneville in early August. This run segment primarily consists of fish of ten pounds or less that have spent one or two years in the ocean before heading to tributaries of the upper Columbia, including the Snake River. B-run summer steelhead are generally larger fish that have spent two or three years in the ocean, and their passage of Bonneville usually peaks some time in mid-September. Because of the extra time spent feeding in the ocean, B-run fish often grow huge, with fish of twenty pounds or more somewhat common. B-run steelhead are primarily headed to spawning grounds in Idaho's Clearwater and Salmon river systems.

By any standards, the Columbia is a giant of a river. For the uninitiated, the task of choosing where and how to fish the big river can be a daunting one. But summer steelhead migrate in such a manner that we can immediately eliminate most of the water from our attention. Unlike chinook salmon, that prefer to swim in deep channels as they move upstream, summer steelhead prefer shallower water that is 8-20 feet deep. This makes summer fish extremely shore oriented, therefore, most seasoned summer steelhead anglers concentrate their efforts close to the bank. Summer steelhead will make use of any structure that breaks up the current and provides a cushion in which to rest. Current seams created by rocks, tributaries and points of land are often excellent places to intercept fish. Wing dams, or pile

dikes as they are sometimes called, are designed to direct the current in order to reduce erosion and enhance flushing of a channel. These structures create a perfect seam in which steelhead often travel.

Diagram 1 This shows a boat strategically located along such a seam on the downstream side of a wing dam. It is permissible to tie-off to a wing dam as long as there is no navigational device attached to it. If a wing dam has a day board or some other such device, steer clear of it or risk a hefty fine. Also, it is advisable to use a "dike anchor" or "dike ring" to fasten to the piling rather than actually tying off the boat with a knot. In case of emergency or if you have to follow a hot fish, these devices allow for a quick departure from your mooring. A dike anchor can be any heavy object that can be tossed over the dike's cross member in order to hang the boat; old-fashioned window weights are excellent for this. A dike ring is a large metal hoop tied to a rope that can be slipped over an individual piling and easily removed in order to leave quickly.

The mouths of cool-water tributaries are also excellent places to concentrate your angling efforts. Because the slow pools created by dams allow the Columbia to become superheated

Diagram 1

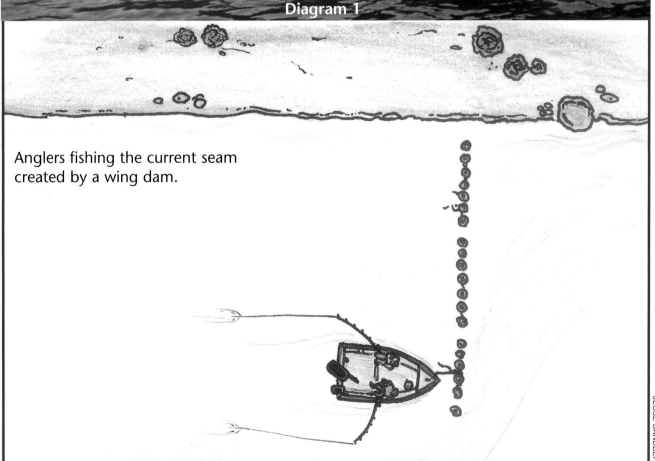

Anglers fishing the current seam created by a wing dam.

JESSE SANDBERG

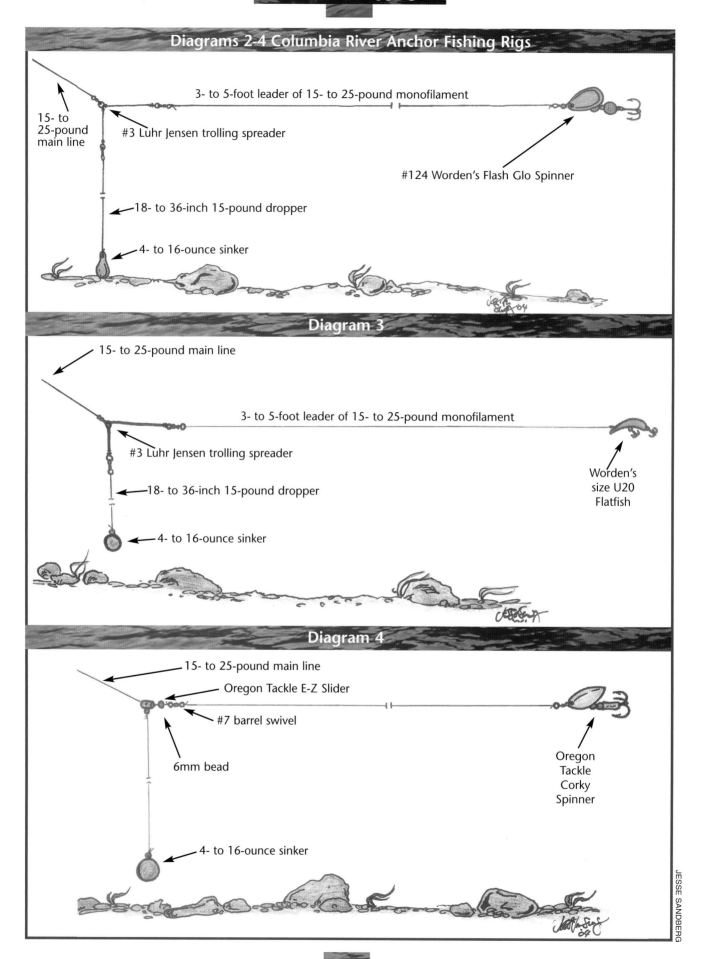

Diagrams 2-4 Columbia River Anchor Fishing Rigs

3- to 5-foot leader of 15- to 25-pound monofilament

15- to 25-pound main line

#3 Luhr Jensen trolling spreader

#124 Worden's Flash Glo Spinner

18- to 36-inch 15-pound dropper

4- to 16-ounce sinker

Diagram 3

15- to 25-pound main line

3- to 5-foot leader of 15- to 25-pound monofilament

#3 Luhr Jensen trolling spreader

Worden's size U20 Flatfish

18- to 36-inch 15-pound dropper

4- to 16-ounce sinker

Diagram 4

15- to 25-pound main line

Oregon Tackle E-Z Slider

#7 barrel swivel

6mm bead

Oregon Tackle Corky Spinner

4- to 16-ounce sinker

during the dog days of summer, the main river often reaches temperatures inhospitable to steelhead. When the Columbia's water temperature reaches the high sixties, steelhead begin to seek out the relief provided by the cooler water of tributaries. Unlike winter steelhead, summer fish are not sexually mature for some time and are not urged on their migration by the need to immediately spawn. Therefore, they can afford to dally. Oregon's Deschutes River is famous for the number of "strays" it attracts, and an incredible troll fishery exists where it enters the Columbia. The mouth of the Sandy River, Eagle Creek and Herman Creek also attract fish on the Oregon side. In Washington, try the mouths of the Cowlitz, Kalama, Lewis, Washougal, White Salmon, Wind Rivers and Drano Lake.

There are three primary techniques employed for summer steelhead on the Columbia: Anchor fishing, trolling, either forward or back, and plunking from the bank. There are other techniques that are somewhat location specific, so pay attention to what other anglers are doing when fishing new water. Anchor fishing is probably the most popular method because it is so effective. By anchoring a boat in a known fish traveling lane, anglers vastly increase their odds of a hook-up. By positioning a boat where the fish are moving through, it's possible for hundreds of fish to see your offering on any given day, and maybe, just maybe, some of them will be biters. Begin by anchoring in moderate to heavy current in 8-20 feet of water. Then bounce back your rig, put the rod in the holder and wait for it to fold over. The amount of lead you use is critical because you want to be able to bounce the rig a good distance from the boat, yet still have it hold bottom once it's there. Bounce the set-up out at least thirty yards from the boat. With this much line out the rig will not be dragged around or lifted off the bottom when the boat bobs or swings due to wind or wake. The idea is to keep the set-up independent from the movement of the boat in order to keep the lure working uninterrupted in the strike zone.

Diagrams 2, 3, 4 These illustrations depict popular Columbia River anchor fishing rigs. In slow to moderate flows use a wobbling plug like a Worden's Flatfish or Luhr Jensen Kwikfish, or a spinner. In really fast water a spinner is the best option. When anchoring on the Columbia, exercise caution at all times. The current can be misleading and downright dangerous. Hazards are many and conditions can change in the blink of an eye. Boats are lost every year due to accidents or inexperience. Outfit your boat with the appropriate gear and be familiar with its proper use BEFORE venturing out on the water. Beginners should go with someone more experienced in order to safely learn the river and its ways. Short of that, consult with the staff of a local tackle shop or pick up the video "Anchor Fishing For Salmon and Steelhead" with Eric Linde and Carmen Macdonald, published by Frank Amato Publications.

Diagrams 5 & 6 Trolling is another technique used to pursue summer steelhead on the Columbia. Early in the season when the water is still cool, say sixty degrees or less, anglers can use a diver and bait rig like that pictured in Diagram 5 to slowly back or forward troll in order to cover large expanses of water. When the water warms over sixty degrees, forget the bait and fish hardware like spinners or plugs. Many plugs on the market dive down 6-10 feet or more, so an angler is able to achieve the proper depth without the use of added weight or a diver. This technique is called "flatlining" and is a lot of fun because it allows one to uselighter gear. Diagram 6 illustrates three effective plugs used for trolling for steelhead.

Popular summer-steelhead troll fisheries include the mouth of the Deschutes and Drano Lake. As with all fisheries, pay attention to what the other anglers are doing and stick with the program. There are often trolling patterns adhered to by everyone in order to avoid chaos. Learn what they are and stick to them or become extremely unpopular in a hurry!

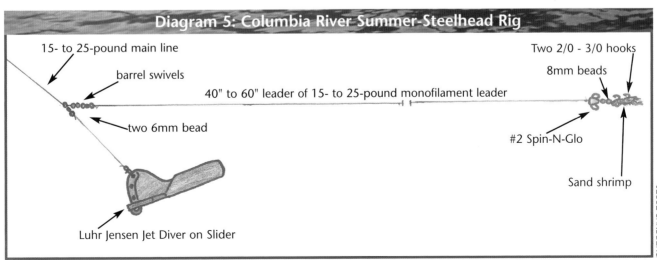

Diagram 5: Columbia River Summer-Steelhead Rig

15- to 25-pound main line

barrel swivels

Two 2/0 - 3/0 hooks

8mm beads

40" to 60" leader of 15- to 25-pound monofilament leader

two 6mm bead

#2 Spin-N-Glo

Sand shrimp

Luhr Jensen Jet Diver on Slider

JESSE SANDBERG

Fly anglers can use clear intermediate lines and small flies to catch summer steelhead like this near the mouth of Herman Creek.

Diagram 7 A float set-up used to present a prawn, sand shrimp or roe. This is a popular technique at several of the tributary mouths, for in the cooler water steelhead are still receptive to bait. This method is extremely effective at Drano Lake in Washington and at the lagoon at Herman Creek on the Oregon side. Fix the bobber stop knot so that the bait is suspended 1-2 feet off the bottom in water of ten feet deep or less. In deeper water it's necessary to determine at which depth the fish are cruising before setting the knot, for steelhead will often suspend in deep water. In the absence of good electronics, start shallow and gradually lengthen the line beneath the float until success is realized. The last thing you want is for your bait to be below the fish, as steelhead will often rise to a bait; rarely will they dive for one.

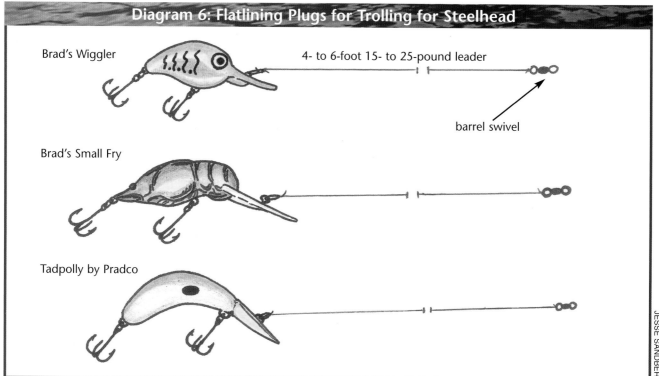

Diagram 6: Flatlining Plugs for Trolling for Steelhead

Brad's Wiggler

4- to 6-foot 15- to 25-pound leader

barrel swivel

Brad's Small Fry

Tadpolly by Pradco

JESSE SANDBERG

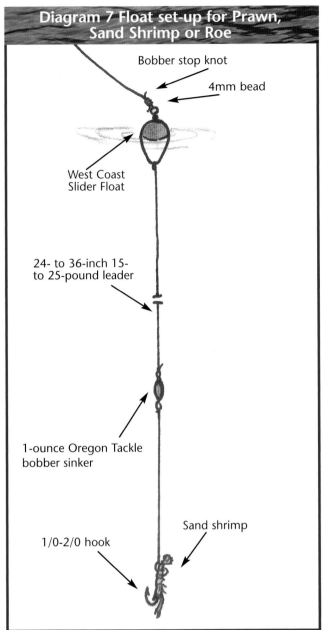

Diagram 7 Float set-up for Prawn, Sand Shrimp or Roe

Bobber stop knot

4mm bead

West Coast Slider Float

24- to 36-inch 15- to 25-pound leader

1-ounce Oregon Tackle bobber sinker

Sand shrimp

1/0-2/0 hook

JESSE SANDBERG

Diagram 8 Another effective and somewhat controversial set-up used at the tributary mouths for summer steelhead. In the hands of a conscientious angler, this rig is deadly for fair-hooking actively biting fish. In the hands of a low-life scumbag posing as a fisherman, it is deadly for snagging fish everywhere but in the mouth. The Corky or other such drift bobber keeps the bait off the bottom where the fish can see it. Unfortunately, this also can put the bait right in the zone where the fish are cruising and they sometimes make contact with it as they pass by. True fishermen learn to discern between a line bump and an actual take and refuse to set the hook on a line bump because they know it will result in a foul-hooked fish. Snaggers set the hook at every little tick of the line and bring their fish in backwards. There is nothing like a snagger to put the fish off the bite and make a bad name for real fishermen. One nice thing about fishing the Columbia is that a state cop is often close at hand. If you see someone setting the hook every thirty seconds in a blatant attempt to snag fish, make the call. Herman Creek used to be infamous for low-life snaggers, but not anymore. If someone starts jerking his rod here, the jerk gets run off. Washington State has purportedly outlawed this rig in some locations, so if you should choose to use it, be sure to check the regulations to make sure you are legal.

The aforementioned techniques are not the only ones used for taking summer steelhead. Bank fishermen do well plunking Spin-N-Glos and Flatfish from beaches, tributary mouths and near Bonneville Dam. Anglers casting spinners like a number four Blue Fox Vibrax or Rattle Spin in chartreuse or green hook aggressive fish near tributaries like the Sandy and Deschutes. Fly-fishermen at Herman Creek, the Wind River and Drano Lake often outfish gear anglers with clear intermediate lines and slow sinking flies. Whichever technique and location you choose to fish, be safe, fish well, carefully release all wild fish and have fun!

Diagram 8 Set-up for Drift Bobber

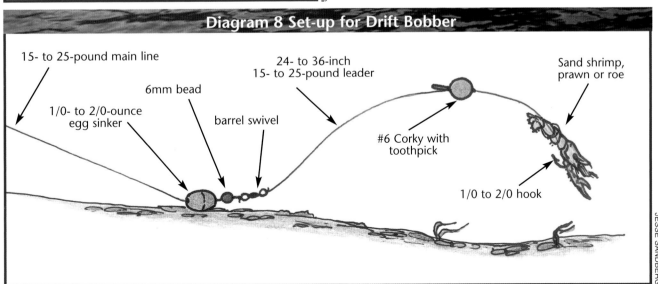

15- to 25-pound main line

24- to 36-inch 15- to 25-pound leader

Sand shrimp, prawn or roe

6mm bead

1/0- to 2/0-ounce egg sinker

barrel swivel

#6 Corky with toothpick

1/0 to 2/0 hook

JESSE SANDBERG

Natural Steelheading Techniques

The author with an immaculate native hen caught while gliding in clear water.

Perhaps one of the most intriguing aspects of steelheading is the constant change inherent in the sport. Each season brings us a treasure trove of new stuff to consider. New boats, new rods, new reels, new lines, lures, waders, clothing, polarized glasses—you get the picture. And while much of this is often just eye candy designed to make us open our wallets, plenty of it is actually new or improved gear that makes our fishing more enjoyable, and sometimes more productive. Last January I received permission from my "accountant" (also spelled Katherine) to purchase a Lamiglas spinning rod I had been oggling for some time. And while the rod was not new to the Lamiglas line, it was new to my rod rack at home. The EC 96 LS has the perfect balance of power and sensitivity for my steelhead float-fishing needs, and I don't know how I lived without it for so long. It was one of my best purchases of 2004, and it did make a difference in my fishing.

Our gear is not the only thing that changes with the seasons. Quite often, sometimes without even realizing it, we ourselves change. Maybe it's something simple like our casting skills. All of a sudden you're pitching your Little Cleo spoon way back under the cedar branches and hooking a steelhead in his house. You fish all day with the same spoon without losing it, and hook two more steelhead. Higher up in the cedars two of your Little Cleos still decorate the branches, reminders of last year's casting ability, or inability.

Or maybe it's something more complex, like reading water. Now you're catching fish out of runs where you went fishless before. Your presentations are more purposeful, and there is confidence behind every cast. You eye a current seam near the far bank and launch a perfect cast. Your slinky taps bottom once, then something taps back. The hook set is suddenly instinctive, and ten pounds of chrome erupts from the water, pissed off and hell-bent on crushing your will. Somehow, you have figured it out. Now you are thinking like a steelhead, now you blend in with your surroundings. And now you are one of the ten percent. On your way to the next run, you realize for the first time that an ouzel can actually walk upside down under water on a fallen tree. "Nothing at all like last winter," you think.

The one aspect of steelheading that changes the least is technique. New methods are few and far between, with breakthroughs limited by the nature of our rivers and fish. The old standbys of drift fishing and back-trolling plugs are still very much in the mainstream, but in recent years, techniques that offer a more natural presentation have garnered much attention from anglers. A natural presentation is one where the bait, lure or fly drifts along at or near current speed, with no indication to the fish that the object is suspect due to unnatural drag or interference from the line or the fisherman. The fact that your offering is tied to the line prohibits it from looking 100% natural in the first place. Think about it. If you were to toss a gob of eggs in the river unattached to your line, devoid of any human interference, they would tumble and roll along as they drifted freely, moving and reacting to each nuance of the constantly changing current. By rigging these eggs on a hook and tying off to it, we have already restricted the natural movement of the bait in the water. A friend of mine once illustrated this point to me by tossing a dry fly—unattached to a line—onto the surface of a creek we were fishing. The fly bobbed and swirled in each micro-current, appearing just as a real insect would. He then tied the same fly to his tippet and we watched as it floated by. There was no comparison. It looked like the fly was tied off to a steel cable. Understanding that steelhead often prefer a naturally presented bait to all else, it is up to us to make our offering look as "untethered" as possible. There are several steelhead angling techniques that make this impossible goal almost obtainable.

Float-fishing for steelhead is a technique that has received a lot of attention in recent years. When executed properly, this method allows for a wonderfully natural presentation. The key to float-fishing is to eliminate any drag on the bobber which causes it to move at a speed dissimilar to the current's. This is accomplished by positioning the line above the float so that a belly does not form in it, which is the major cause of drag. It may be necessary to mend the line upstream several times during one presentation in order to maintain a drag-free drift. Once the technique of mending is mastered and the concept of the dead drift is fully understood, float-fishing becomes a deadly weapon in the steelhead angler's arsenal.

In float-fishing, the bait or jig is shown to the fish very near to current speed, and this is exactly what a steelhead expects to see when an intruder drifts into its lie. Most quality steelhead jigs are constructed of either marabou or bunny fur, and these materials undulate enticingly in the current, seemingly coming to life as the jig drifts down river. Steelhead are extremely territorial and can't stand to have another living creature invade their space. Jigs that come alive in the water are great for annoying steelhead, and an annoyed steelhead is a hooked steelhead.

Diagram 1 Three different ways to rig up for float-fishing. The first is a simple fixed bobber with a marabou jig. This set-up takes less than a minute to set-up and is great for the leisurely fisherman who would rather fish than mess around with gear. The second rig shows a novel jig designed and sold by Over The Edge Tackle. The dropper jig has an additional eye on the bottom of the jig head that allows for a second bait or lure to be rigged below the jig, which allows the fisherman to fish two different levels of the water column at once, while offering twice the annoyance factor. The third set-up illustrates a slip float set-up used when fishing the deepest of steelhead holding water, because casting a fixed float in this situation would be awkward due to the length of leader between the float and jig or bait. But because most steelhead are caught in water between three and eight feet deep, a slip float is seldom a necessity.

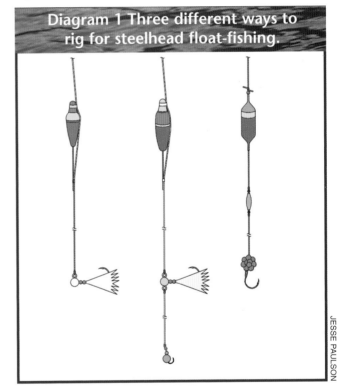

Diagram 1 Three different ways to rig for steelhead float-fishing.

JESSE PAULSON

Side-drifting is another technique that provides a natural presentation. Side-drifting is most often practiced from a drift boat or jet sled, and is a great technique to cover large expanses of water quickly. The skipper begins by positioning the boat to the side of the most promising looking water, then gets the boat moving downstream very near to current speed. Usually, the boat is moving just slightly slower than the current. Then the angler the furthest upstream in the boat casts across stream and slightly up, then the remaining anglers cast in order until all the baits are in the water. The idea is to stagger the baits at different distances from the boat in order to cover all of the best holding water while drifting through.

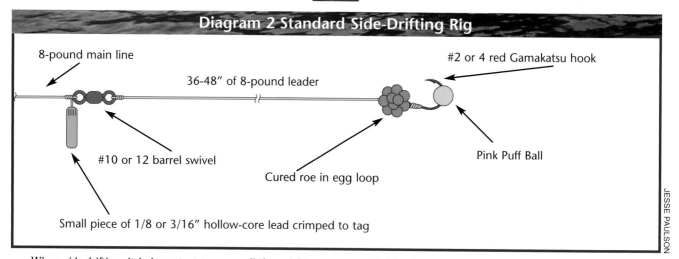

Diagram 2 Standard Side-Drifting Rig

8-pound main line

#2 or 4 red Gamakatsu hook

36-48" of 8-pound leader

#10 or 12 barrel swivel

Cured roe in egg loop

Pink Puff Ball

Small piece of 1/8 or 3/16" hollow-core lead crimped to tag

JESSE PAULSON

When side-drifting, it is important to use as little weight as necessary in order to achieve the desired drift. The bait should glide along one to two feet off the bottom, the weight hitting only occasionally, say every fifteen to twenty feet. When the lead does hit bottom, pull up by gently raising the rod tip so that it continues to glide as it is swept down stream. In this fashion, the baits are presented in an incredibly realistic manner and the fish respond accordingly. When a steelhead picks up the bait, it is important not to set the hook too soon. Because the boat is drifting rapidly down stream and the fish is not, the hooks are usually pulled into the corner of the mouth by the boat's progress, resulting in a solid hook-up. For this reason it is important to use a rod 9 to 10 feet long with a soft tip. The long rod gives just enough shock absorption to provide the split second that it takes the hooks to work back without being pulled jerkily away from the fish.

While side-drifting out of a boat is the most practical way to use this technique, it is possible to side-drift from the bank. The angler merely casts out and begins walking down stream at a pace near to the current's. This provides for a much longer, more natural presentation than the drift fisherman's standard swing. Obviously, don't try this method when there are other anglers down stream of you, for this will certainly interfere with their fishing. Also, be very careful when walking or you may just wind up flat on your face. Some anglers have difficulty walking a stream bank in the first place, add the distraction of maintaining a drift and anticipating a take and you have a train wreck in the making.

Diagram 2 A standard side-drifting rig. In order to minimize the river's pull on the line, it's typical to downsize to 8- or even 6-pound line and leader. The thinner diameter has less surface area and is not pushed down stream as rapidly as a larger line size would be. This may seem like light line to use while steelheading, and it is, so be careful. But fishing from a boat gives the advantage of being able to chase down a fish, and using the lighter line is somewhat critical in attaining the natural presentation

provided by this method. In this rig, the hollow-core pencil lead is attached by crimping it on a short tag of monofilament hanging from the swivel. When snagged on the bottom, this allows the lead to be pulled from the tag without losing the entire rig and facilitates a quick return to fishing. Use 1/8- or 3/16-inch pencil lead and keep it small. Usually, a half to one inch is enough. There is much debate regarding proper leader length when using this technique, but 36-48 inches is ample. You'll want to incorporate some type of small drift bobber in the set-up to maintain at least a slight buoyancy so that the bait does not settle on the bottom. A simple way to do this is to add a Puff Ball onto the bend of the hook as pictured here.

Diagram 3 Another way to rig for side-drifting. Here, a double-hook set-up is shown, as many anglers believe this results in fewer lost fish. Between the two hooks is a #10 or 12 Cheater for buoyancy. Flame and pink are popular colors. When side-drifting, it is important to use the proper-sized hooks. Excessively large hooks are too heavy and will continuously hang on the bottom. Therefore, size 2 and 4 are standard, and make sure they are ultra sharp.

Gliding was first covered by Bill Herzog in *Color Guide to Steelhead Drift Fishing*. Gliding is a method to use when water visibility is good and water temperature is warm— 45 degrees. In this technique, the weight is reduced so that the rig glides along just off the bottom, letting the rig travel at or near current speed, quite similar to side-drifting. On some days this is just what the fish are looking for, as the standard drift-fishing swing just doesn't look natural enough. Every time the weight hits bottom in drift fishing it slows the rig down, signaling to the steelhead that there is something unnatural occurring. In clear water it is not necessary to slow the bait down so that the fish can see and follow it, and here is where gliding really shines. Also, the clearer the water, the spookier the steelhead will be. The more natural the presentation is under these conditions, the more successful you will be.

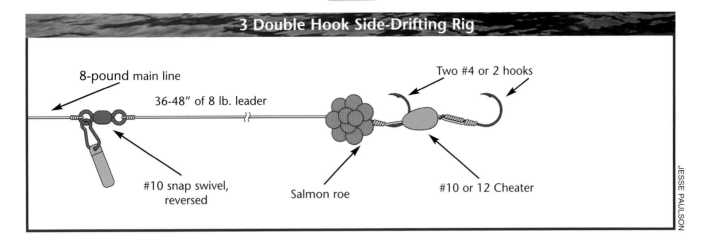

3 Double Hook Side-Drifting Rig

8-pound main line

36-48" of 8 lb. leader

Two #4 or 2 hooks

#10 snap swivel, reversed

Salmon roe

#10 or 12 Cheater

JESSE PAULSON

I first tested this method on Clackamas River coho several years ago with good effect. Clackamas coho are notoriously tight-lipped and tough to get to bite when water conditions are low and clear. On one particular day I drift-fished for several hours to a pod of fresh fish to no avail. Having only drift gear with me I began to experiment and reduced the amount of weight on the rig so it would just skim along, uninterrupted just off the bottom. The results were eye-opening. Why such a subtle difference in presentation matters so much to the fish is beyond me, but the more natural appearance of the glided bait was all it took to trigger a response from the fish.

When gliding, it is important to maintain tension on the line so that the weight remains off the bottom, drifting freely. This is done by reeling slightly or gently raising the rod, or a combination of both. In effect, this method is the equivalent of the fly-fisherman's tight-line nymphing technique, using tension on the line to swim the fly through a lie instead of letting it bounce bottom on the dead drift.

Diagram 4 A stealthy rig used for gliding when rivers are low and clear. Use just enough lead to keep the rig down but not on

bottom. Pictured here is a Jensen Egg that is deadly on low-water steelhead. To rig the egg, back the egg loop from the eye of the hook and thread it through the Jensen Egg, then run the leader back through the eye and tie it off to the swivel. It is not necessary to always use a buoyant drift bobber with this technique, as the rig is kept from the bottom by applying tension to the line.

In really slow water, it may become necessary to use a drift bobber because there is not enough force from the current on the line to keep the set-up gliding. Diagram Five shows such a set-up. Here, a Cheater is used to provide buoyancy. The Cheater is a fantastic drift bobber, that, when rigged this way, wobbles as it drifts along. This added movement imparts a life-like action to the rig, and, as stated before, steelhead hate any other living creature invading their space.

Other techniques are great for steelheading when rivers have color and are in prime shape, but as they drop and clear a more natural presentation will always get better results. The next time you're on the river and the fish are being difficult, try lightening your weight or float-fishing to achieve a more realistic presentation. I'm sure that you will be pleased with the results of going natural.

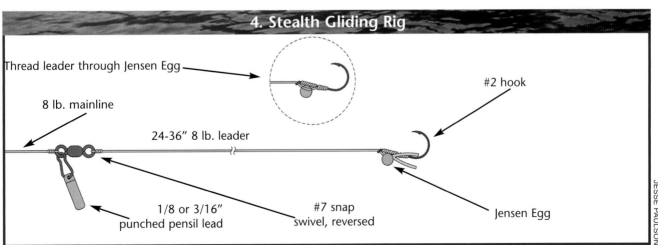

4. Stealth Gliding Rig

Thread leader through Jensen Egg

#2 hook

8 lb. mainline

24-36" 8 lb. leader

1/8 or 3/16" punched pensil lead

#7 snap swivel, reversed

Jensen Egg

JESSE PAULSON

Float-Fishing For Steelhead

These intrepid anglers will certainly attest to the effectiveness of steelhead float-fishing.

As we drifted into yet another beautiful tailout on a Willamette Valley steelhead river, I said to Jim Martin, "Wow! Look at that one."

"He must go twelve pounds," I exclaimed as the chrome steelhead spooked from its lie and bolted upstream into the safety of deeper water. So far, it had been a slow day. The river was absolutely choked with steelhead and chinook, yet between the two of us we had yet to have a hook-up. The sun was glowing brightly in the afternoon sky and the visibility of the water was somewhere near infinity—conditions not exactly conducive to good steelhead angling. So Jim and I had resigned ourselves to fish-watching as we drifted on, he on the oars and I haphazardly casting a jig-and-float set-up as we scattered fish like a pair of orcas scattering sea lions.

As we floated through the tailout, I delivered a lazy cast to a deep trough running down the middle and went back to scanning for fish. A few moments later I glanced up to check the progress of my float and was alarmed to see that it had disappeared. "Where the hell is my bobber?" I shouted to Jim in a panic. Just then a lovely eight-pound hen erupted from the river with my jig in its mouth and answered that question. Jim just shook his head and smirked. "Rookie," he must have been

thinking. Luckily, the fish had taken the jig so hard that it had pinned itself in the absence of my own hook set. A few minutes later Jim netted the fish for me. Later, I would net one for him that was also taken on a jig-and-float set-up.

Although a relative newcomer to float-fishing, these were not the first steelhead I had hooked by using this method. But considering the impossible conditions under which they were encountered, these two fish went a long way in further cementing in my brain the efficacy of float-fishing for steelhead.

Using a float to suspend a bait, jig or lure while fishing for steelhead is a technique pioneered by Canadian fishermen back in the 1970s. Later on, savvy Midwesterners began to realize its effectiveness for steelhead on Great Lakes tributaries. Here in the steelhead mecca of the Pacific Northwest, it has taken a little longer for die-hard steelheaders to catch on, or, to at least accept it as a legitimate tactic. I guess for many of us the idea of using a bobber reminded us more of fishing for bluegills on a farm pond than for noble steelhead on a brawling Northwest river; more of regression than progress. It took awhile, but eventually us soggy-brained North-westerners caught on, and over the last decade float-fishing for steelhead has entered the mainstream, so much so that it is the go-to tactic for many anglers under a variety of river conditions.

Float-fishing for steelhead is incredibly effective for a variety of reasons. First of all, it is a fairly simple method that even a novice can execute with a little instruction or practice. All that is needed to get started is a rod and reel, a couple of floats, a simple weight system, and bait, lure or jigs. In float-fishing, the bobber serves two primary purposes: That of delivery system and strike indicator. The float carries the bait or jig through prime holding water, allowing the offering to drift at or near current speed, which is critical in triggering a steelhead to take. The more natural the presentation, the more often a steelhead will bite. Because the bait or jig is suspended off the bottom, snags are infrequent, thus extending fishing time. More time in the water equates to more steelhead landed. Most of us who began steelheading by drift fishing are all too familiar with the frustrating scenario of casting out only to get snagged, breaking off the rig, then having to re-tie another set-up. Then, casting out only to get snagged, breaking off the rig, then having to re-tie another set-up. Sound familiar? In float-fishing, this agonizing occurrence is reduced drastically, if not eliminated altogether. After an angler learns to read water and is accomplished at judging depth,

it is possible to fish for days without ever losing a rig, a fact appreciated by "accountants" everywhere.

When properly rigged, a jig or bait will suspend anywhere from six inches to several feet off the bottom. How far off the bottom is determined by several factors. Water clarity is one. In really clear water, say that with four feet of visibility or more, steelhead can see extremely well and will move great distances to intercept a bait, therefore, an angler can rig an offering farther from the bottom and still expect good results. In more colored water, it may be necessary to present the rig nearer to the bottom so the fish get a good look at it. Water temperature plays another role. When the water is between 42 and 50 degrees, steelhead are extremely active and willingly move to intercept the bait. In water temperatures above or below this, steelhead may become lethargic and it may become necessary to rig the bait or jig so that it taps the fish right on the nose. Either way, the offering is still suspended and the fish must rise to grab it, and this is when the float becomes a strike indicator.

Usually, when a steelhead grabs the bait or jig when using this technique, the float is immediately pulled under water as the fish dives back down to its lie. It is here that a quick response is needed from the angler. Quickly reel up any slack line that may

Tim Rooney displays a fine steelhead taken on a jig-and-float set-up from an Oregon coastal river.

be on the water and set the hook firmly before the fish senses something is wrong and spits the bait. Because the float acts as a visual strike indicator, one of the most frustrating elements of learning to fish for steelhead is eliminated for the neophyte—learning what is and what isn't a take. Most beginners spend several seasons drift fishing before they can readily discern between bouncing the bottom and an actual bite, but this guesswork is eliminated when float fishing. Occasionally, a dour or timid steelhead may only rattle a float or make it bob or twitch subtly, but this is still an obvious take to the angler who is paying attention. If you are prone to gawking at water ouzels or watching other anglers fish—as I am—then you will miss some bites when float-fishing because the hook set came too late. Not to worry, the natural presentation of this method is so unobtrusive that a missed fish can often be made to bite again.

Another advantage of float-fishing for steelhead is that the method allows you to extend your drift. In drift fishing, your bait swings in an arc and only allows for a limited presentation through the best water. In float-fishing, the rig more or less travels in a straight line downstream, allowing for excellent control of the presentation. By feeding out line as the rig floats down stream of you, much more water can be covered on one cast than by drift fishing. Just remember that the more line you have on the water the more delayed the hook set will be, and this may cost you a fish or two.

Begin by casting up, across or down stream as the water dictates, and allow the rig to float stealthily through the best water. It is advisable to hold your rod tip high to keep as much line off the water as possible, for the line will often move down stream faster than the rig. This results in the line forming a belly, which will eventually begin to drag the set-up down stream faster than the current is moving. This creates an unnatural drift that all but the most suicidal of steelhead will ignore. Remember, we want the whole affair to progress down stream at a dead drift, at or near current speed, with as little interference from the line as possible. If a belly of line does begin to form down stream of the float, it becomes necessary to mend the line to preserve the natural presentation. Mending is accomplished by lowering your rod tip to the water, then abruptly raising it to lift the line off the surface. As the line rises through the air, the rod tip is then flipped upstream so that the line follows it and is repositioned above the float. This results in several more yards of a drag-free float. Perhaps no other facet of float-fishing causes as much confusion to the beginner than the concept of mending. Really, it's quite simple.

All we are doing is using the rod to reposition the line upstream of the float so that the line does not belly and pull the set-up down stream at an unnatural clip. On a particularly long drift, it may be necessary to mend the line several times during the presentation in order to maintain the desired effect.

To better hold the line off the water and to facilitate effective mending, most float-fishermen use rods that are considered long in the world of steelheading. Anglers in British Columbia often use rods of twelve feet or more in length coupled with center-pin reels. In the Oregon and Washington, rods of 9 1/2 to 10 1/2 feet are more common. G. Loomis, Lamiglas and St. Croix are manufacturers who have paid special attention to the needs of Northwest float-fishermen and have designed rods specifically to match our varying needs. I am particularly fond of the Lamiglas EC 96LS, and G. Loomis has created an entire line of steelhead float-fishing rods to suit any condition. St. Croix has entered nicely into the mix with two rods from its Avid Series, the AS 96MLF2 and the AS 96MF2. Xstream brand rods are more affordable than the above and offer a couple of nice actions as well.

The floats used for this method come in all manner of shapes and sizes, so selecting the proper set-up can often be daunting. Because the current in a river is often swifter at the surface than down where your bait or jig is, it's advisable to use the smallest float possible for the conditions at hand. A smaller float has less surface area for the water to grip onto, therefore the float will not be dragged down stream of the bait at an unreasonable rate. Also, a smaller float is more sensitive and will better transmit the subtle take of a lethargic steelhead. Because many floats are made of balsa or EVA foam, and are therefore light in weight, casting them with a bait-casting reel can be difficult at best. For this reason, many veteran float-fishermen have turned to spinning reels for their float-fishing outfits. If you are fishing heavier water that requires a bigger float and an additional weighting system to the bait or jig, then by all means use the bait-caster if that is your preference. In choppy or roily water, it is necessary to use a larger float to maintain visual contact as it bobs in the current.

In recent years many anglers have turned to synthetic super-braided lines for their float-fishing needs. These fine-diameter lines float well and therefore aid in proper line control and mending; it is an exercise in frustration to try to lift from the water a line that has sunk! They also have very little stretch, which can be a huge benefit when you have two hundred feet of line out and a fish takes your bobber down. Less stretch results in a quicker, more positive hook-set when there is a lot of line on the water. Western Filament's Teflon-coated Tuf Line XP is an excellent choice as a superbraid for spinning reels, as is Berkley's Fireline. Monofilament line is still widely used in float-fishing, but because it can absorb water and sink, it is advisable

Mending the Line to Avoid Drag

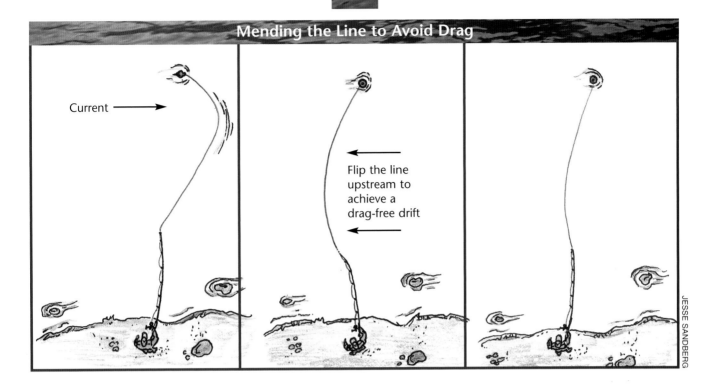

Current →

Flip the line upstream to achieve a drag-free drift

JESSE SANDBERG

to treat it with mucilin or a silicone fly floatant. A limp line like Trilene XL, Stren Easy Cast or Stren Clear Blue works great on spinning reels.

The various combinations of floats, baits, jigs and lures that can be employed in float-fishing is endless. In recent years, manufacturers have really stepped up to offer anglers an incredible assortment of gear to use for this tactic. Just remember, it's important to match the set-up to the water you intend to fish, and some experimentation may be needed to find the right combination. The accompanying diagrams are just a small sample of effective float rigs in use today.

1. Pictured here (page 34) is a high-quality float from Thill called the Turbo Master #3. The chartreuse and flame finish make this float easy to track in most lighting conditions. This float balances perfectly with an 1/8-ounce jig without using any additional weight. The wire peg helps telegraph to the angler exactly where the jig is at all times. Equipped with two silicone sleeves, the line is merely threaded through each and tied to the jig. Insert the float into the sleeves and you're fishing. The sleeves allow for easy adjustment for varying depths by merely sliding the float up and down the line.

The jig is a Beau-Mac SMJ2, one of the best-selling steelhead jigs of all time. The pink and white marabou really comes to life under water, providing a very realistic motion that steelhead can't resist. The eye-catching beads provide good contrast and stand out well in colored water. On a recent fishing trip with Nick Amato, Nick stated that one of the reasons he so likes jig

fishing is the simplicity of the rigging. It doesn't get any simpler than this, folks!

2. The West Coast Float pictured here is constructed of EVA foam and is nearly indestructible. West Coast has gone to the trouble of assigning a weight rating to each of its floats that makes it easy for fishermen to match the proper weight gear to the float. This is a slip float that is ideal for fishing deeper runs where it may be difficult to cast a fixed float set-up due to the length of line hanging below the float. The jig is from Rainbow's End Fly Company and is made with a uniquely translucent yarn that looks really good in the water. Step up to a 1/4-ounce jig in deeper water to get it down faster.

3. The Steelhead Stalker Float pictured here comes in two sizes that are designed to float either an 1/8-ounce or 1/4-ounce jig. Like the Turbo Master 3, this float has an extended peg that helps show when the presentation is right, that is, with the float riding vertical or slightly tilting up stream. The jig is a Beau-Mac SMJ10. Tied with an extremely bright cerise marabou body, this 1/4-ounce jig is a real killer under a variety of water conditions.

4. A jig is not the only offering to be fished beneath a float. While jig fishing draws mostly a sight-oriented response from fish, certain water conditions may call for a bit more enticement to get a steelhead going. In water with color, the use of bait like roe or sand shrimp can enhance your success by providing a scent trail that leads right to the end of your line. The West Coast Slip Float provides both an effective delivery system and strike indicator, and The Oregon Tackle Bobber Swivel Weight is both a weight and a swivel.

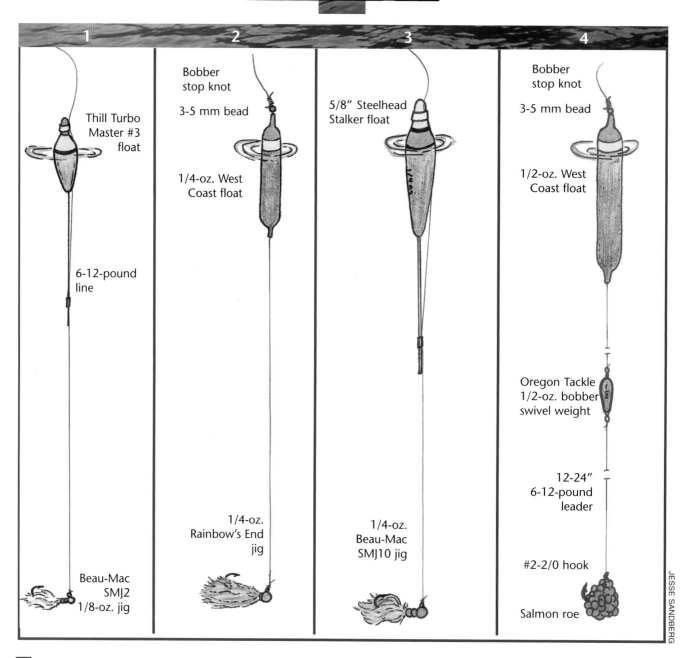

1
Thill Turbo Master #3 float

6-12-pound line

Beau-Mac SMJ2 1/8-oz. jig

2
Bobber stop knot

3-5 mm bead

1/4-oz. West Coast float

1/4-oz. Rainbow's End jig

3
5/8" Steelhead Stalker float

1/4-oz. Beau-Mac SMJ10 jig

4
Bobber stop knot

3-5 mm bead

1/2-oz. West Coast float

Oregon Tackle 1/2-oz. bobber swivel weight

12-24" 6-12-pound leader

#2-2/0 hook

Salmon roe

JESSE SANDBERG

5. This is a really cool set-up that promises double the trouble for Northwest steelhead. The float is a two-inch Thill Balsa Steelhead Float that comes with a single sleeve that slides over a hook that the line runs through to secure it. Rigged as intended, this float serves well in moderate to slow currents. But being the innovative sorts they are, steelheaders learned that this float rides better and allows for improved mending if they added an additional sleeve to the top peg as well. Like all Thill floats, this one has a high-quality finish that won't crack or chip unless badly abused.

The real gem of this rig is the Over The Edge Dropper Jig that borrows from the fly-fisherman's practice of offering a two-for-one deal to the fish. The jig head has an eye on the bottom as well as the top, which allows an angler to fish the second offering of his/her choice as a dropper. This lets the fisherman effectively cover two different levels of the water column at once, a trick that fly-fishermen long ago realized enhanced their success. It's no surprise then, that this jig was created by a group of accomplished bug flippers from the Spirit River Fly Company in Roseburg, Oregon. I spoke to factory rep Derrick Fergus regarding their new approach.

"In 2001 I fished with Nick Amato and witnessed first-hand how effective this whole jig thing is," he explained, "and realized that this was something we should get into. Our main idea was to take the innovativeness of the fly-tying world and apply it to the jig-fishing realm. Our parent company, Spirit River, already offered some radical materials for tying flies, and applying them to tying jigs was a no-brainer. The Dropper Jig and

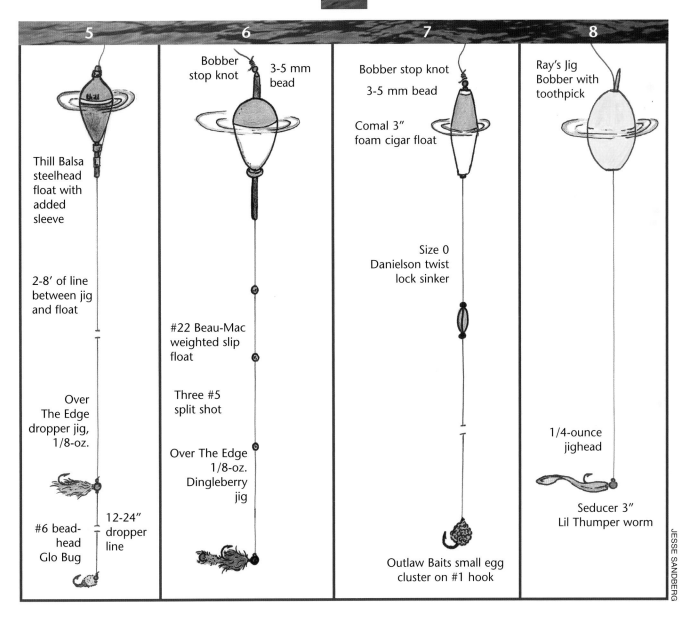

5 — Thill Balsa steelhead float with added sleeve

2-8' of line between jig and float

Over The Edge dropper jig, 1/8-oz.

#6 bead-head Glo Bug

12-24" dropper line

6 — Bobber stop knot

3-5 mm bead

#22 Beau-Mac weighted slip float

Three #5 split shot

Over The Edge 1/8-oz. Dingleberry jig

7 — Bobber stop knot

3-5 mm bead

Comal 3" foam cigar float

Size 0 Danielson twist lock sinker

Outlaw Baits small egg cluster on #1 hook

8 — Ray's Jig Bobber with toothpick

1/4-ounce jighead

Seducer 3" Lil Thumper worm

JESSE SANDBERG

Dingleberry are our best sellers, but there are others that serious steelhead fishermen should check out." You can find Over The Edge Jigs, formerly known as Osprey Tackle, at tackle shops throughout the Northwest. If you have no luck finding them in your area, contact the author at (503) 557-3313.

6. Here is another slip-float rig for fishing deeper water. Pictured is a #22 Beau-Mac weighted slip float with an Over The Edge Dingleberry Jig hanging beneath. In between are three #5 split shot that help keep the jig running at depth. When using split shot in this manner, do not crimp them so tightly that they damage the line or you will regret it when that 15-pounder climbs on. Space them evenly down the line or all together 12-16 inches from the jig. Any greater distance between the last split shot and the jig will increase tangles when casting.

7. Yet another variation on the theme. A deep-water slip-float rig using a Comal brand three-inch cigar float and size 0

Danielson twist lock sinker. On the hook is an imitation egg cluster from Outlaw Baits. This particular cluster comes in a color very similar to the old fingernail polish pink Oakie Drifter—now that got your attention, didn't it?

8. The Ray's Jig Bobber pictured here is a bait-caster's delight, as this float is HEAVY but buoyant. If you need to reach that seam on the far side of the river, this is the float for you. This bobber has a hollow core to thread the line through for easy rigging, and comes with toothpicks to peg the rig to set depth. Easily adjustable by sliding float up or down line. In recent years, the popularity of pink rubber worms rigged below a float has steadily migrated south from Canada. Featured here is a Seducer 3" Lil Thumper rigged on a jig head. Over the past several seasons, this soft plastic bait has proven very effective for taking steelhead when rigged under a float. It also works well when drift-fished for coho.

Soft Plastics for Steelhead

For well over a decade, savvy steelhead anglers have turned to the soft plastic baits traditionally associated with bass fishing in order to increase their angling success. While some were just looking to add another weapon to their arsenal of steelheading trickery, others began to realize that plastics will sometimes trigger a strike when nothing else seems to work. It all started back in the late 1980s when innovative Canadian fishermen began fishing pink worms under floats with excellent results. Word gradually spread, and these baits are now used virtually anywhere steelhead are found, and for good reason.

Soft plastics are extremely pliable and provide life-like action even in a subtle current. Whether fished under a float, drift-fished, attached to a jig, plunked or even cast and retrieved, plastics will writhe, twist and undulate like a live creature, and, as most steelhead anglers know, old metalhead hates to share his space with other living things. Plastic baits are incredibly versatile and may be used for a variety of angling techniques, such as those listed above. This furthers their appeal because one technique might be more effective than others under certain river conditions.

In recent years, manufacturers have taken note of the demand for quality plastic baits for steelhead angling, and there now exists an endless array of worms, grubs, jigs and imitation roe. Color choices have improved as well, and plastics for steelhead are now easy to find in nearly any shade of pink, red or orange.

Another important aspect of fishing plastics is their novelty. While each passing season sees more fishermen turning to these baits, they are still underutilized compared to other more traditional set-ups, for instance, the venerable Corky and yarn drift-fishing rig. I am a firm believer that steelhead, especially under heavy pressure, will sometimes become accustomed to a certain bait or presentation and after time will not react to it as aggressively, or not at all. This seems particularly true after the fish have been in fresh water for a while and have seen countless baits presented in the same fashion. Every river has its own "local favorites" when it comes to method, colors and rigging, and it only stands to reason that a #12 pearl pink Corky drift-fished on a 32-inch leader by 99% of the fishermen will lose its appeal to the fish after said fish have seen this set-up drift past their snouts hundreds of times over the course of several days. Or maybe, some of the fish eagerly grabbed on to this rig and were pricked before getting loose and have "learned" to stay away from the offending bait. Depending on the scenario, you have a bait that has become either benign and commonplace, or one that the fish may view as dangerous. Each day, a certain number of fish will fall to the go-to technique before the bite seems to fall off. It is here when it pays to be different. Try dead-drifting a six-inch pink worm under a float in this situation and see what happens.

Because none of the other anglers on the river are fishing this technique with this peculiar offering, the whole affair is quite novel to the fish. Because the pink worm is a new type of intruder to the steelhead's lair, and because it is squirming like a live critter, it may trigger a violent reaction when the same old song and dance did not. Another advantage to plastics is that they are soft and squishy, just like something a steelhead may have eaten at one time. Therefore, when the fish grabs the bait, it might hold on longer because it feels natural, thus affording the angler more time to first detect the bite, and secondly, to set the hook.

Technique and Rigging

Probably the most common way to fish a plastic bait is under a float, and this goes back to the method our northern neighbors pioneered on British Columbian streams. There are as many ways to rig soft plastics for float-fishing as there are baits available to try, but the threaded pink worm still rates the most popular when using this technique. Use a darning needle or bait threader to push the leader through the length of the worm, and be sure to rig some sort of bumper between the eye of the hook and the worm to keep the hook from being pulled into the bait and tearing it. A sequin, piece of yarn, puff ball or even a small drift bobber works well for this. When using a drift bobber or puff ball, the buoyancy of the lure serves a dual purpose, helping to float the tail of the worm thus providing a more horizontal presentation to the fish, and therefore a better silhouette. This presentation also allows for improved hook placement as the fish is nearly always hooked in the corner of its mouth as it turns to return to its lie.

There are an insane number of float designs and sizes from which to choose. As a rule of thumb, use the smallest float you can get away with for the conditions at hand. A smaller float will not be pulled downstream as quickly as a larger float, allowing for a more natural delivery. Choosing a float with a thin profile like a Dink, cigar or pear-shaped will also aid in achieving a dead-drift. When fishing "power water" where more weight is needed, it might be necessary to use a larger float to maintain buoyancy and to help visually track it through broken water.

Diagram 1 This illustration shows an Outlaw Baits 5" Ripple Worm rigged under a Rainbow Plastics A-Just-A-Bubble, a fixed float that can be easily adjusted for depth to suit ever-changing conditions. The weight in this system is several split shot crimped to the line in 4- to 5-inch intervals in order to reduce

Diagram 1   Diagram 2   Diagram 3

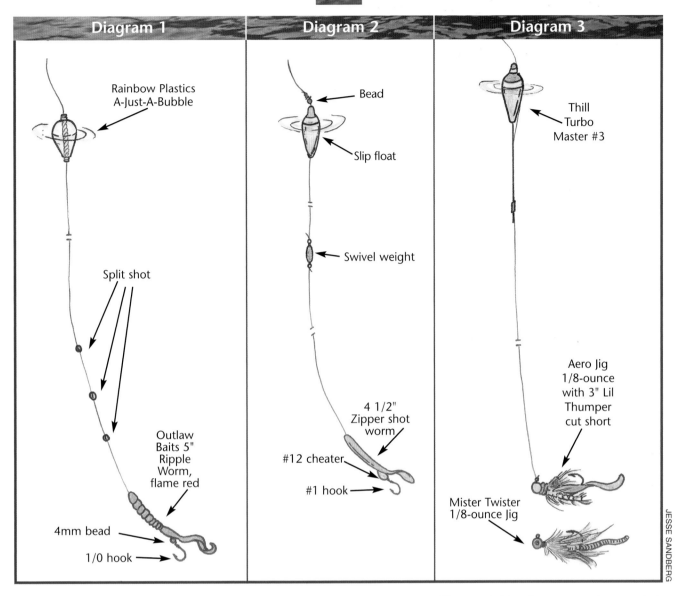

Diagram 1: Rainbow Plastics A-Just-A-Bubble; Split shot; Outlaw Baits 5" Ripple Worm, flame red; 4mm bead; 1/0 hook

Diagram 2: Bead; Slip float; Swivel weight; 4 1/2" Zipper shot worm; #12 cheater; #1 hook

Diagram 3: Thill Turbo Master #3; Aero Jig 1/8-ounce with 3" Lil Thumper cut short; Mister Twister 1/8-ounce Jig

JESSE SANDBERG

tangles when casting. Hook size varies depending on the size of the worm being used and the size of the fish to be encountered, and the 1/0 shown here is a good match for the 5-inch worm.

Begin fishing this rig by casting just upstream of the best holding water so that by the time the float reaches it, the worm has settled to depth and is already squirming in the current as it passes through. It is important to hold as much line off the water as possible when float fishing in order to reduce drag and therefore avoid a bogus presentation, and a longish rod of 9 to 10 1/2 feet will aid in this endeavor. A long rod also helps in mending the line when a downstream belly has formed, an occurrence that will pull the rig down and across the river in a glaringly unnatural presentation. When this happens, all an angler need do is flip the line back upstream of the float in order to maintain the dead-drift. Keep your eyes trained on the bobber so you will know the instant that a fish takes and pulls it under. Usually, a steelhead will hit a pink worm so viciously there is no doubt

what is going on. When the bobber disappears, reel up any slack and set the hook.

Diagram 2 Here is a different type of float set-up employing a slip float from Thill. Slip floats are most often used when fishing deeper steelhead holding water, say eight feet or more, because it becomes difficult to cast a fixed float rig when there is that much line between the float and the worm. Tie a UNI-Knot around the mainline to act as a bobber stop. Cortland Micron braided fly line backing works excellently for this and comes in a bright chartreuse color, making it easy to see the knot under most conditions. Always put a small bead between the float and the bobber stop to keep the knot from getting lodged in the opening on the float. The weight system used here is an Oregon Tackle Bobber Swivel Weight with barrel swivels molded into each end of the weight, which reduces line twist and allows the bait more freedom of movement. The worm pictured here is a 4 1/2-inch Zipper Shot Worm with a widened tail that provides an action all its own.

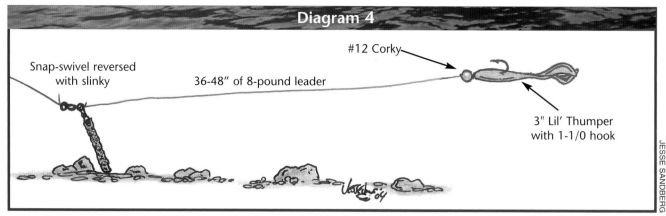

Diagram 4

Snap-swivel reversed
with slinky

36-48" of 8-pound leader

#12 Corky

3" Lil' Thumper
with 1-1/0 hook

JESSE SANDBERG

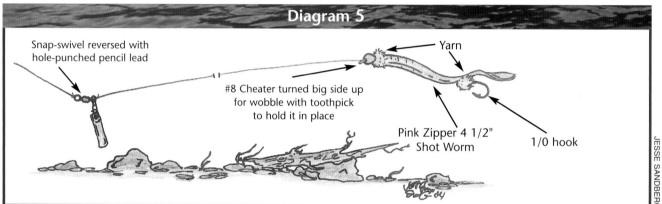

Diagram 5

Snap-swivel reversed with
hole-punched pencil lead

Yarn

#8 Cheater turned big side up
for wobble with toothpick
to hold it in place

Pink Zipper 4 1/2"
Shot Worm

1/0 hook

JESSE SANDBERG

Diagram 3 This illustrates the marriage of two proven steelhead getters to make one fantastic offering. Steelheaders have long realized the effectiveness of float-fishing with jigs, so combining the suppleness of plastics with the attraction of fur and feathers was a no-brainer. The float pictured here is a Thill Turbomaster 3, an awesome float to use with 1/8-ounce jigs and no additional weight. The jig is a 1/8-ounce Aero jig with a 3-inch Seducer Lil' Thumper attached to the hook for added attraction. The Lil' Thumper has a paddle tail that provides a unique swimming action to the jig. Just make sure to cut about a half inch from the head of the worm so that it fits better on the jig hook and lessens the occurrence of short strikes. The lower jig/worm combination is manufactured by Mister Twister and comes ready to fish with the worm already attached.

Under most situations when float-fishing, the desired presentation is that of the dead-drift, which occurs when the set-up is drifting downstream at or near to current speed, as though it isn't tethered to a fishing line. Under some conditions it may be effective to fish a float set-up by using a somewhat different technique. When the water is extremely cold or off-color, it sometimes helps to slow the progress of the rig so that it moves downstream slightly slower than the current, giving fish a better chance to see it in colored water or more time to react to it in colder flows. This is accomplished by applying tension to the line and holding back on the float while feeding just enough line to keep the rig creeping downstream. You'll know when this is happening because the float will tilt upstream, signaling that it is moving slower than the current. By applying this tension to the line, the soft materials in a jig or the curly tail of a worm really come to life, and this may be just what it takes to a get a lethargic steelhead to rise to the jig in 38-degree water.

Diagram 4 While float-fishing is the most common method used to fish plastics for steelhead, anglers have gradually figured out that these baits work well for a variety of techniques, including drift-fishing. Here is a simple rig that employs a Lil' Thumper for drift-fishing. Use a pair of scissors to cut the tail in two so it's split, as this will add more action to the bait as it is swinging through the current. It is also helpful to add a drift bobber in front of the worm in order to provide floatation so the rig remains just off the bottom during the presentation.

Diagram 5 Here is another worm rig set-up for drift-fishing. The #8 Cheater is pegged with a toothpick to keep it against the worm where it belongs. Rigged with the fat end forward like this, the Cheater acts as a baffle and really wobbles as the current pushes against it. This wobbling action is then transmitted to the worm, which drives steelhead crazy. Yarn is attached to both serve as a bumper between the hook and worm and to spruce things up and provide contrast. Because this is a sizeable rig, it works great in green to off-color water because it provides so much visual stimulation, and steelhead are extremely sight oriented.

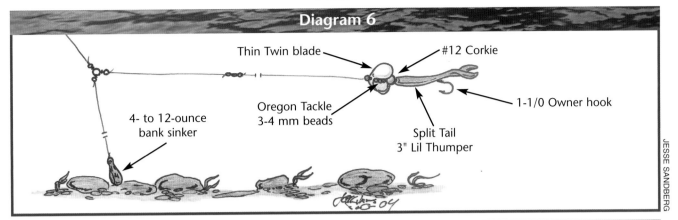

Diagram 6

Thin Twin blade — #12 Corkie

Oregon Tackle
3-4 mm beads

4- to 12-ounce
bank sinker

Split Tail
3" Lil Thumper

1-1/0 Owner hook

JESSE SANDBERG

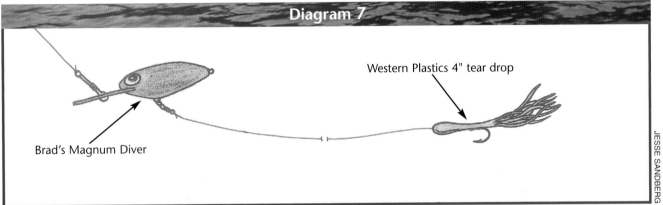

Diagram 7

Western Plastics 4" tear drop

Brad's Magnum Diver

JESSE SANDBERG

Diagram 6 Plunking is another tactic in which anglers have begun to experiment with plastics. Near my home in western Oregon there is a popular area for plunking on the Willamette River called Meldrum Bar. Here, a huge gravel bar extends out into the river and fish follow the edge of it as they migrate upstream to the Clackamas River or some other Willamette tributary. This unique geography brings the fish close to the bank where anglers get a good shot at them as they pass by. It is here where I first saw an angler plunking with a pink worm incorporated in his rig.

The plunking rig pictured here is just one example of the endless variations available to the creative fisherman. The Thin Twin blade from Martin Tackle is a popular, lightweight blade that adds flash to the set-up without weighing it down. Use several beads between the blade and the Corky, which is tied in to add floatation so that the rig stays up where the fish will see it. Pictured here is a Lil' Thumper, but just about any worm can be used when plunking. Plunking is sometimes derided by some anglers as a lesser tactic, but accomplished plunkers are some of the best anglers around, using their vast knowledge of fish movement, travel lanes and tidal affect to pull salmon and steelhead from big water. They are also extremely patient.

Diagram 7 Back-trolling with plugs or a diver-and-bait set-up is a proven technique for catching steelhead, and this is yet another method in which soft plastics can be employed. In this technique, boat anglers let out 40-50' of line, allowing their plugs or diver to dive down to depth while allowing the boat to slowly slip downstream. By doing so, a group of anglers can effectively cover vast amounts of water while their offerings are continuously fishing, and more time in the water usually equates to more fish being caught. The rig pictured here merely substitutes a pink worm—in this case a Western Plastics 4-inch Tear Drop—for the bait. The Brad's Magnum Diver takes the bait down to where the fish are, and the constant wiggle provided by the plug imparts an enticing action to the worm.

As you can see, there are endless ways to utilize soft plastic baits when steelhead angling. Because manufacturers have taken note of the rising popularity of using soft plastics for steelhead, there is now available a vast assortment of these baits suitable for just about any angling method or river conditions. Just make sure to check the regulations for the water you intend to fish, as some states actually consider soft plastics as bait. In the General Regulations for the State of Oregon, for instance, it is stated: "Molded soft plastic or rubber imitation worms, eggs, or other imitation baits are considered bait." So don't head off to the Deschutes with a bag of pink worms, and check other rivers for bait restrictions. Soft plastics are yet another alternative for the fisherman to turn to in timesof need, and their effectiveness makes them deserving of a place in any angler's tackle box.

Low-Water Summer-Steelhead Techniques

A Skamania summer-run nymphed out of "heavy structure" under low-water conditions.

The meager snow pack and below-average rainfall of last winter have left many Northwest waterways flowing unusually low, clear and warm for this time of year. As many anglers learned during the 2004/2005 winter steelhead season, these factors are not exactly optimum for good steelhead angling. But for those anglers who were willing to adapt their tactics to the conditions at hand, some successful days on the water were still realized. The same should ring true for summer-steelhead fishermen who switch from more traditional methods to low-water techniques.

Summer steelhead in low flows behave much differently than they do in higher water. First of all, they get spooky. In water with good color and current, steelhead feel secure because predators can't see them as easily, and therefore they remain aggressive and willing to bite. In low water they may lose this aggressiveness if bothered, or even bolt at the slightest disturbance in their vicinity. I recall fishing one day for summers on

the Collawash River back when it was legal to do so. Getting in position to cover several fish that were holding amongst some boulders in gin-clear water, I was well below the fish where they could not possibly see me. Then, a raven flew overhead and relieved itself upon the water. When the poop plopped, every fish in the hole scattered, when they calmed down and resumed their former lies, they could not be made to bite.

Low stream flows in the summer months usually equate to higher water temperatures, and summer steelhead will hold in different types of water than their winter counterparts. Jim Martin is a retired Chief of Fisheries for ODFW. He is currently the Conservation Director for Pure Fishing, the parent company of Berkley, Fenwick and Abu Garcia, among others. Jim is also a specialist when it comes to catching summer steelhead under tough conditions, and he had this to say about angling for summers in low, clear water: "Where a steelhead holds under low-water conditions is dependent on water temperature. In winter the steelhead may lurk in the deeper holes that chinook often frequent because the depth provides cover and the water has good oxygen content because it is still cold. Under low-water situations in the summer, however, the steelhead will crawl up into the riffles at the top of the holes and runs. Because the water is warmer in the summer it generally holds less oxygen, and steelhead need plenty of oxygen. The choppy surface of riffle water helps infuse more oxygen into the water, and it also provides cover because it is difficult to see the fish.

Jim continues, "Summer steelhead can commonly be found holding in water only two feet deep. They'll nose up into the riffles and hold in the nooks and crannies that provide relief from the fast current. These fish can be aggressive if undisturbed, but will still be spooky due to the shallow, clear water. The biggest mistake I see anglers make in this situation is that they boat into a hole before fishing it. This only spooks the fish into scattering as the boat drifts near to them, moving the fish out of their comfort zone where they might not be as willing to bite. Clanking an aluminum drift boat on rocks as it enters a hole is a sure way to turn previously aggressive fish into non-biters. That's why it's so important to stalk summer fish in skinny water to keep from disturbing them. I'll anchor the drift boat in the tailout upstream of the next riffle I want to fish, then walk down to the head of the next hole. Ideally, you don't want the fish to know you are

present, so approach the fish from below where they can't see you as easily and keep a low profile. Be conscious of where your shadow falls and wear drab-colored clothing—leave that bright red shirt at home!

"Another point I would like to make," continues Jim, "is that adult steelhead holding in riffle water seem to revert back to a juvenile mind-set. Now mind you, I'm speaking here as a fisherman and not a biologist, but juvenile steelhead are riffle fish that spend two, three or even four years in this river environment before heading out to the salt. They share this water with other young steelhead in what becomes a serious fight for survival, because food supplies in any stream are limited, and the young fish must gain as much size as possible while still in the river in order to have a better chance of survival when entering the ocean. That's why I believe adult steelhead returning to this type of water can be extremely aggressive biters despite the seemingly poor angling conditions, as long as the fish remain undisturbed.

"When fishing under such conditions I prefer to float-fish because it provides a natural presentation and I don't have to cast right on top of the fish. I can also use a downstream presentation by standing far enough upstream that the fish can't see me while feeding line into the drift. I use jigs much of the time, but a cocktail shrimp tipped with a Jensen Egg can also be dynamite,

Why a 3-inch-long, bright pink worm works well in clear water is anyone's guess, but the fish love 'em.

Diagrams 1, 2, 3, & 4

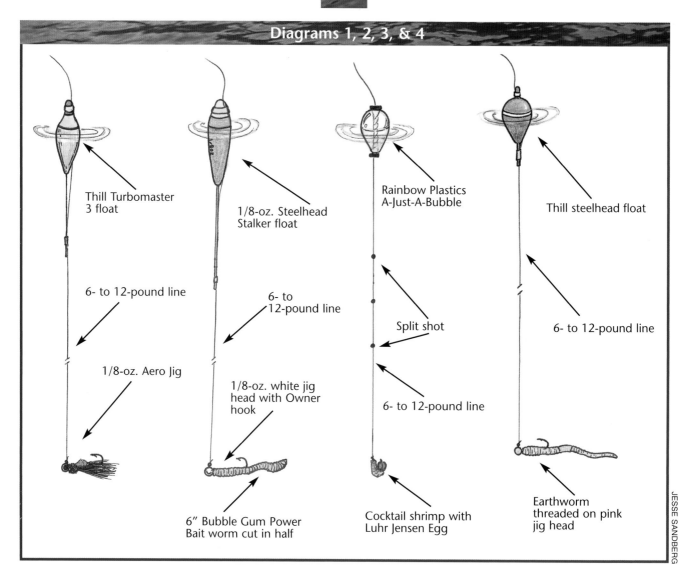

Thill Turbomaster 3 float

6- to 12-pound line

1/8-oz. Aero Jig

1/8-oz. Steelhead Stalker float

6- to 12-pound line

1/8-oz. white jig head with Owner hook

6" Bubble Gum Power Bait worm cut in half

Rainbow Plastics A-Just-A-Bubble

Split shot

6- to 12-pound line

Cocktail shrimp with Luhr Jensen Egg

Thill steelhead float

6- to 12-pound line

Earthworm threaded on pink jig head

JESSE SANDBERG

and earthworms are an excellent bait that remain mostly ignored by Northwest steelheaders. On the Rogue and Klamath rivers in Southern Oregon, wise fishermen commonly use earthworms to catch steelhead, and for good reason. We've all been taught to tone down our gear when fishing low, clear water and to use more natural colors—it doesn't take rocket red in low flow—and what is more natural than a worm? They have natural color and natural scent. Can you imagine a young steelhead allowing a worm to drift through a riffle unmolested? Believe me, many an adult steelhead holding in riffle water will react to a naturally presented earthworm, just as it did as a youngster!"

Diagram 1-4 Thanks Jim, that's all great stuff. Like Jim, I can't stress the importance of sneaking up on the fish under such conditions. Walk softly on cobble to prevent the noise and vibration of rolling rocks (actual rocks, not the beer) from being transmitted to spooky fish in shallow water. Also, leave the drift boat at home and invest in a small inflatable pontoon boat for fishing slim water in the summer months; they're much easier to get

around in and are much more quiet. For some killer float-fishing set-ups refer to Diagrams 1-4.

As Jim mentioned, summer steelhead in low flows often concentrate in riffles because of the oxygen content and cover. Riffles also tend to have slightly cooler temperatures due to the mixing that occurs. But riffles are not the only type of water that summer steelhead will hold in. In fact, some anglers have come to realize that steelhead are inexplicable critters that will sometimes do the opposite of what they're supposed to. I remember floating a certain Willamette Valley stream in high summer with a friend who had never been on that river before. As we launched the boat I told Jason to be on the lookout for fish holding in odd places. Later in the day with the sun beating down on the water, we drifted up to a fish lying tight to the bank in less than a foot of water. The fish was reluctant to bolt because the boat was between it and the safety of deeper water, and did so only when Jason's oar was hanging right over its head. What was this fish doing holding in such an unlikely locale? Closer

Diagram 5 Where to Find Low-Water Steelhead

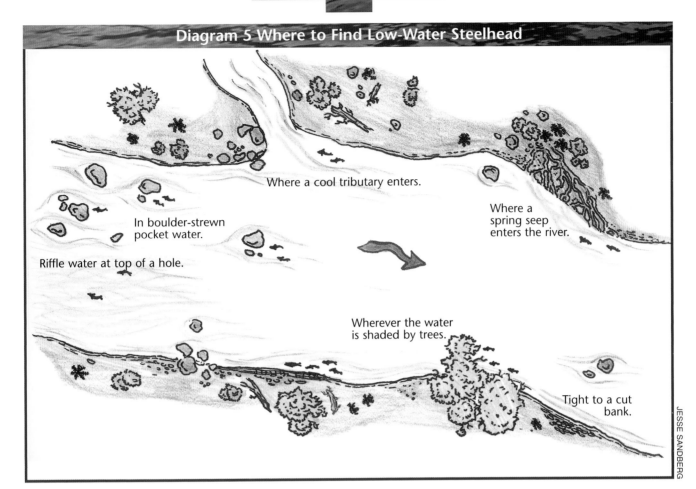

Where a cool tributary enters.

In boulder-strewn pocket water.

Where a spring seep enters the river.

Riffle water at top of a hole.

Wherever the water is shaded by trees.

Tight to a cut bank.

JESSE SANDBERG

examination revealed that the smallest of spring seeps entered the river right where the steelie's head had been, providing cool, oxygenated water under the blazing July sun. Now, I'm not claiming that fish would have been catchable if we had known of its presence and not spooked it, but then again, you never know.

Diagram 5 This illustrates the many types of water where summer steelhead may orient during low, clear flows. At the top of the hole, fish may hold in the riffle water as Jim mentioned earlier. Boulder-strewn pocket water also affords good cover and oxygen content. The current seam created where a cooler tributary enters the river is always a sound place to target fish as well.

Summer steelhead will also hold tight to a cut bank, especially if there is good current, shade and structure present. Sometimes all it takes to attract fish is shade from the hot summer sun. Finally, anywhere a cold spring trickles into the main river will attract fish as well, even if it is only inches deep in that location. Part of the great fun in fishing low-water conditions for summers is spotting the fish before they see you, carefully stalking within casting range without spooking the quarry, then executing a natural presentation that fools the fish. Sight-fishing to clearly visible fish is a challenge held in high regard by many

avid steelheaders. A quality pair of polarized sunglasses is invaluable in this endeavor.

Float-fishing is not the only method used on summer steelhead, but it is perhaps one of the deadliest. In pocket water or runs with good current, drift-fishing can still be effective, especially if you scale down your gear. Tie your rigs with lighter leader or experiment with fluorocarbon material that nearly disappears in water. Use smaller drift bobbers than normal and size your hooks accordingly to maintain buoyancy. A #12 Corky rigged on a 2/0 hook will be an exercise in snagging bottom and tying rigs. Mix things up and don't be afraid to be different. Try plain yarn balls without a drift bobber, drift-fish a Jensen Egg, or, in froggy pools and runs, free-drift a shucked crawdad tail with no weight at all. The latter is a favorite low-water tactic of my father, Ted Campbell, and he's caught a fish or two in his time!

Diagram 6 I've found that fishing hardware in dehydrated rivers is a 50/50 proposition at best, but there are few cooler sights than a 10-pound chromer chasing a spinner across a riffle only to catch up to it right at your feet! In shallow water you will most likely hook a visible fish on the first cast or scare the living hell out of it. Back when we used to fish the Collawash we would often find the fish kegged up in deep plunge pools because this is a mountain river and remains cool enough for the

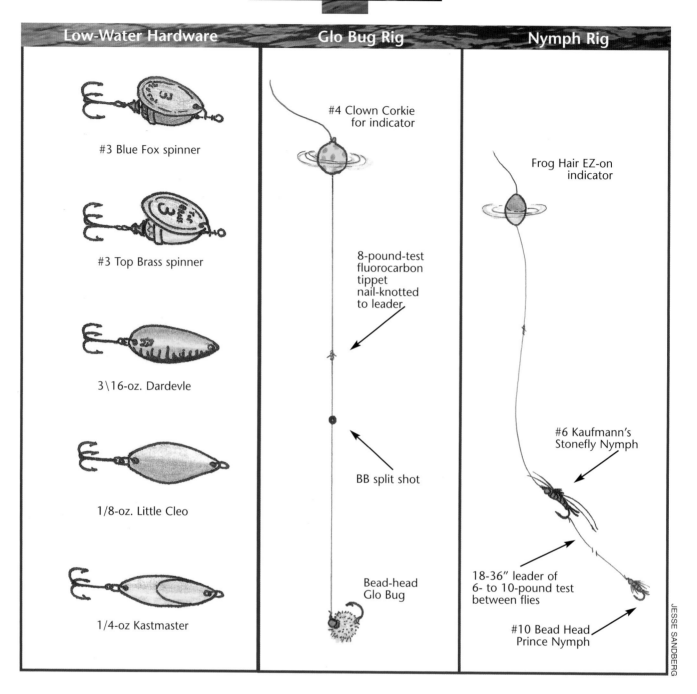

Low-Water Hardware

#3 Blue Fox spinner

#3 Top Brass spinner

3\16-oz. Dardevle

1/8-oz. Little Cleo

1/4-oz Kastmaster

Glo Bug Rig

#4 Clown Corkie
for indicator

8-pound-test
fluorocarbon
tippet
nail-knotted
to leader

BB split shot

Bead-head
Glo Bug

Nymph Rig

Frog Hair EZ-on
indicator

#6 Kaufmann's
Stonefly Nymph

18-36" leader of
6- to 10-pound test
between flies

#10 Bead Head
Prince Nymph

JESSE SANDBERG

fish to use such water. A favorite tactic was to cast and retrieve an 1/8-ounce black Rooster Tail just under the surface in water 10-15 feet deep. If we could see fish in the hole we would keep varying the retrieve until we somehow triggered the fish into striking, and they would rise, rise, rise—all in plain view—to smash our tiny spinners on the surface. We lost a lot of fish due to the wimpy hook on this trout spinner, but it was great fun just to watch such a drama play out. When using hardware in skinny water, just remember that smaller is often better, such as the lures pictured in Diagram 6.

Fly-fishing in low water can often be exciting, too. Swing a traditional hair-wing pattern or a Bunny Leech through riffle water and watch what happens. Often you will see "old ironhead" follow your fly several times before finally pouncing on it. Good stuff. I've also had great luck nymphing smallish bugs in riffles where steelhead ignored the swung fly. I think the effectiveness of this method goes back to what Jim was explaining about steelhead in riffle water exhibiting juvenile fish behavior. Nymphing works extremely well on dour fish that have been around awhile and have seen a lot of other gear, some of it grossly outlandish for clear-water fishing. A single-egg or small nymph pattern is often just the ticket for a fish that has once again adopted a trout-like mindset.

The author used a Fisher Jig to take this Nestucca River summer steelhead under less-than-ideal conditions.

One mistake I've often witnessed streamside is that some anglers use too much additional weight on their nymph rigs. I've found that I get the best results with just one or two BB split shot above a bead-head nymph. Remember, we want a natural presentation here, the bug gliding down the river reacting to every nuance of the current, just like a real bug at the mercy of the river. Too much weight and the whole affair tap, tap, taps along the bottom like a rod tip against sheet metal. We don't necessarily need the fly presented near the bottom like we would for sluggish winter fish; summer steelhead can be quite active in warmer water and will often rise to take a fly or jig, or even a black Rooster Tail near the surface.

I like a longish fly rod for nymphing because it helps mend ridiculous lengths of line and aids in distance casting on big rivers like the Deschutes. My favorite nymphing rod is the G. Loomis FR1206 GLX, which is a ten-foot for a six-weight. Yes, a six-weight for steelhead! Use the proper weight leader (8-10-pound) and you will have no problem subduing even Herculean steelhead on this stick. Last winter I caught my largest-ever fly-caught steelhead, an 18-pound wild hen, and this rod never blinked.

So there you have it, a few tidbits on angling for summer steelhead in thin water under a bright sky. The rest is up to you, folks. And remember, walk softly and carry the right stick. Bonk the amputees and kiss the wild ones adieu before gently releasing.

Trophy Steelheading Revisited

*Robert Kratzer of Anglers Guide Service and Bob Haldermen with a 43.5" X 22.5"
27-pound winter steelhead caught in the Bogachiel River on a jig.*

For most avid steelheaders the pursuit, capture and release of a twenty-pound steelhead is the goal of a lifetime. Some skilled anglers often repeat this rare feat several times in one season, while the rest of us struggle to make it happen at all. Then there's the story of the first-time steelheader who hired a guide and caught two twenty-pounders on his/her first time on the water. Tales such as these are enough to make crazy the life-long steelhead fisherman who has yet to realize the same accomplishment. (Although some would argue that all winter steel-headers are irreversibly insane!)

In thirty-plus years of steelhead fishing Northwest rivers and streams, I have been privileged to see many a trophy steelhead caught and released by fellow anglers. I've even been lucky enough to hook a few myself over the years, but these contests always ended in the fish's favor. When it comes to landing a trophy steelhead, I have been truly vexed by bad luck, bad decisions, bad skills, and probably, bad karma.

More than once I've been spooled by a giant steelhead. When I was nineteen I fought a steelhead for nearly an hour that I estimated to be an honest twenty-five pounds before it managed to saw my leader in two on a basalt ledge. When the leader parted, I slumped to the earth and bawled like a baby. Then there was the twenty-pounder that I had near the surface and nearly bested before it decided to take one last charge at freedom. The fish sliced across the surface, ran headlong into the side of the drift boat and dislodged the Hot Shot from its mouth. No kidding. On March 29th of this year, I had the good fortune to be humiliated by two trophy steelhead in one day. The first fish parted my twelve-pound leader as if it were sewing thread when it jumped and cartwheeled through the air. The second took me around a huge boulder in fast water, then around a stump with a protruding root wad, then got sideways in a rapid as it left the hole and took most of the line from my reel before I intentionally broke it off. Good times. Aside from the trouncing by the two monsters,

Fly-fishing big steelhead water on a coastal stream.
Below: Coastal rivers are a great place
to target trophy steelhead late in the season.

we caught a bunch of steelhead that day, and March 31st found Nick Amato, Mark Laplant and myself too sick to make it to our respective offices. The remedy? Fresh coastal air, rejuvenating rainfall and rowdy native steelhead.

We began the day leap-frogging upriver on the small Oregon coastal stream. Because the river was in prime shape and this was the last day of the season, many anglers passed us on their way to reliable water upstream. This little river has walk-in access only, and by mid-morning we had covered the lower couple miles of stream and caught a few fish. Knowing that there were a bunch of fishermen above us, and likely some more steelhead below us, we decided to turn around and fish our way back to the truck.

Nick and I had lost track of Mark when we stopped on a bridge over the river and scanned the hole below for fish. Nick spotted several in the tailout and I wondered aloud if that was a big steelhead holding in the swift, deep water in the gut of the hole. We were debating whether or not to fish the run again—Nick had already caught and released a chromer there earlier—when a hoot and holler came from directly below us. Mark had inched his way out to the middle of the river on a narrow concrete ledge at the base of the abutment and was now fighting a steelhead from that precarious perch. Nick and I scrambled down to the river and watched Mark skillfully land and release his fish, then the three of us took turns working over the hole.

Big steelhead water.

Nick went through with a float and marabou jig combo, I drift-fished a Corky and yarn and tried floating a pink worm, and Mark showed them his ever-reliable yarn ball—all to no avail. I was kicking myself for once again forgetting my spoon box at home, for the ornery native fish in this river love to smash 'em. I resigned to making one more pass through the hole as Mark and Nick resigned to conversation.

I made a few half-hearted casts and gave up, too. I joined the others. The conversation they were having centered on—what else?—steelheading. Mark is a former Minnesotan transplanted to Oregon who has fished just about everywhere steelhead swim, an admirable trait that he shares with Nick. I decided to slip into shut-up-and-learn-something mode, hoping to glean some useful information from these two masters. As Mark gave an in-depth instructional on proper yarn-balling technique, I gazed up at the alder branches overhead and saw it—there, hanging from a broken line, was a spoon!

I had to have it. The spoon was a good fifteen feet off the ground and I decided the only way to retrieve it was to get a hook through the tip guide of my 9 1/2-foot spinning rod and gently pull it down. Now, this was a gross miss-use of such a fine piece of equipment and both Nick and Mark let me know it. "What are you doing?" asked Nick incredulously.

"You'll break your rod," cautioned Mark.

But I defended my lame-brained actions by muttering something about Bill Herzog, "his book" and catching big steelhead

on spoons. Soon, I had in hand what at first I thought was a SteeLee. It turned out to be a Danielson brand super-deluxe BlackHawk StreamLure Spoon, but a spoon nonetheless. I cut off the 30-pound Maxima that was attached directly to the spoon, added a snap swivel and tied it to the mainline on my fifteen-pound outfit. Next, I took out my file and went to work on the half-rusted stock treble hook. All of this provided much amusement to my counterparts, who seemed to revel in my optimism, or foolishness. Whatever.

On my first cast with the spoon I hooked and landed a ten-inch cutthroat trout, and I distinctly recall someone behind me commenting—without sarcasm, I'm sure—something about spoons catching big fish. Unshaken, I continued casting, and the ridicule continued to rain down. "Wow, look at that presentation," called Mark, "Just like in the book." I continued to cast and step, cast and step. Nick and Mark forgot about me and went back to chatting. As I reached the gut of the hole, I pitched the trusty BlackHawk down and across, allowed it to sink, then tightened up to let it thump through the sweet spot. The take was not extraordinary but it was powerful. The rod tip bent over and stayed there. The fish didn't move. I should have set the hook then, but I didn't. I glanced over my shoulder to see that Nick was eyeing me quizzically, wondering if I really had a fish or if I was just hooked on bottom, messing with him. The rod pulsed with each swipe of the fish's tail, but only the guy holding the rod could know for sure whether it was a fish or a log. I smiled at Nick, for I knew that the serenity of our coastal rainforest setting was about to be shattered.

At first, the big fish stayed down and slowly moved around the hole. Testing. After a few minutes, though, he determined, "Yep, I'm hooked solid, better do something about it," and launched into a series of catapulting jumps that I was certain would tear out the hook or snap the line. Miraculously, they both held. Nick and Mark shouted encouragement as I hung on for dear life. I was higher than Al Pacino in *Scarface*. Who needs cocaine when we have steelhead! Walter raced around the hole and threw the book at me. Several times he went to the lip of the tailout and hung there, threatening to slip into the rapids below. Probably trying to see if he could make a grown man cry. Had he gone over, I likely would have. Walter did figure-eight death rolls and plowed gravel with his snout. Then, he'd jump some more. I wondered, "How can a fish that big jump so high?"

Eventually, Walter began to tire and I began to entertain the thought of actually landing a twenty-pound steelhead. But when I worked him in close and he got a good look at Nick and Mark's faces, he went ballistic all over again. This close-in tug-of-war

Target gnarly water for big steelhead.

lasted an eternity, but everything held. Finally, I lead the brute into the shallows where Mark was able to tail it for me. What a creature! This was a different animal altogether. His sheer size and girth was amazing. The fish was somewhat dark but I didn't care. His head and snout were battle-scarred from fighting the river and other twenty-pound steelhead, but I would never call him ugly. What a day! Good fishing on a pristine coastal stream with good people and a twenty-pounder to boot. Definitely a highlight of my angling career.

Trophy steelhead behave somewhat differently than average size fish so an angler needs to adjust his/her game in order to increase the likelihood of an encounter. Always remember that giant steelhead are extremely rare and should be handled quickly and gently in order to limit mortality. Lee Darby is a highly

successful salmon and steelhead guide who targets winter steelhead on the Oregon Coast. I asked Lee to share some tips on improving our chances of hooking into a monster steelhead.

"The first thing you should do," begins Lee, "is target different water than you would for average fish. Big steelhead like to hang in bigger, faster, heavier water, the type of water chinook like to frequent. Water with a choppy, swirly or boiling surface provides the type of cover big steelhead are drawn to. If there's additional structure in the area such as submerged boulders, even better. My dad was a master at catching trophy steelhead from the East Fork Lewis River, and he'd tell me that to consistently catch the bigger steelhead in a system, you had to target bigger water."

Lee continues, "Looking at the river, fish the same areas for trophy steelhead that you would back-bounce for salmon. But don't back-bounce eggs for steelhead. The last thing you want to do is gut-hook a native trophy steelhead and end up killing it. Same goes for diver and bait combos. These techniques allow the fish to take the bait deeply and should be reserved for fish you intend to legally harvest. I like to drift-fish such water because this technique usually results in the fish being hooked in an area that facilitates a quick release with little or no harm done to the fish.

"In these faster, deeper runs, it may be necessary to use heavier lead to get down to the fish," says Lee. "Also, it may be necessary to cast further upstream than normal to allow your rig more time to sink before the drift begins. When specifically targeting large steelhead, it's advisable to upsize your gear," continues Lee. "Twelve- to fifteen-pound line and leader is not too heavy as long as the water has color to it. In low, clear water it may be necessary to drop down to as light as eight pound test to get a spooky fish to hit, but then you have to cross your fingers and hope for the best if a big one climbs on.

"It's always important to match your gear to the water conditions. Pick a stretch of river and learn where the fish hold at different water levels. I often see anglers who fail to adapt to the conditions at hand. For instance, a guy catches a nice fish from a shallow tailout when the river is high and green. He returns to the river a few days later when it is low and clear and proceeds to pound that tailout all morning. Under these conditions the fish usually hold higher in the hole where increased depth provides more security. You certainly won't find a twenty-pound steelhead holding in a shallow tailout in gin-clear water.

"There are so many variables in steelheading," continues Lee, "that a person needs to be able to put it all together. Steelheading is like a jigsaw puzzle—whether fishing low, medium or high water—you've got to be able to put all of the pieces together to get the big picture. Time spent on the river under varying conditions is the best way to solve the puzzle."

Thanks, Lee. (Lee's Guide Service: (503) 351-0547.)

Diagram 1

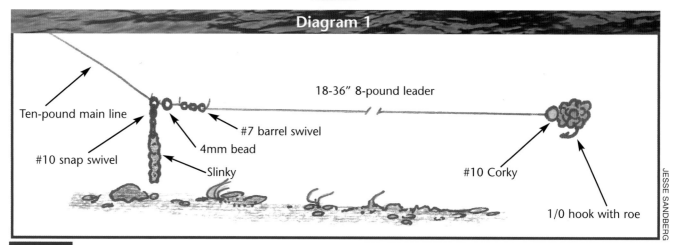

Ten-pound main line

18-36" 8-pound leader

#7 barrel swivel

4mm bead

#10 snap swivel

Slinky

#10 Corky

1/0 hook with roe

JESSE SANDBERG

Diagram 1 Low-water drift rig. This rig is tied on light line and leader to help hook spooky fish in low water. In ultra-clear water, try fluorocarbon material that allows you to use a heavier leader while maintaining invisibility. Sea Guar, Izorline, P Line, Maxima and Umpqua all produce reliable fluorocarbon leader material. In low, slow flows, try rigging the slinky on a snap swivel that slides on the mainline. This aids in detecting a subtle bite in calm water. When targeting trophy steelhead in low water, focus on the fast water at the head of the hole and the deepest water in the hole.

Diagram 2

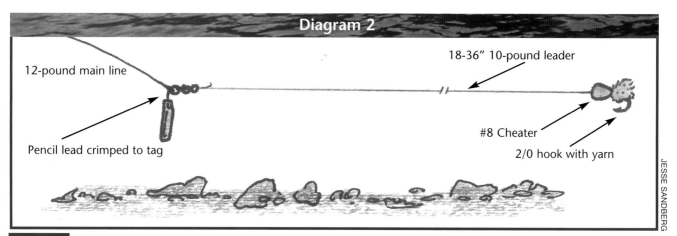

12-pound main line

18-36" 10-pound leader

#8 Cheater

2/0 hook with yarn

Pencil lead crimped to tag

JESSE SANDBERG

Diagram 2 Medium-water drift rig. In this rig, the mainline is tied to the barrel swivel and a long tag end is left to attach hollow-core pencil lead to. Slide the tag into the core of the lead and crimp with needlenose pliers. When fishing water where snagging bottom is common, this allows the angler to gently pull the rig away from the lead. Reel in, attach new lead and you're fishing again. The Cheater is a great drift bobber that wiggles seductively when rigged with the fat end forward and fished in the heavy current big steelhead prefer. For added attraction put a few drops of your favorite scent on the yarn.

Diagram 3

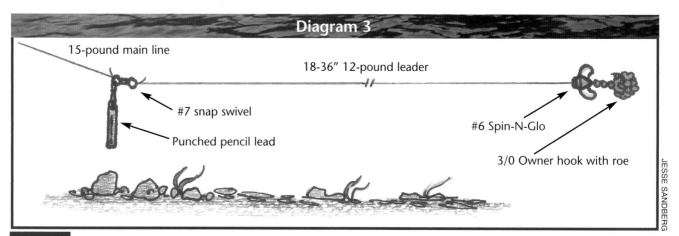

15-pound main line

18-36" 12-pound leader

#7 snap swivel

Punched pencil lead

#6 Spin-N-Glo

3/0 Owner hook with roe

JESSE SANDBERG

Diagram 3 High-water drift rig. Tied on heavier line for fighting big fish in big water. The Spin-N-Glo creates noise and vibration as it spins which may help a big fish to easier locate the offering in colored water. Always use a couple of beads between the Spin-N-Glo and hook so that the drift bobber spins effortlessly and independently of the hook, thus avoiding line twist and a fouled leader.

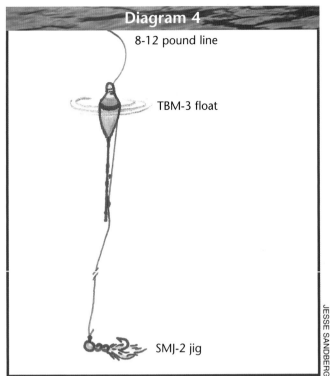

Diagram 4

8-12 pound line

TBM-3 float

SMJ-2 jig

JESSE SANDBERG

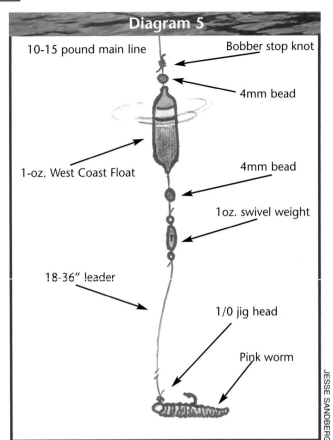

Diagram 5

10-15 pound main line

Bobber stop knot

4mm bead

1-oz. West Coast Float

4mm bead

1oz. swivel weight

18-36" leader

1/0 jig head

Pink worm

JESSE SANDBERG

Diagram 4 Low-flow float and jig rig. The Thill Turbomaster III float pictured here is a favorite among low-water steelheaders because it telegraphs exactly where the jig is at all times. It also slips easily under water when a fish grabs on, which may cause the fish to hold onto the jig a little loner allowing more time for the hook-set. Be careful when adjusting for depth that the end of the wire shaft doesn't abrade your line and therefore weaken it. For this reason, I like the end of the shaft to protrude from the sleeve about 1/16" so that I can be sure it's not chaffing the line. The Beau Mac SMJ-2 is perhaps the best-selling steelhead jig of all time. It has it all: good color combination, hi-vis beads for contrast, undulating marabou and a sharp hook.

Diagram 5 High-water float rig. Here is a float set-up to use in higher flows where more weight is needed to keep your offering down where the fish can see it. This rig also casts better in windy conditions where a light balsa float may not work so well. West Coast Floats are nearly indestructible and slip under easily with little resistance. The Oregon Tackle Swivel Weight kills two birds with one stone.

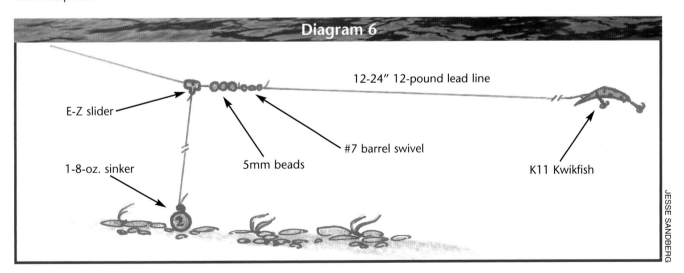

Diagram 6

12-24" 12-pound lead line

E-Z slider

#7 barrel swivel

1-8-oz. sinker

5mm beads

K11 Kwikfish

JESSE SANDBERG

Diagram 6 Lots of trophy steelhead have been caught on plugs, but sometimes it's difficult to get a plug down where the fish are in certain types of water. Borrowing from the salmon angler's playbook, rig the plug with a lead dropper and back-bounce it through the gnarly water at the top of a hole, or drop it down amongst those big boulders that big steelhead like to hold around. Luhr Jensen has recently introduced the new Kwikfish K11, a plug that swims true without tuning and promises to be a good lure to tempt a trophy steelhead.

Side-Drifting Rigs For Steelhead

The author with a big native caught while side-drifting on an Oregon coastal river.

ide-drifting is a term that represents a variety of related angling techniques that share one fundamental element that defines their effectiveness: The extended presentation of a bait, lure or fly on a long, uninterrupted, drag-free drift that maximizes fishing time and increases the odds of a hook-up. On the West Coast, side-drifting from a drift boat is commonly referred to as side-gliding. In this technique, anglers use just enough weight to sink their offerings to the fish but not so much that it constantly dredges the bottom and interrupts the natural drift of the bait. Most commonly practiced on small to medium-sized rivers with snaggy bottoms, properly executed side-gliding minimizes contact with the bottom allowing for a drag-free drift while decreasing hang-ups and break-offs on the river bed.

To begin a side-gliding presentation, the boat handler lines up parallel to the water to be targeted and begins to row or motor the boat downstream at or near current speed. As he does so, the anglers cast out, usually slightly upstream of the boat's

position, and if everything is timed correctly, the baits settle to depth and begin fishing just as the boat reaches the proper speed to maintain an extended drift. Ideally, the baits are gliding along just downstream and to the side of the boat, and the boat is progressing downstream at the exact speed that the baits are. In this fashion, expanses of water can be covered without having to reel in and re-cast. The oarsman then cants the boat toward the baits so he can better monitor their progress downstream. (Refer to Diagram 1) The key to any side-drifting method is proper boat handling to ensure that the craft is moving downstream at the same rate that the baits are. Many novice side-drifters err by always trying to match the boat's speed to that of the surface current. But much of the time the current on top is much faster than it is down where the baits are, and this results in the baits being pulled downstream at an unnatural clip. The best side-drifters I know are always acutely aware of where the baits are by watching the angle of the lines and by having a keen familiarity with the different runs on the rivers they fish.

In side-gliding, it is imperative that all of the rods are rigged the same so that all of the baits drift downstream at the same speed. Reels should all be spooled with the same mainline to ensure consistency. Leader lengths and terminal tackle—right down to the size of the hooks and bait clusters—should all match so they perform the same in the water. It is difficult enough for the boat handler to maintain proper speed in a constantly changing river when all of the rods are rigged the same, and if they are not, side-gliding becomes a hair-pulling exercise in futility.

Experienced side-drifters prefer longish spinning rods in the 9- to 91/2-foot range for several reasons. First of all, spinning gear aids in casting the lighter weights employed in this method, as does a longer rod having a soft tip that loads easily. Also, these longer rods fish with the rod tips further out from the restrictive confines of a drift boat where the oarsman can better see them in order to gauge what the baits are doing and maneuver the boat accordingly. Lastly, long spinning rods with soft tips bend easily when a steelhead climbs on and may afford you an extra second or two to set the hook because the fish doesn't immediately feel the rod, sense something is wrong, and drop the bait. The G. Loomis STR 1141S is a rod designed specifically for side-drifting techniques and remains at the top of its class. Lamiglas, St. Croix, Rogue and Shimano also provide excellent choices in rods.

As with any steelheading technique, reels should be the best quality that you can afford because winter steelhead and winter steelheading conditions will certainly test them. My personal favorite spinning reel for steelhead and light salmon is the Shimano Symmetre 2500. You get great bang for the bucks on

Mike Kostel with a Sandy River chromer caught side-floating.

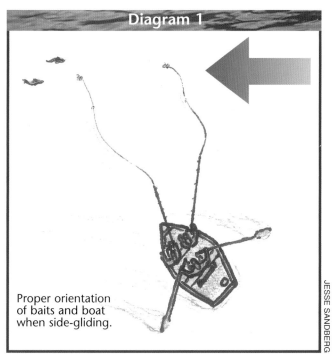

Diagram 1

Proper orientation of baits and boat when side-gliding.

JESSE SANDBERG

this one, folks. The 2500 has good line capacity without being overly heavy, has a strong, smooth drag, and comes with an extra spool. Guide Chris Vertopoulos sold me my first Symmetre back in 1996 when he was selling tackle for Fisherman's Marine and Outdoor in Portland, Oregon. Since then, the reel has been used, misused, abused—and it still works great. There are many other great spinning reels available to the steelheader, just be sure to invest in a quality reel that will provide years of service without failing you while on the water.

When it comes to line for side-drifting everyone has their own preference and there are many excellent options available. Some prefer a soft, limp monofilament with low memory that casts well on spinning reels and is less susceptible to twisting and tangling. Others prefer "harder" lines that have good abrasion resistance to better handle the rigors of your typical steelhead river. High-visibility lines are also popular so the boatman

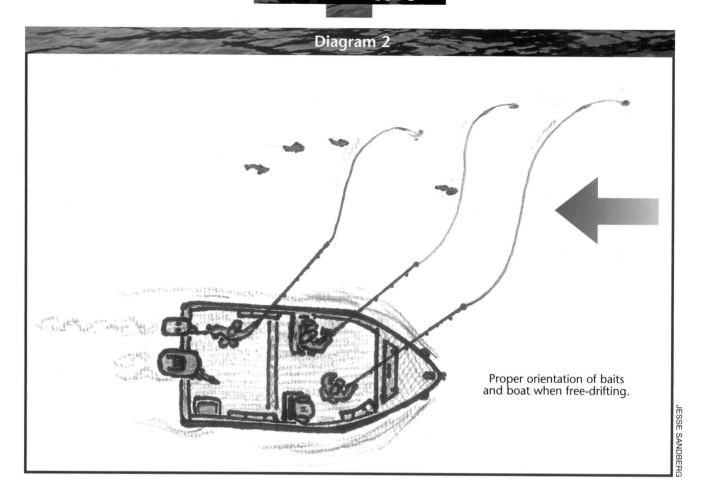

Diagram 2

Proper orientation of baits
and boat when free-drifting.

JESSE SANDBERG

can better track the bait's progress and operate the boat accordingly. Many experienced side-drifters are turning to braided lines for their superior strength. When side-drifting, you can hang up and break off a lot due to the amount of time you are in the water, thus burning through a ton of line. When using thirty-pound braid with eight-pound mono leader, the mainline rarely breaks and your reel stays full and functional all day. Whatever line you choose, just make sure it's the right line for YOU, and that you have extra spools or a back-up reel on hand if needed.

Last fall I was fortunate to join author Gary Lewis for a morning of walk-in coho fishing on the Sandy River. Gary had a good laugh when he saw that I carried an extra baitcasting reel and two extra spinning reel spools in my backpack for only a few hours of fishing, and I admit that this may seem excessive. But I'm a firm believer in the old "stuff" happens axiom, and that if it's going to happen, it's going to happen to me. How many of us ever, aside from Nick Amato, get to go fishing as much as we would like to? It makes sense to me to be geared properly so that you don't get sidelined during the time you do have streamside. Avoid disappointment, carry extra line.

The most popular rigging for side-drifting techniques is undoubtedly cured roe and some form of drift bobber, be it a Corkie, Cheater, Puff Ball, Fish Pill, etc. The drift bobber provides enough buoyancy to float the rig just off the bottom in the strike zone, as long as the egg cluster is sized according to the bobber. Therefore, use small baits. The generally accepted size of the bait is roughly the same diameter of a penny. Veteran side-drifters will tell you that having quality bait is second only to good boat handling for success; just don't expect them to cough up any of their own egg cures without extensive bribery or blackmail. If you are new to steelheading and would like a line on some good commercial egg cures, visit your local tackle store or read Scott Haugen's book, *Egg Cures*.

Don't fall into thinking that eggs are the only good bait to use when side-drifting. Nightcrawlers, sand shrimp tails, cocktail shrimp, crawdad tails, and small chunks of prawn tails work great, too. Personally, I don't often use bait for steelhead unless fishing with a guide or friend who demands it. (Remember, all rods must be rigged the same.) But I am a huge fan of scent, and bottled scents provide most of the allure of bait without the mess and time spent rigging them. Save your cured roe for fall chinook and springers and try one of the many killer scents available. Use a Corkie and yarn rig or plain yarn fly and load up that yarn with scent. The scent travels downstream faster than your rig and alerts the fish that, "Hey, something tasty is coming down the pipe, so be ready!" I'll tip my hand here and say that the best commercial scent I have ever used for steelhead, hands down, is Catcher Company's Sticky Liquid shrimp. The fish go absolutely nuts over it, and when applied to white yarn, turns it the fishiest steelhead peach color you'll ever see, which works great in low, clear water.

As mentioned earlier, side-gliding is but one of many related side-drifting techniques. Another highly effective technique is called free-drifting. This method is usually employed on larger rivers—like Washington's Cowlitz—where anglers use power boats to control the drift of their baits while covering miles of water. In free-drifting, the boat is pointed upstream and backed down river with the baits being positioned upstream and to the side of the boat. (See Diagram 2) I asked Mike Perusse, sales representative for G. Loomis Rods and former Cowlitz River guide, to explain the history of this technique on Northwest rivers.

"You know, the free-drifting thing started way back when I was still roller skating," begins Mike. "Fishermen began 'drift fishing' from their boats but were using the oars to control the boat.

The guys were catching plenty of fish but they still let the boat stay upriver of the baits. Anchoring and pulling plugs was very effective, but the Skagit boys always out-fished us by side-drifting with their 'sticks.' I guess the reason was that they slowed the presentation down to a point that the fish couldn't resist.

"Then came along the 'Sacramento King,' Clancy Holt. Clancy was the one who took a look at this mess and said, 'Why can't I use my kicker motor to keep the boat straight?' I'm sure there were a couple of people out there that were free-drifting by accident," continues Mike, "But Clancy perfected it.

"About the same time, Gary Loomis was looking for a way to hook more summer steelhead on the North Fork of the Lewis River. The river would get skinny and crystal clear so you had to be stealthy to catch fish, so Gary took some of his fly rod blanks and turned them into casting and spinning rods. What he found out was these rods fished much better with lighter gear and you could have ten times the amount of fun with way more hook-ups. So you take those two guys and put their ideas together and come

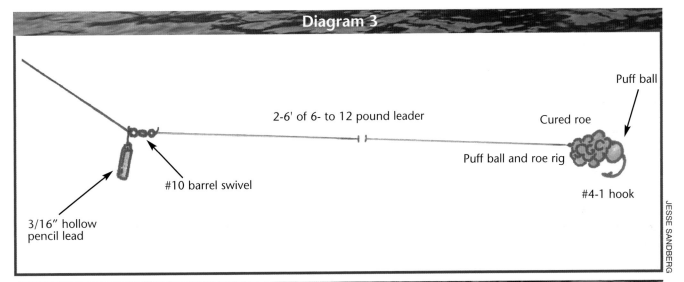

Diagram 3

2-6' of 6- to 12 pound leader

Cured roe

Puff ball

Puff ball and roe rig

#4-1 hook

#10 barrel swivel

3/16" hollow pencil lead

JESSE SANDBERG

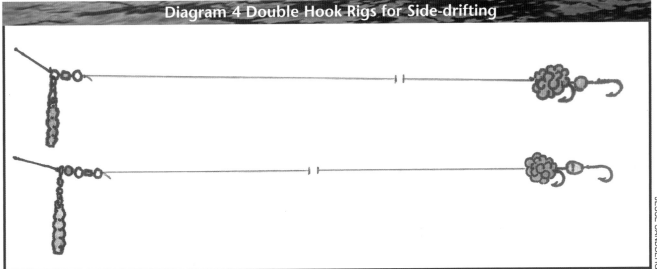

Diagram 4 Double Hook Rigs for Side-drifting

JESSE SANDBERG

Diagram 5 Corky and Yarn Rig for Side-Drifting

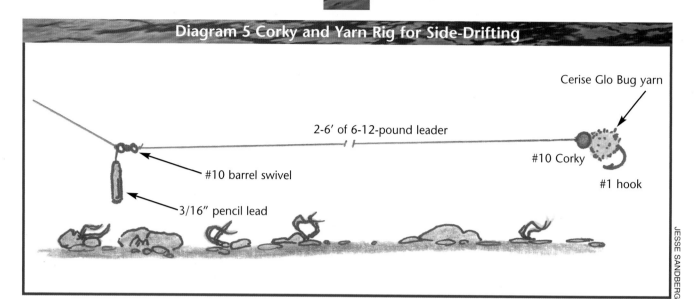

Cerise Glo Bug yarn

2-6' of 6-12-pound leader

#10 barrel swivel

#10 Corky

#1 hook

3/16" pencil lead

JESSE SANDBERG

Diagram 6

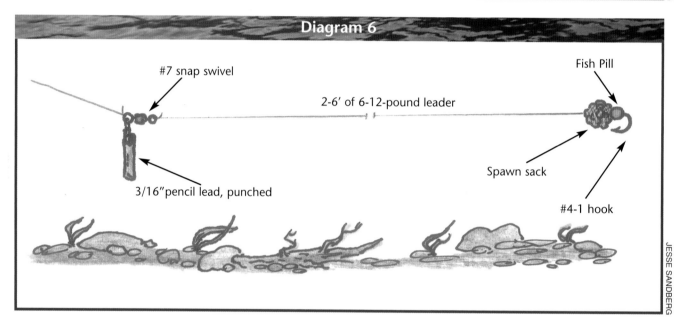

#7 snap swivel

Fish Pill

2-6' of 6-12-pound leader

3/16"pencil lead, punched

Spawn sack

#4-1 hook

JESSE SANDBERG

Diagram 7 Pink Worm Rig

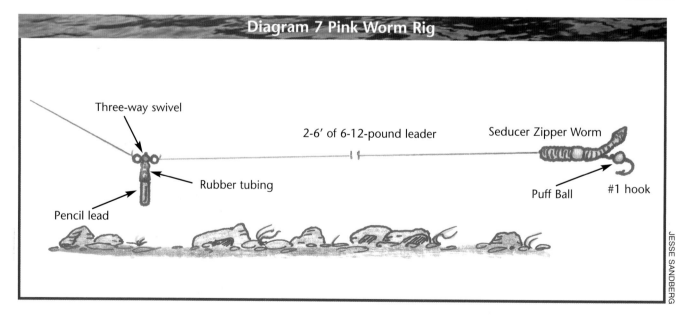

Three-way swivel

2-6' of 6-12-pound leader

Seducer Zipper Worm

Rubber tubing

Puff Ball

#1 hook

Pencil lead

JESSE SANDBERG

Mike Kostel of White's Outdoor in Spokane, Washington shows off a nice hen that fell for side-drifted roe.

up with the STR 1141S and free-drifting." Thanks Mike. For a more detailed examination of free-drifting technique, check out the DVD "Side-drifting for steelhead," hosted by Nick Amato, Mike Perusse and Travis Price.

While side-drifting techniques are mostly employed by boat anglers, it is by no means impossible for bank anglers to cash in on the effectiveness of this presentation. Find a long run with a cobble or sandy bank, cast out the properly weighted rig, and walk downstream keeping pace with the bait. Side-walking, or "walking the dog" as we call it, can be just as effective as side-drifting from a boat. Just be courteous of other anglers and don't try this technique at a crowded hole. Side-floating involves using a float and jig or bobber and bait combination to accomplish the same extended, drag-free drift. When fishing from a boat, anglers can use a float set-up to cover tons of water by fishing upstream, downstream or to either side of the boat without tangling lines. A friend of mine calls this technique "boon-bobbering." Also, don't be afraid to try alternative offerings when side-drifting such as flies, pink worms or yarn balls.

Side-drifting techniques seem somewhat simple on paper but have many nuances that take time and practice to master. Preparedness and organization are essential to success when rapidly moving with the river. Rods and rigs should be pre-tied and at the ready. Hook-setting is a much debated topic by side-drifting experts. Some say that you should never set the hook when side-drifting, some say you should pause and hit the fish only after it has turned away from the boat, and some say you should set the hook if a fish even looks at your bait. I'll leave it to you to decide who's right. Side-drifting is a method that takes up a lot of space on the river and can interfere with other anglers using different techniques if proper river etiquette is not observed. When side-drifting, give bank anglers the right-of-way. Power boats should always yield to drift boats. Don't cut off a boat pulling plugs and fish through the water directly below it; wait your turn. When in doubt, ask. It's amazing how many conflicts can be avoided by using common courtesy and communicating with your fellow anglers. Who knows, you may even end up making a friend or two.

Plug-Fishing Alternatives

Classic plug water on the Sandy River. Unfortunately, regulations prohibit fishing from a boat on this section of the river. No worries. Put to shore and try swinging a plug through such water.

Back-trolling plugs was one of the earliest techniques developed for consistently catching steelhead on rivers across the West. In fact, during the early days of steelheading, anglers who weren't flinging feathers basically had two established methods to choose from—pulling plugs or drift-fishing. As pioneers like Buzz Ramsey and Bob Toman experimented with

Diagram 1 Casting & Retrieving Plugs from a Boat

JESSE SANDBERG

Diagram 2 Swinging a Plug on a Broad Flat

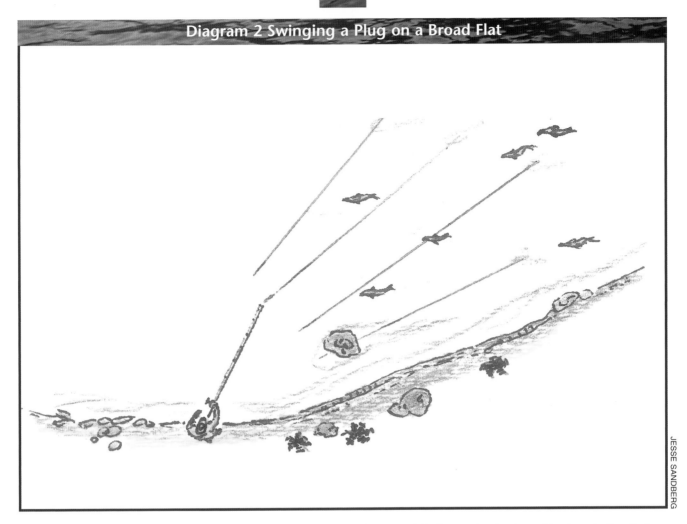

JESSE SANDBERG

back-trolling plugs and tweaked the lures to perform better, the efficacy of this technique became apparent to many fishermen, and, by the mid 1970's, the plug-fishing craze was full-blown.

Back-trolling plugs is an effective technique for many reasons. First of all, it allows a group of anglers to cover vast reaches of water and fish through all of the potential holding areas in a given stretch. Under varying river conditions, steelhead will hold or rest in certain locations that appeal to them because the current is just right and there is cover nearby in the form of a logjam, boulders, undercut bank, drop-off, etc. Because these "lies" may be somewhat limited in number in the typical steelhead river, competition for them can be fierce. A steelhead that has taken up a particular lie becomes territorial and defends its area from intruders, mainly other steelhead, trout, leafs, twigs or any other item that drifts into its area and doesn't seem too formidable to attack.

Your typical steelhead plug is designed to look alive in the water. Backing such a miniscule threat into a known steelhead lie where a defensive fish is already on guard will likely elicit a violent response from the fish. Back-trolling provides a presentation that keeps the lure in front of the fish for extended periods

of time, and the longer the plug is working in a steelhead's face, the better chance there is of triggering a strike. Once a steelhead has been in the river awhile it may become accustomed to the constant parade of baits, jigs and lures passing through its lair and may no longer view these items as threats. But hanging a slow-moving plug in front of a steelhead and keeping it there may result in a strike from a fish that may not have responded to another method. While most steelhead plugs were undoubtedly developed with back-trolling as their intended means of employ, it stands that most plugs are versatile lures that may be utilized for a variety of angling techniques. Let's investigate some alternative methods for fishing plugs for steelhead.

While some steelhead plugs, like the Hot Shot 30, may be too light to cast effectively on typical steelhead gear, others are weighted well enough to cast and retrieve. When fishing from a boat, an angler can cast and retrieve a plug to fish water that can't be covered by back-trolling. There are some areas on the typical river where a drift boat or sled just can't go—at least not safely—and these are great places to cover by casting and retrieving plugs. Try pitching a plug up under overhanging brush and crank the reel to make the plug dive down to depth. A

Diagram 3 Swinging a Plug Through a Narrow Slot

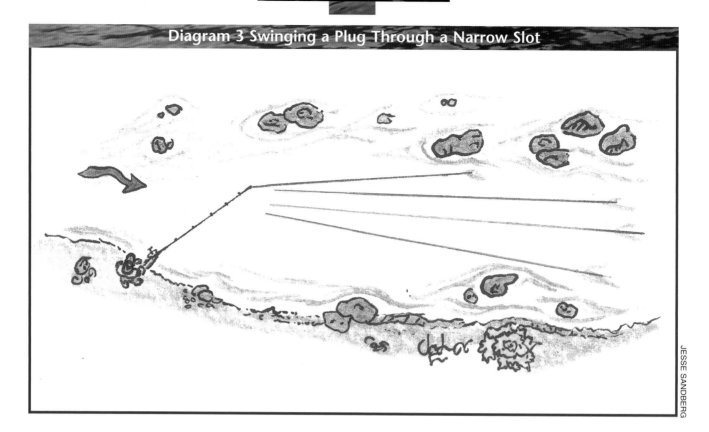

JESSE SANDBERG

favorite spot of mine to target is anywhere a western red cedar hangs over a slot that's 3 to 5 feet deep. In my experience, cedar trees seem to attract steelhead; perhaps it's the pleasant aroma!

Try casting plugs to any other tight spot where it isn't safe or realistic to reach the fish by back-trolling. Pockets behind the many boulders that make up a rock garden are also excellent places to try, as is the seam behind a log jam or root wad. When the water is low and clear and steelhead stack up in deep, chinook-type water with minimal current, try anchoring and casting downstream, then slowly retrieve a deep-diving plug through the holding fish. This can be a great way to surprise a lethargic steelhead into striking and can also be an effective technique for taking silvers and kings under the right conditions. Good plugs to use for casting and retrieving include the Heddon Tadpolly, Storm Wiggle Wart, Worden's Fatfish, Norman Sand Shrimp, and Luhr Jensen Hot Shot S.E.

Casting and swinging plugs is a method that can be used with great success to cover tons of water and coax active steelhead into smashing your lure. This method borrows from fly-fishing's classic down-and-across swing. Begin by casting the lure downstream at an angle, then merely let the plug dive and swing across the potential holding water. The speed of the current will dictate how far down to place your lure, and the faster the flow, the farther downstream you will want to cast in order to control the speed of the swing. Ideally, you want the plug to swing through the holding water as slowly as possible so that a steelhead

views the plug as an intruder, not just a passerby. In moderate to faster flows it may be necessary to lead the plug with your rod tip to keep a downstream belly from forming in the line and speeding up the plug's progress due to drag. In slower water, you may want to do the exact opposite and allow a belly to form to speed up the lure and allow it to dive better. Because a swinging plug is moving through a steelhead lie at a fairly good clip, this technique works best in warmer water temperatures where a steelhead is more likely to follow or chase down your lure. Swinging plugs is the go-to method for summer steelhead on Oregon's Deschutes River, but for winter fish this works best when the water temperature is forty-five degrees or warmer.

"Feeding" plugs to fish is a method I began using as a kid fishing small western Oregon streams for cutthroat trout. The idea was to place yourself upstream of a fishy-looking spot and allow an F4 Frog Flatfish to slowly work into the strike zone. This was a highly effective technique for catching the biggest, most territorial trout in the stream, and it wasn't long before I started applying the same principle to steelheading.

On really small steelhead streams, it may not even be necessary to get your feet wet in order to properly feed a plug to the fish. Merely hold the rod out over the current and allow the line to slowly slip from the reel so the plug is gradually working through the best water just as it would be if you were back-trolling from a boat. Baitcasting reels work best for this method because you can leave the reel in free-spool and use your thumb to control

Diagram 4 Feeding a Plug on a Small Stream

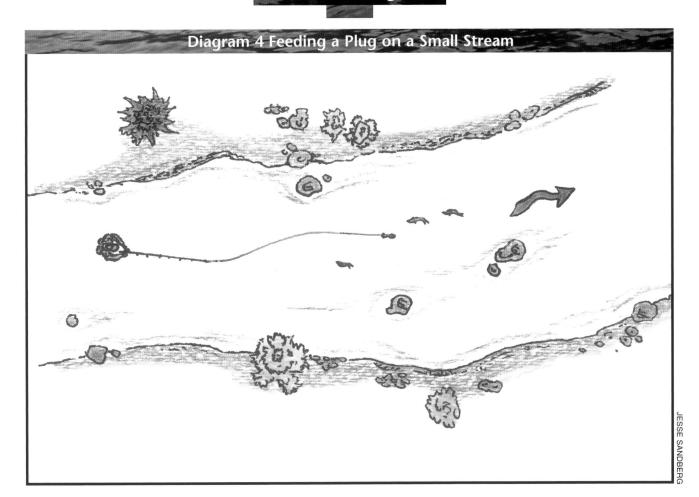

JESSE SANDBERG

Diagram 5 Feeding a Plug from a Strategic Location

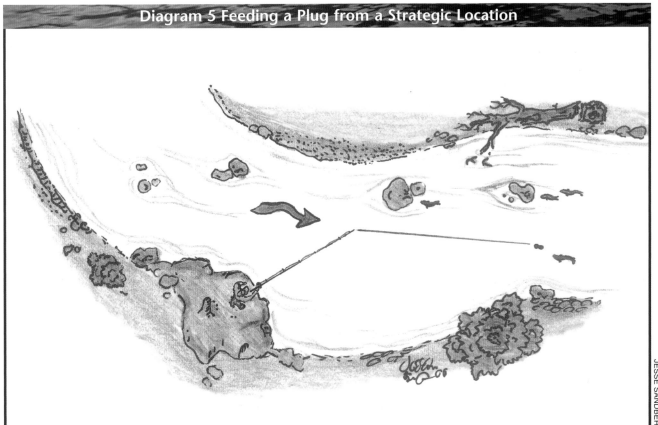

JESSE SANDBERG

the smooth release of the line. Just don't be caught off guard when a fish strikes or you will experience a backlash like no other.

On small to medium rivers it may be possible to wade out at the top of a hole and feed a plug down into the holding water, especially if a run begins with a classic riffle at the top end. As you remain stationary and feed line into the presentation, you can stop the plug and let it hang in a particularly sweet looking spot in hopes of aggravating a steelhead into climbing on. Another effective trick is to slowly sweep your rod tip from one side of your body to the other, allowing the plug to swing from one side of a slot to another and covering the most water possible. Think about it. If using an 8 1/2-foot rod, an angler can cover a 17-foot swath of water by holding the rod tip to either side. By extending his/her arms several more feet of water can be covered. That's a lot of water to be fished by standing in one place.

By being observant and creative, the shore-bound angler can feed plugs to steelhead in a variety of situations just as effectively as a boater may back-troll them. On big rivers, look for geological features or a river contour that positions you above good water where all you have to do is release line and let the plug work down to the fish. I know of just such a spot on the lower Deschutes where a chunk of basalt juts into the river directly above a stretch of good steelhead water along an otherwise impenetrable, brushy bank. Over the years I've hooked plenty of

fish in this spot by feeding a metallic green size-30 Hot Shot down under the trees. Look for places you can access by wading or rock-hopping, and pay attention to bends in the river that may allow you to wade out and feed a plug down the inside seam. Boat anglers can use this method to fish behind boulders and other restricted confines where it may not be possible to place the boat.

Another tactic that allows the shore-bound angler to fish plugs requires the use of a clever gadget created by Luhr Jensen Company of Hood River, Oregon. The Hot Shot Side Planer is a device that attaches 20-40' above the plug and planes away from the angler out into the stream so that a plug may basically be back-trolled down through a run. This allows the bank angler to present a plug just as a boater would by reaching water he/she wouldn't otherwise be able to and by keeping the lure fishing that water in an extended presentation. By reeling in or letting out line, or by slowly walking downstream, the angler can manipulate this set-up to cover water as far as 100' from the bank. When a fish grabs on and you set the hook, a trip mechanism allows the planer to slide down the line to the barrel swivel so you can fight the fish and land it. When using a Side Planer, try to keep the line between the device and your rod tip out of the water to minimize drag.

Bank anglers can sometimes clean-up on steelhead by using a Side Planer with a plug on rivers where angling from a boat is

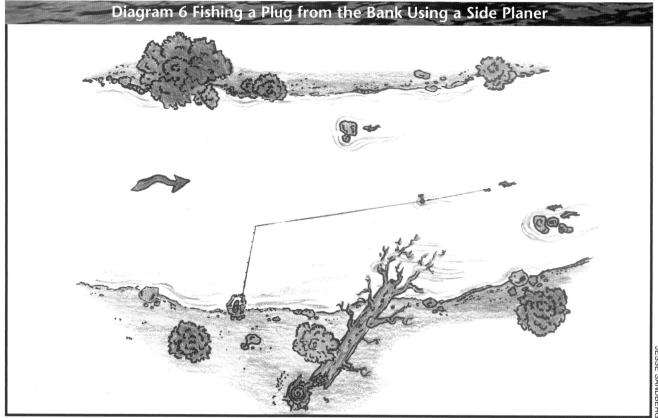

Diagram 6 Fishing a Plug from the Bank Using a Side Planer

JESSE SANDBERG

Bill Mathews teamed up with Bob Toman to catch this Deschutes summer steelhead by swinging a plug from the bank.

not allowed. This can also be a great tactic to try on holes that get pounded by the masses. Wait until the crowds have gone home after the bite has died, then run a plug through the hole where everyone was drift-fishing and see what happens. Don't try this technique under crowded situations as it requires a lot of room to execute properly. When in doubt ask your neighbor if he minds if you try the method; he may want to try it too.

Back-bouncing is a technique usually associated with fishing bait for chinook, but under certain situations lends itself well to steelhead plug fishing. Targeting fish around heavy structure where pinpoint accuracy of presentation is one place. You can use heavy weights to slow down the presentation in heavy water and have better control and placement around boulders, ledges and submerged logs. When fishing for trophy steelhead, back-bouncing a plug will allow an angler to more effectively fish the deep, roily water that big steelhead favor. Just don't use bait to back-bounce for steelhead where wild fish are prevalent, as this may result in deeply hooked fish that have little chance of surviving.

While back-trolling is still the preferred method for fishing plugs, it is not the only one that will bring fish to the net. Try any of the aforementioned techniques under the right circumstances and you may discover the versatility of these lures.

Plug Tuning and Maintenance According to Bob Toman

Few anglers have spent as much time on the water chasing salmon and steelhead as professional guide Bob Toman. Bob began guiding on Northwest waters in 1968 and has worked hard at it since. Although Mr. Toman will use bait to coax a bite when he feels it necessary, he is truly a diehard lure fisherman. "I consider catching fish on lures a purer form of trickery," he explains. Over the years Bob has been involved in the research, design and development of some of the tackle industry's most effective salmon and steelhead lures.

A tireless experimenter, Bob never relaxes from altering and tinkering with a lure until he feels that the action is just right for the fishing conditions at hand. Bob's laboratory consists of the Northwest's greatest salmon and steelhead rivers and estuaries, and his experimentation often results in the design of a proven fish-getter like the Bob Toman line of spinners available from Worden's Lures. Another dividend of his work with lures is the vast number of satisfied clients who return to fish with him time and again, as well as the incredible streaks of success he's had, like the time he went 596 consecutive trips landing at least one fish for his clients.

In March of this year I was fortunate to be invited onto Bob's boat for a lesson on tuning, maintaining and fishing plugs for steelhead. In just a few hours of schooling I learned a ton about fishing plugs and how the slightest alteration of a plug

Here's Bob Toman in September, 1968, his first year as a guide. Bob began his summer at the Babine River Resort mowing lawns and doing maintenance for former owner, Bob Wickwire. By summer's end he was guiding clients into fish like these two giant steelhead. A five-year-old Judd Wickwire lends Bob a hand.

A six-year-old Bob Toman displays his third steelhead in what was the beginning of a great angling career. "When this photo was taken," says Bob, "I had just graduated to a big stick! I learned in a hurry that when fishing with this kind of gear, when you hooked a fish, there was a helluva lot of splashing going on!"

can make a huge difference in its action. Subtle changes in hook size, fasteners and orientation of hook hangers had a huge effect on how a plug behaved in the water, and therefore, how the fish reacted to it. I asked Bob to share some general tips on tuning plugs to catch more fish and he agreed to do so.

"First of all," Bob explains, "tuning a plug isn't merely making a lure go straight through the water. Tuning is the act of altering a plug to achieve the best action for that lure under the conditions present at a given time. Some plugs have good action and fish well right out of the package, but others need to be changed—or tuned—to achieve better results. What I'm looking for in a plug's action for salmon and steelhead is a somewhat

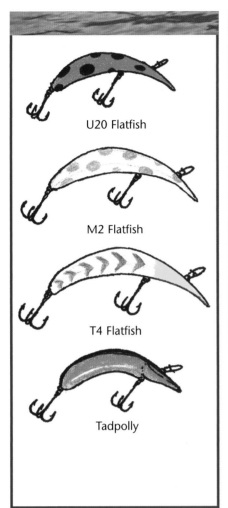

U20 Flatfish

M2 Flatfish

T4 Flatfish

Tadpolly

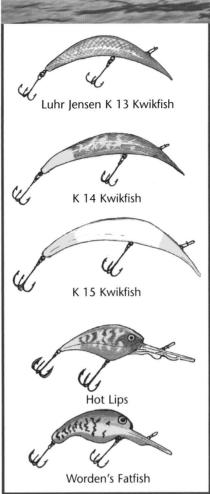

Luhr Jensen K 13 Kwikfish

K 14 Kwikfish

K 15 Kwikfish

Hot Lips

Worden's Fatfish

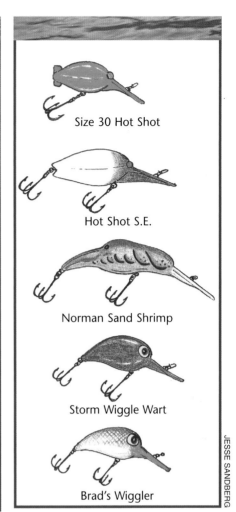

Size 30 Hot Shot

Hot Shot S.E.

Norman Sand Shrimp

Storm Wiggle Wart

Brad's Wiggler

JESSE SANDBERG

wide wiggle where the lure tracks true but occasionally darts from side to side in what bass fishermen refer to as a 'hunting' action. In my experience, lures that have a tight wiggle out of the package have more of a bass action and are not as effective on Northwest salmon and steelhead.

"I have found," continues Bob, "that salmon and steelhead respond best to the vibration created by a plug having a wider action. A plug tuned to vibrate approximately 120 times per minute, as shown by the vibrating rod tip, is usually extremely effective on salmon and steelhead. It's also important to remember that there is no single plug or action that works great under ALL conditions, so it's important to keep experimenting and mixing things up to see what the fish want. On my home river, the Clackamas, spring chinook seem to favor a different plug type and color every year. One year they may prefer a metallic blue Wiggle Wart, another year it may be the Green Pirate Hot Shot, and in another a Worden's T4 Flatfish in gold.

"There are several steps to effectively tuning a plug. Before you put the plug in the water to check its action, examine the hooks. Most treble hooks are constructed by welding a single

shank to the double shank that has the eye on it. If not attached properly, this slight variance in weight distribution can cause the lure to pull to one side. On plugs that have more than one treble hook, I make sure that the welded shank on one hook is on the opposite side of the lure from the other. This counterbalances the plug and helps it run straighter.

"Hook selection is a very important aspect of tuning a plug because hook size and how they are attached to the lure have a big impact on the action of the plug," continues Bob. "Hooks are like the tail on a kite. A kite's tail controls the action of the kite in different types of wind, and hooks do the same for a plug in different types of water. In varying current speeds, it is necessary to change the hook size and sometimes the way they are attached to the lure in order to attain the best action for the plug you are using. Bigger hooks slow down the action in heavy water and stabilize the lure so it doesn't wash out. Conversely, smaller hooks don't overweight a plug in lighter flows and allow the lure to move more freely in less current.

"A good example of this aspect of plug tuning can be exhibited by the way I rig the old Storm half-ounce Wiggle Wart for

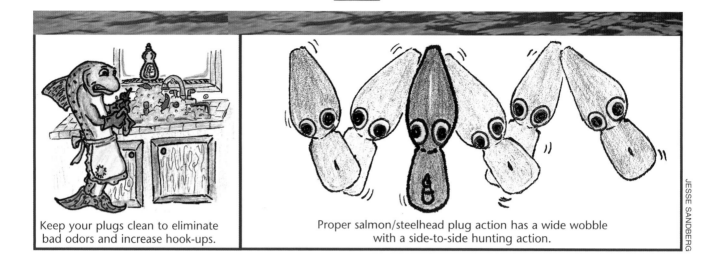

Keep your plugs clean to eliminate bad odors and increase hook-ups.

Proper salmon/steelhead plug action has a wide wobble with a side-to-side hunting action.

JESSE SANDBERG

varying water conditions. In heavy flows—what I would call ten-ounce water—I rig the plug with two #2 VMC treble hooks. In medium current I'll hang a single #3 treble from the tail and leave the belly hook off. Then, in more moderate flows like typical steelhead holding water, I'll use two #4 trebles so the plug has the action I expect the fish to respond to.

"The next thing to look at when tuning a plug," states Mr. Toman, "is the point where the line attaches to the lure. This is really the key to the whole lure. I always use a duo-lock snap to attach my lure to the line because it has a rounded snap that allows the plug to move freely. A swivel with a pointed snap doesn't allow the plug the same freedom of movement. Next, I never attach a barrel or bead-chain swivel directly to the lure, instead, I tie it four to six feet above the plug where it still reduces line twist, but doesn't negatively affect the action of the lure. Before putting the plug in the water, make sure the eye on the plug is straight.

"Now we're ready to check the plug's action in the water. Select a spot on the river that has current similar in speed to that of the location you intend to fish. The water you choose should have a steady, even current so you can properly view the plug's action. You don't want to check the plug's action in a boil or swirl, because this type of water is going to make the plug behave erratically anyway and you will have no idea whether it is tuned correctly." Bob continues, "Lower the plug into the water next to the boat and just let it sit for a moment so it begins working. Once the lure is wobbling and starting to dig, use the rod to pull the lure steadily upstream to see if it pulls to one side or washes out. If it does, adjust the eye of the plug to make it swim straight. Turn or bend the eye in the direction you want the plug to travel. Change out the hooks if necessary to achieve the action you want. Now your plug is tuned and you're ready to catch fish.

"Remember that the current is always changing in a river and that you may have to tune your plugs for different water types. If the current changes through a hole, as it often does, tune the plugs according to the water where the fish are holding or where you expect them to be caught, whether it be at the head of the hole, the gut, or the tail-out. Also, try to devise a system of consistency when tuning plugs so you always know what to expect when altering a plug. Use the same size snaps, split rings, hooks, etc. so that the changes you make are consistent on each plug you tune. And don't forget the role that your line plays in your plug's action. Most of the time we don't want our plugs diving down to where they're smashing into the rocks as this presentation rarely elicits the best response from the fish. Therefore, use line that is heavy enough to provide the lift necessary to keep the plugs up where the fish can see them. In a situation where you want a plug to dive deeper you obviously want to use a thinner line that cuts through the water allowing the plug to reach maximum depth. Also, you'll want to match the diameter of the line to the size and action of the lure. For instance, a #50 Hot Shot rigged on a stiff twenty-pound monofilament line doesn't provide the best action for that lure; use lighter line for smaller lures to allow freer movement."

The next aspect of plug fishing that we will explore is referred to by Mr. Toman as "plug maintenance." Before I got to know Bob and before he began teaching me different aspects of plug fishing, I thought I had a fairly good grasp of what it takes to catch a salmon or steelhead on a plug: Choose a plug type and color that suits both the fish and water type I'll be fishing, be on the river when it's in good shape and the fish are present, back-troll a tuned plug through the sweet spot and Slammola, fish on! Seems like a fairly straightforward technique, right? Wrong! According to Bob there are many facets to plug fishing that go ignored by the vast majority of salmon

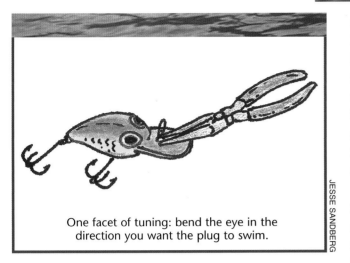

One facet of tuning: bend the eye in the direction you want the plug to swim.

JESSE SANDBERG

and steelhead anglers, and it is these very small, seemingly unimportant details that set Bob apart from most other plug fishermen. When Bob first began sharing these details with me I was somewhat defiant in my acceptance of them, and I would argue that I had never done this or that before and still seemed to catch some fish. But then Bob would smirk and reply, "Yes, I'm sure you did, Robert, but just think how many fish you could have caught!"

Plug maintenance is nothing more than paying attention to all of the details that could result in more success when plug fishing, and Bob has agreed to share a few points on this particular aspect of fishing for salmon and steelhead with plugs.

"The two most important facets of plug maintenance are proper plug action and proper color," begins Mr. Toman. "You can have the correct action on a plug but the wrong color and not do so well. Color selection can be made according to experience, experimentation, watching what other anglers are using or researching effective colors for a particular fishery. If you know you have the correct color for a fishery but aren't catching, then tweak and tune the lure. Once I have determined that I have the right color and action for a given situation, I feel that ALL of the plugs of that color should fish, not just the "sweet" one that I caught fish on yesterday, which brings me to another aspect of maintenance.

"When you catch a salmon or steelhead on a plug, something happens to the plug—I don't know what exactly—but I feel that the fish give off a scent or pheromone that gets on the plug and begins to repel fish. That's why it's so important to continually clean your lures. I typically start each day fishing with at least one brand-new lure and several that have been cleaned. On the brand-new lure that doesn't have any bad scent on it, I always land the first two fish that hit it because they do so with authority because the color and action are

right, and there is no bad smell present to repel them. However, I usually lose or miss the third and fourth fish that hit because now there is bad scent on the lure and they don't take it with the same enthusiasm as the first two. If I continue to fish the plug without washing it, soon the fish are just half-heartedly mouthing and nipping at the plug because they're still attracted by the color and action, but are turned-off by the bad odors. If I then bring the plug in and wash it, the next fish once again slams it with authority and is usually boated.

Bob continues, "But soon there's more bad scent on the lure than you can keep up with and no amount of washing will seem to remove it. At this point it's best to wash the lure, retire it for a time, and use it again sometime down the road. I know this sounds odd, but through years on the water I have tested this theory and it seems to hold water. I think the bad odor that is placed on a plug is why so many fish are lost when fishing with Kwikfish, no matter how the hooks are rigged. Once this odor is on the plug, the fish just don't hit in a manner that results in a solid hook-up. I've also tested this theory by filming how fish react to a 'dirty' plug in my underwater videos. Even when the action and color is right, the fish are only mildly interested, or, they completely ignore the 'dirty' plug and just swim right by it. But if I replace it with a clean or brand-new plug, whammo, fish on!

"Typically," continues Bob, "Every plug I've ever fished goes through the same scenario where the effectiveness of the plug begins to decline. On the Clackamas, I usually catch two fish on a brand-new plug before I see a decline. On the Deschutes it usually happens at about four fish, and on the Nushagak, at about seven or eight. I always carry either Lemon Joy dish soap or Crest Original toothpaste to clean my plugs with because I know from experience that the fish don't mind the smell of either.

"Other plug maintenance issues are more obvious but still receive little attention from anglers. For instance, always check your lure after catching a fish. Inspect the hooks and sharpen if necessary. Also, make sure the split rings, hook hangers and eyes are straight and in good condition. Re-tune your plug after catching a fish if necessary, and wash it to keep bad odors to a minimum. Also, try not to handle your plugs too much. And whatever you do, don't bring any fried chicken on board. Nothing turns off a hot salmon bite like the smell of fried chicken in the water!"

Author's note: Thank you to Bob Toman for his time and insight. Check out Bob's DVDs "Underwater Salmon 101 and 201" for some great info on salmon fishing, and some rare underwater footage of how and why salmon take a bait or lure. To book a guided trip with Bob, phone Bob Toman's Guide Service at (503) 705-3959.

Plunking Rigs for Salmon and Steelhead

rom *Webster's New World Dictionary:* Plunk—to throw or put down heavily. Picture a ten-ounce pyramid sinker sailing through the air only to crash through the surface of a Northwest river, and it's not hard to see where the technique of plunking got its name. Plunking for salmon and steelhead is a technique often maligned by some anglers for being boring or requiring little skill. Other fishermen embrace the method, both for its leisurely nature and its effectiveness in bringing fish to the bank. The throngs of anglers who amass at popular plunking locations like Meldrum Bar on the Willamette River or near Bonneville on the Columbia, are testimony to the popularity of this technique. Whatever one's opinion may be, let there be no doubt that plunkers catch their fair share of salmon and steelhead from Northwest waterways.

Plunking is a method that utilizes a heavy sinker to hold a bait or lure in the travel lane of migrating fish. It is most often practiced in large rivers in locations where salmon or steelhead swim close to the bank on their push upstream. Anywhere a gravel bar or point extends into the river is a good place to start, as proven by the hundreds of fish caught each season from Meldrum Bar. Another good place to try is anywhere fish congregate in a bottleneck created by an obstruction like—oh, I don't know—let's say a dam. Since the Columbia re-opened to spring chinook fishing several years ago, plunkers have waylaid thousands of springers from the bank near Bonneville, often out-fishing boat anglers as the fish migrate in the margins near shore, avoiding the powerful current of the main river.

Veteran plunkers have an uncanny ability of knowing when and where to be to intercept passing fish. Over the years, they take note of river conditions, tides and moon phases to have a better understanding of what effect these variables have on run timing. Savvy anglers keep journals or remember when fish were caught during previous years and under what conditions. Plunkers can be a great "indicator species," providing valuable information to anglers who fish on smaller tributaries. Clackamas River fishermen, for instance, would do well to pay attention to what is going on in late December or early January at Meldrum Bar. When plunkers start catching winter steelhead there, it's a signal that the Clackamas will soon pick up as well.

The gear used in plunking is as varied as the type of water conditions and bottom structure to be found. Sinker type and size, dropper lengths and leader size are all determined by various factors. The following diagrams should help the beginner get started in plunking, but keep in mind that there is nothing like local knowledge to accelerate the learning curve. If just starting out, fill up the thermos and spend some time at the local fishing hole. Hang out at the campfire and swap fishing stories with the locals. Most plunkers are quite social or they wouldn't be plunking in the first place, and it shouldn't take long before they are sharing their secrets and helping you catch fish.

Diagram 1 This is a basic plunking rig that can be employed just about anywhere this technique is used. The Luhr Jensen salmon spreader helps keep the dropper line from tangling in the leader when casting. Dropper length is determined by bottom structure

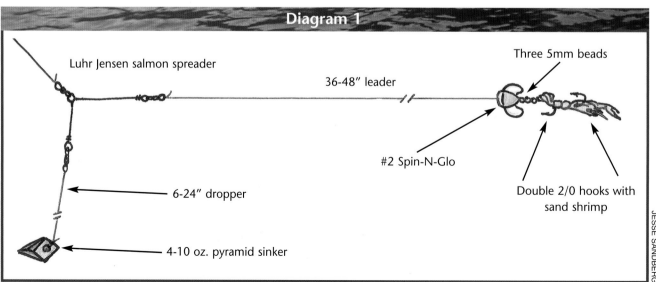

Diagram 1

Luhr Jensen salmon spreader

36-48" leader

Three 5mm beads

#2 Spin-N-Glo

6-24" dropper

4-10 oz. pyramid sinker

Double 2/0 hooks with sand shrimp

JESSE SANDBERG

Diagram 2

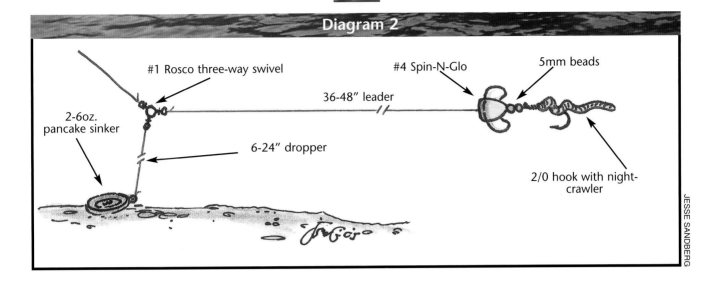

#1 Rosco three-way swivel

#4 Spin-N-Glo

5mm beads

36-48" leader

2-6oz. pancake sinker

6-24" dropper

2/0 hook with night-crawler

JESSE SANDBERG

and depth. If the bottom is cobble or sand, fish will be closer to it than they would be if it was comprised of large boulders, so a short dropper of 6"-2' may be in order. In deeper water with a bottom structure of larger rocks, it is necessary to lengthen the leader to keep the offering above the boulders where the fish are.

Leader length with this rig is determined by depth, and in general the shallower the water the shorter the leader should be. A buoyant drift bobber is used to keep the bait off the bottom where fish can see it. Because it has wings that make it spin and give action to the set-up, the venerable Spin-N-Glo is the plunker's lure of choice. Size of the Spin-N-Glo depends on water conditions, size of bait being used and the type of fish being targeted. Size #4-#0 are used most commonly for salmon and steelhead.

Diagram 2 Pictured here is a rig to use for summer steelhead off lower Columbia River beaches. The type of sinker to be used when plunking depends on bottom structure, and the pancake type shown here works well on a sand or mud bottom. Migrating steelhead on the Columbia are extremely shore-oriented, and many are caught from water less than ten feet deep, especially from beaches on or near Sauvie Island. When fishing shallower water like this, a short dropper is needed as the steelhead will be hugging the bottom as they make their way upriver. Make sure to use a couple of beads between the Spin-N-Glo and hook, as these help eliminate line twist and therefore keep the leader from becoming tangled. Nightcrawlers are an excellent bait for steelhead that, for some reason, are seldom used.

Diagram 3 Plunkers long ago figured out that they could double their odds of a hook-up by using a double rig. This particular set-up was shown to us by Cory Reid, an experienced plunker from Oregon. Cory uses this rig on both the Columbia and Willamette rivers primarily for steelhead, but will sometimes catch a chinook on it as well. Cory believes that the fish aren't always on

the bottom and are at times suspended. By using the double set-up, Cory covers much more water and drastically improves his success rate. He also stresses the importance of keeping the leader lengths a short 28-30" in order to reduce tangles when casting. Cory likes cured prawn tails for bait and secures them to the hook with Miracle Thread, and says it sometimes helps to inject the prawn with scent.

Diagram 3

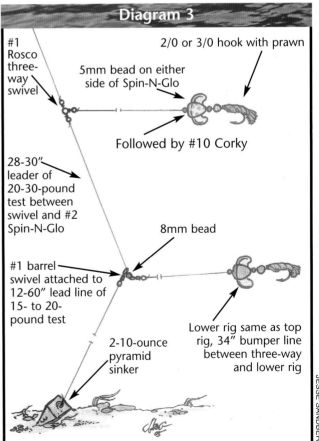

#1 Rosco three-way swivel

5mm bead on either side of Spin-N-Glo

2/0 or 3/0 hook with prawn

Followed by #10 Corky

28-30" leader of 20-30-pound test between swivel and #2 Spin-N-Glo

8mm bead

#1 barrel swivel attached to 12-60" lead line of 15- to 20-pound test

2-10-ounce pyramid sinker

Lower rig same as top rig, 34" bumper line between three-way and lower rig

JESSE SANDBERG

Diagram 4

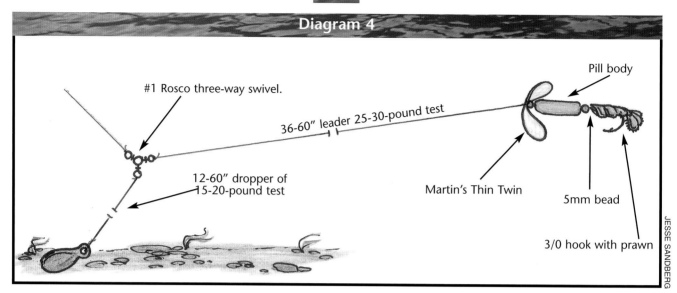

#1 Rosco three-way swivel.

Pill body

36-60" leader 25-30-pound test

12-60" dropper of 15-20-pound test

Martin's Thin Twin

5mm bead

3/0 hook with prawn

JESSE SANDBERG

Diagram 5

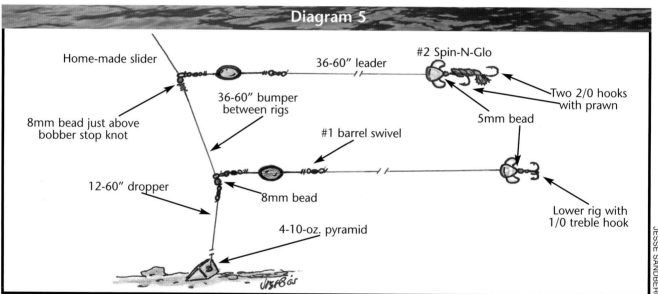

Home-made slider

#2 Spin-N-Glo

36-60" leader

8mm bead just above bobber stop knot

36-60" bumper between rigs

Two 2/0 hooks with prawn

5mm bead

#1 barrel swivel

12-60" dropper

8mm bead

Lower rig with 1/0 treble hook

4-10-oz. pyramid

JESSE SANDBERG

Diagram 6

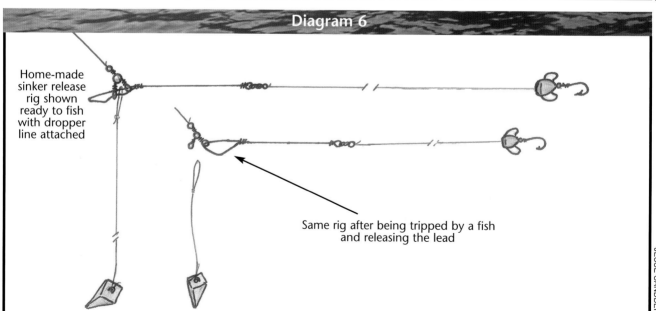

Home-made sinker release rig shown ready to fish with dropper line attached

Same rig after being tripped by a fish and releasing the lead

JESSE SANDBERG

Diagram 4 Here is another basic plunking rig that incorporates the Thin Twin Spinner from Martin's Tackle Company. The Thin Twin works well in slow to moderate current and provides a lot of flash but little weight. The Pill body shown here provides the buoyancy to hold the bait up from the bottom where fish can see it. Tear drop, or bank sinkers as they are sometimes called, work well in moderate flows with a somewhat rocky bottom structure. If this type of sinker doesn't hold where you are fishing, try a pyramid sinker or a railroad spike.

Diagram 5 Here is a trick double set-up shown to us by Scott Harris, an experienced plunker on the Columbia River, of Fisherman's Marine and Outdoor. Clever plunkers developed this rig to combat one of the headaches involved in using a double rig—the constant tangles that can occur when casting. The homemade sliders pictured here are built by sliding a piece of stainless-steel spinner wire through the hollow core of a 1/2-ounce egg sinker. On one end, twist on a #3 interlock snap swivel, on the other, a #1 barrel swivel. Tie the Spin-N-Glo rig to the barrel.

Go ahead and attach the lower rig to your line by clipping the snap swivel onto your mainline, but leave the top rig off for the time being. Cast the single rig out and let the whole thing settle, then put the rod in a rod holder and clip the second rig onto the mainline. The weight of the sinker will pull the second rig down the line to the bobber stop and bead, and now you're fishing two different levels of the water column without having to wonder whether or not your rig is tangled. Many anglers will use this set-up to run a Kwikfish or other wobbling plug down the line in order to pick-up suspended fish.

Scott also offers the following sagacious advice for springer fishing near Bonneville: "When the water is high the fish will swim close to shore, and when it's low they swim close to shore. So, cast close to the shore! Seems obvious, I know, but the last thing you want to do at Bonneville is cast out too far and have the current sweep your rig downstream into other anglers' lines. Needless to say, you won't be popular.

"Another thing to keep in mind when fishing near Bonneville is that the bottom structure is often made up of huge boulders, and many a fish has been lost when the long lead dropper became snagged up on bottom. So be sure to use a light lead line of 15- or 20-pound line so it's easy to break the dropper and recover the fish. It also helps to tie an overhand knot in the dropper to create a weak point where the line will break more readily."

Diagram 6 Using a light lead line is one way to fight the problem of losing a fish to the bottom, but pictured here is another. Mel Weseman is an experienced Northwest angler, who also works at Fisherman's Marine, and he showed us this homemade sinker release set-up. Begin by cutting a 16" piece of #12 or larger spinner wire and twisting on a #1 barrel swivel to one end. On

Tom Gordon with a winter steelhead. The best time to plunk in small streams is during and right after high flows.

the other end, run the wire through one eye of a #3/0 Rosco three-way swivel. Fashion a triangular loop with the wire and twist back onto itself to secure the loop. Tie your mainline to the top eye of the three-way. Then tie a loop on the end of your dropper line and place it over the wire loop. Follow by sliding the third eye of the three-way over the end of the wire loop, and the rig is ready to fish.

With this rig, there is enough tension provided by the wire loop to cast and retrieve without losing the sinker, but when a fish grabs on there is enough weight to pull the eye of the three-way off the wire loop, releasing the sinker so that it does not get snagged during the battle.

Whether or not plunking is for you, there is no denying that it is an effective method for catching Northwest salmon and steelhead. Locations for plunking are endless and will keep you and your family busy searching for the best of them.

Salmon Rigs

*Captain Mike Scheehean and the boys search
for their pot-o-gold, err, silver—on the
Columbia River near Astoria, Oregon.*
Photo by David Johnson

Columbia and Willamette River Spring Chinook Salmon Rigs

Dick Holmes displays a giant Willamette River springer. This whopper went 42 pounds! A springer this size is a rare treat.

The annual arrival of spring chinook to Northwest waters is a much anticipated event, and not just for the excellent sport they provide for fishermen. For centuries, springers have been considered a harbinger of, well, spring. When the first spring chinook of the season is landed, Northwest residents know that it won't be long before winter, ever so slowly, will begin to loosen its frigid grip on our region. Suddenly, the rain doesn't seem quite as cold. It is no longer pitch black when we get home from work. Also, there is a suspicious rumor floating around Clackamas County that someone actually caught a glimpse of the sun the other day. And somewhere down my street, in the driveway of a man who does not fish, a lawnmower sputters to life. Yes, to us wet-headed Northwesterners, spring chinook mean much more than great fishing and gourmet dinners. Springers are a symbol of renewal,

of sustenance anew, of life itself. Springers speak to us of the great fishing to be had in the new year. They tell us of acrobatic summer steelhead and tasty brook trout from high-mountain lakes. They talk of shad, of bass, of sturgeon, of that trip to Alaska in July, and finally, of fall chinook and winter steelhead. Spring chinook kick-off our angling year. Perhaps that is why they are so dear to us. I used to laugh at the fishermen who brought out their boats in mid-January in a foolhardy attempt to catch the first springer of the year, but not anymore. Now I understand. What an honor, indeed, to be the sole person responsible for announcing the spring!

It appears that this honor goes to Jack Howell of Newburg, Oregon, for 2004. Jacked weighed in a beautiful 25-pound springer at the Oregon City Fisherman's Marine and Outdoor Store on January 24th. The fish was reportedly caught on a Wiggle

Wart from the Willamette River near Oregon City. If someone caught a springer earlier than Jack's, they sure weren't talking about it. Jack's salmon was the first of over 100,000 forecasted to enter the Willamette System this year, another bumper crop, folks. With numbers like this, anglers should once again enjoy an excellent season for springers on the Willamette and its tributaries, as long as water conditions cooperate. The Columbia River is also expected to have another robust run, with one estimate calling for over 450,000 hatchery fish to return to the big river.

Anglers can choose from a myriad of tactics and techniques to pursue these awesome game fish. The Columbia and Willamette are both huge rivers, so boat anglers have a distinct advantage over bank anglers most of the time, but there are exceptions to this. Bank anglers on the Willamette congregate at Meldrum Bar and do very well plunking Spin-N-Glos and bait from the rocky shore. Plunkers also have good success at several beaches on the lower Columbia, and can out-fish the boat anglers near Bonneville Dam when the flows are high and the fish travel near shore. However, fishing from a boat usually provides an advantage. The following illustrations should help boat anglers realize greater success when targeting spring chinook this season. Keep in mind that the following leader lengths, lead line lengths and sinker sizes are generalized, and should be altered by the fisherman whenever deemed necessary to better suit the conditions at hand.

Diagram 1 This set-up is used to slowly troll for springers and incorporates a Luhr Jensen Eric's Prawn Rig to help draw attention to the bait. In the spring, large rivers like the Columbia and Willamette are often high and somewhat colored due to heavy rains and/or snow melt. The flash and vibration emitted by the spinner blade on this rig is sometimes just the ticket to bring a big chromer in closer for a sniff of your bait. Early in the season the water is still chilly, and salmon in cold water love bait. Cured prawns are one of the top baits for springers, and you can either buy the cure and prepare them yourself, or purchase them ready to go at an area tackle shop. The Eric's Prawn Rig comes with a small rubber band which should be placed around the bait's head after it is rigged. This keeps the cheek plates from flaring in the current and causing your bait to be shredded before a big 'nook has a chance to eat it.

Diagram 2 Here is another trolling rig for spring chinook. The plug-cut herring is rigged on a Luhr Jensen 101 Herring Rig. Once again, the added attraction of the spinner blade can often spell the difference between success and failure. Herring is a great bait that, when properly rigged, puts a lot of flash and scent in the water. I fish herring for chinook whenever possible, just because I like the unpredictable way the fish take the bait. When a chinook first starts chewing on the herring, it is important not to set the hook or "tighten on" too soon, for the fish will often be missed while doing so. It is advisable to let the rod double over before lifting into the fish for the best hook-up. Sitting on your hands while your rod tip is tapping, bouncing, jerking, ripping or wrenching can be a frustrating exercise in restraint, but it is also one of the most exciting moments in salmon fishing.

Why a chinook salmon eats a herring when in fresh water and not feeding is still a mystery, but I'm glad they do. When

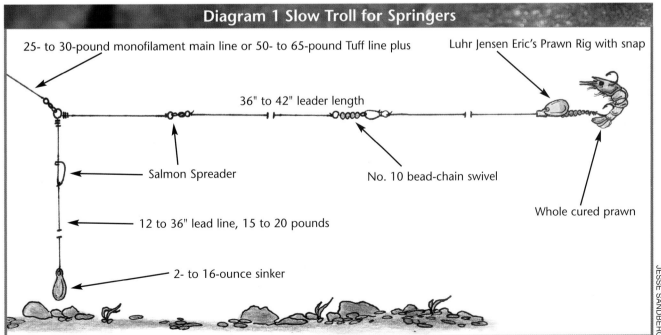

Diagram 1 Slow Troll for Springers

25- to 30-pound monofilament main line or 50- to 65-pound Tuff line plus

Luhr Jensen Eric's Prawn Rig with snap

36" to 42" leader length

Salmon Spreader

No. 10 bead-chain swivel

12 to 36" lead line, 15 to 20 pounds

Whole cured prawn

2- to 16-ounce sinker

JESSE SANDBERG

Diagram 2 Trolling Rig for Spring Chinook

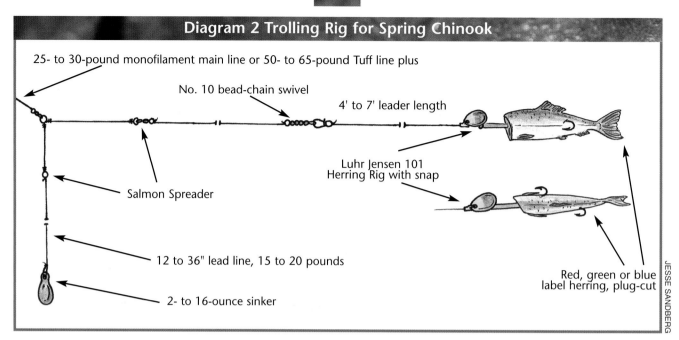

25- to 30-pound monofilament main line or 50- to 65-pound Tuff line plus

No. 10 bead-chain swivel

4' to 7' leader length

Luhr Jensen 101 Herring Rig with snap

Salmon Spreader

12 to 36" lead line, 15 to 20 pounds

2- to 16-ounce sinker

Red, green or blue label herring, plug-cut

JESSE SANDBERG

Diagram 3 Backbouncing for Salmon in Large Rivers

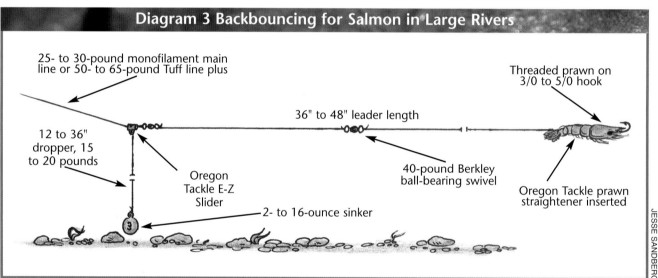

25- to 30-pound monofilament main line or 50- to 65-pound Tuff line plus

Threaded prawn on 3/0 to 5/0 hook

36" to 48" leader length

12 to 36" dropper, 15 to 20 pounds

Oregon Tackle E-Z Slider

40-pound Berkley ball-bearing swivel

2- to 16-ounce sinker

Oregon Tackle prawn straightener inserted

JESSE SANDBERG

fishing the Willamette, you may hear an old myth that states that springers won't hit a herring upstream of the Sellwood area. This is completely bunk! I know many anglers who fish herring in the Oregon City Reach early in the season and do quite well. Personally, I have noticed that later in the season when the water warms, herring is not as effective, but I think this can be said of many baits. If you enjoy fishing herring in the ocean, bay or estuary, don't hesitate to try it in the rivers, too.

Diagram 3 Backbouncing is an effective technique used to take salmon in our larger rivers. Depicted here is a simple rig used to deliver a bait of sand shrimp, roe or prawn to chinook lurking near the bottom. When backbouncing a prawn, thread the leader through the prawn and insert an Oregon Tackle Prawn Straightener into the bait. This will help the fragile prawn stay

intact as it is constantly bounced through the current. When using this technique, it is important to use just enough lead to maintain constant contact with the bottom, but not so much that the sinker keeps getting snagged up. The only way to determine this is through trial and error and the experience that comes with it, for our rivers are constantly changing and a run that required a four ounce sinker yesterday may require six or more tomorrow. I am always impressed by a skilled backbouncer who can look at a stretch of water and say, "That's six-ounce water," because it usually takes me a couple of tries to get it right. Nothing beats experience on the water for angling success, not even luck.

When using this technique, begin by placing the boat at the top or upstream part of a hole or run thought to hold fish. Once the baits are in the water and contact with the bottom is made, the skipper allows the boat to slowly slip downstream as the

Diagram 4 Simple Hardware Rig for Anchored Boat

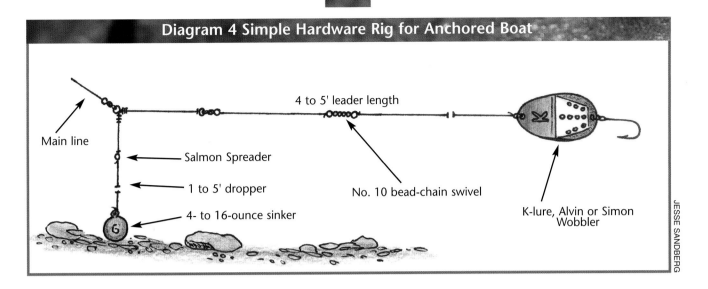

Main line

4 to 5' leader length

Salmon Spreader

1 to 5' dropper

No. 10 bead-chain swivel

4- to 16-ounce sinker

K-lure, Alvin or Simon Wobbler

JESSE SANDBERG

Diagram 5 Simple Rig to Troll, Backtroll, or Backbounce

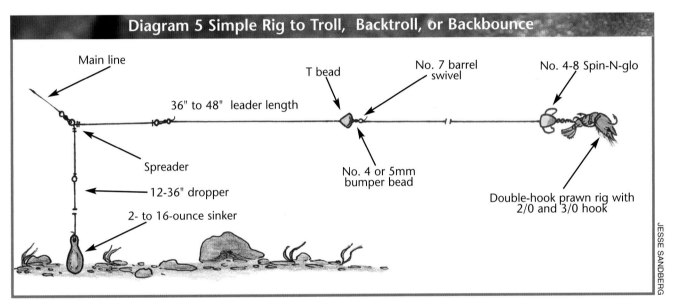

Main line

T bead

No. 7 barrel swivel

No. 4-8 Spin-N-glo

36" to 48" leader length

Spreader

12-36" dropper

No. 4 or 5mm bumper bead

2- to 16-ounce sinker

Double-hook prawn rig with 2/0 and 3/0 hook

JESSE SANDBERG

anglers constantly raise and lower their rods, allowing the baits to "bounce" downstream to a waiting salmon. It is imperative to maintain contact with the bottom on each bounce, as this keeps the bait in the strike zone and lets the angler know that he is fishing effectively. A quality depth finder is an important tool for successful backbouncing, for the skipper can watch the depth and bottom structure and instruct the other fishermen to either reel in or let out line as the bottom changes. This decreases the chances of a frustrating hang-up while increasing the chances of a pleasing hook-up. When a fish takes the bait when backbouncing, allow it to get a good hold on it before setting the hook. When the line grows taught and the fish is pulling well, set the hook sharply and hold on. Sometimes when using this technique you may experience a slack line bite. A fish has picked up your bait and kept moving upstream toward the boat, thus eliminating your contact with the bottom. When this happens, reel like a madman until you catch up to the fish, then stick it!

Diagram 4 Here is a simple rig used to fish hardware while the boat is on anchor. Wobbler fishing is an effective technique employed to fish the traveling lanes fish use when migrating up river, or anywhere numbers of fish may congregate such as the mouths of tributaries, near Willamette Falls or Bonneville Dam. Leader and lead dropper lengths vary widely while using this technique, but on the mainstem of the Columbia or in the deep water of the Lake Line on the Willamette, the "five and five" rule reigns supreme, that is, a five-foot leader to the wobbler and a five-foot dropper to the sinker. This puts the lure just above a moving fish's head where it can see it. Be sure to use enough weight to keep the sinker on the bottom, as heavy spring flows can sometimes create enough drag on your line to lift the rig up and out of the strike zone. The argument of whether to use single siwash hooks or trebles is an old one, but I still prefer to use trebles when wobbler fishing, because I feel that I don't miss as many fish with a multiple point hook. However, there is no

Diagram 6 Rig for Backtrolled Plug with Diver

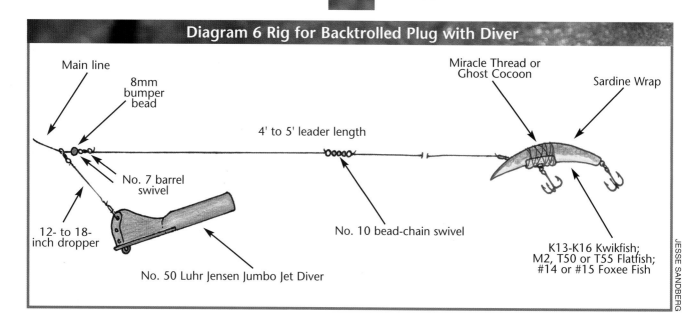

Main line

8mm bumper bead

4' to 5' leader length

Miracle Thread or Ghost Cocoon

Sardine Wrap

No. 7 barrel swivel

12- to 18-inch dropper

No. 10 bead-chain swivel

No. 50 Luhr Jensen Jumbo Jet Diver

K13-K16 Kwikfish; M2, T50 or T55 Flatfish; #14 or #15 Foxee Fish

JESSE SANDBERG

Diagram 7 Simple, User-Friendly Trolling Rig

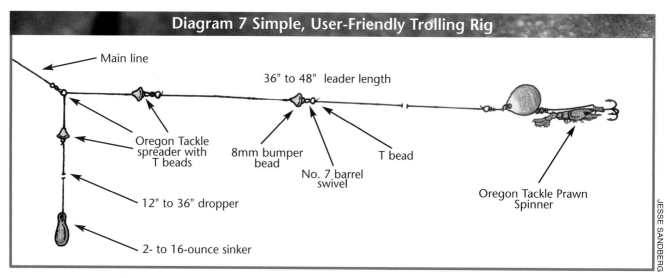

Main line

36" to 48" leader length

Oregon Tackle spreader with T beads

8mm bumper bead

No. 7 barrel swivel

T bead

12" to 36" dropper

2- to 16-ounce sinker

Oregon Tackle Prawn Spinner

JESSE SANDBERG

doubt that once a fish is hooked well on a siwash, there is very little chance of it coming off. Whichever hook you decide to use, make sure that it is extremely sharp in order to increase the odds of a solid hook-up when the fish climbs on.

Diagram 5 This is another simple set-up that can be used to troll, backtroll, or backbounce. The Spin-N-Glo adds color and motion for additional attraction, and helps float the bait up from the bottom. This rig shows a cured prawn as bait, but cured roe and fresh sand shrimp are also popular. Toward the middle of the season when the water begins to warm, undesirable species such as squawfish, peamouth and redhorse chub become active in massive numbers. These fish can be an extreme nuisance as they continuously chowder your bait before a salmon gets a chance to eat it. Because these species are primarily bottom dwellers, it is advisable to lengthen your lead line when faced

with this problem. This allows the bait to ride above the nuisance fish, right where a big springer will be holding.

Diagram 6 Experienced salmon fishermen know that there is nothing like the sight of a rod slamming down in the holder when a big chinook slams a backtrolled plug. Luhr Jensen's Kwikfish and Worden's Flatfish have long been popular lures for this technique. The new Foxee Fish from Blue Fox looks promising as well, and this season we'll get to see if it measures up. The use of a Jumbo Jet Diver makes this set-up extremely user-friendly. Merely let out the desired amount of line, put the rod in the holder and wait for it to bury. The diver is also convenient because it allows an angler to easily cover the water column from top to bottom, and this is important with springers. We know that much of the time chinook are found near the bottom when holding, but when springers are

The author holds a twenty-eight-pound Willamette River spring chinook caught at the "Lake Line," a popular salmon hole at Oregon City, Oregon.

on the move they may swim surprisingly shallow. If the water is turbid from run-off, springers may run as close as five or six feet from the surface.

When using a plug for salmon it is important that the lure is "tuned" so that it runs true. Plugs that pull or dart to one side aren't nearly as effective as those that run straight. Before fishing, lower the set-up into the water to check its action. If the plug pulls to one side, slightly turn the screw eye on the lure's bill the opposite direction that the plug is going. Keep making this adjustment until the lure swims straight. Remember to check the lure's action over the course of the day, especially after landing a fish or pulling on a snag.

For an extremely deadly set-up, use a bait wrap on your plug to put a scent trail into the water. Anchovy, herring and sardine all work, but sardine usually produces the best results. Start by filleting the meat from the bone and then cut into rectangular strips. Leave the skin on and place it against the lure when wrapping so

that the flesh is exposed and therefore dispersing the most scent into the water. Don't cut the bait wrap too large or it could negatively affect the action of the lure. Luhr Jensen recommends a strip measuring 3/4"x 2 1/4" for a K14, 1" x 2 3/4" for the K15, and 1 1/8" x 3" for the K16. Popular colors for Kwikfish include anything with green or chartreuse on it, especially if it is one of the "hot tail" finishes. There are some promising new colors available this year, so be sure to check out the Pacific Watermelon, Thumper, Cricket and Kiwi finishes.

Diagram 7 Here is another trolling rig that is very user-friendly. Some anglers don't like handling bait any more than necessary, and the Oregon Tackle Prawn Spinner really minimizes this. Merely skewer a whole prawn onto the wire shaft and it's ready to fish. Once again, the combination of bait and spinner is often deadly, so don't overlook this type of set-up when targeting spring chinook.

Plug-Fishing for Spring Chinook

BOB TOMAN

Bob Toman and Buzz Ramsey with a Clackamas springer caught in 1978.

The endless assortment of plugs available to anglers is proof of these lures' ability to trigger a strike from one of the most sought-after gems in northwest rivers—the mighty spring chinook. The various plugs on the market today have evolved over time to match a variety of river conditions, angling techniques and the demands of fishermen. Whether flat-lining, trolling forward or back, anchor fishing, or even casting, there exists a plug for most situations an angler may face on any given fishery. Spring chinook will whack a well-presented plug more often than not if you put it right in their face, and anglers theorize that they do this for a couple different reasons.

In the ocean, chinook are gluttonous creatures that feed with reckless abandon until they return to fresh water. Once in the river again, springers feed little, if at all, instead relying on stored fat to provide the energy necessary to complete their life cycles. But old habits are hard to break, and a wobbling plug may appear so similar to the baitfish they once devoured, that many a springer just can't resist the temptation. Another camp suggests that chinook hit a plug solely as a territorial response to having their space invaded, aiming to kill or remove the offender from proximity rather than feeding upon it. Whatever the reason springers may smack a plug, let us give thanks that they do, and examine some techniques for fishing plugs.

Perhaps the easiest way to present a plug to spring chinook is by anchor fishing. This method requires the boat to be anchored in a likely location where migrating salmon may pass. Known travel lanes on big rivers are one place to target, as spring chinook will use the same migration routes year after year. Pay attention to where the fish are being caught to determine which areas to target. On smaller rivers, deep slots along cut banks, the outside of river bends and deeper water in tidal reaches are good places to target migrating fish.

Diagram 1 Pictured here is a basic anchor fishing rig. The M2 Flatfish is just one of a myriad plugs that may be employed with this method. Begin by anchoring the boat in a likely location, then lower the rig into the water, bouncing it back until it is holding bottom with the plug's proper action being communicated by the vibrating rod tip. Make sure the set-up is far enough back that it is not dragged around as the boat bobs or sways in the current. How far back to run your rigs is strictly a matter of experimentation for the particular water to be fished, and it may require anywhere from 40-100' of line out depending on current speed, depth and size of lead being used. When on anchor, use sea anchors off the stern to stabilize the boat and minimize movement.

Always use caution when anchoring in swift water, and use the proper anchor system for your boat. Mistakes in anchoring may cost you much more than that new jet sled. When pulling the anchor with a power boat, always pull the anchor from a bow cleat, never the stern, for if the anchor were to hang up

while doing so, it could sink the boat in an instant. For more information on this technique, check out *Anchor Fishing* with Eric Linde and Carmen Macdonald, available on VHS or DVD from Frank Amato Publications.

Trolling plugs is another technique that accounts for lots of springers each season. In slow to moderate current, plugs can be forward trolled either up or downstream to cover water. But in water with good current, slowly backtrolling is the preferred method. When backtrolling, the boat is held against the current so that it slowly slips downstream, allowing the plugs to remain in the strike zone while covering lots of water. Begin at the top of a hole and back the plugs down through the best water, maneuvering the boat slowly from side to side to place the plugs in the likeliest spots.

Diagram 2 Because most plugs will only dive so far, most anglers use either a diver or lead sinkers to get their lures down to the fish when backtrolling. Pictured here is a Luhr Jensen

Diagram 1 Basic Anchor Fishing Rig

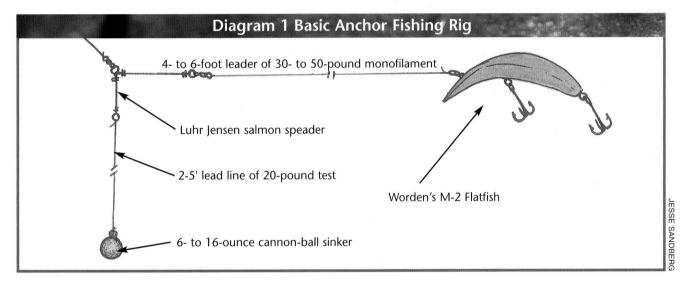

4- to 6-foot leader of 30- to 50-pound monofilament

Luhr Jensen salmon speader

2-5' lead line of 20-pound test

6- to 16-ounce cannon-ball sinker

Worden's M-2 Flatfish

JESSE SANDBERG

Diagram 2 Simple Back-Trolling Rig

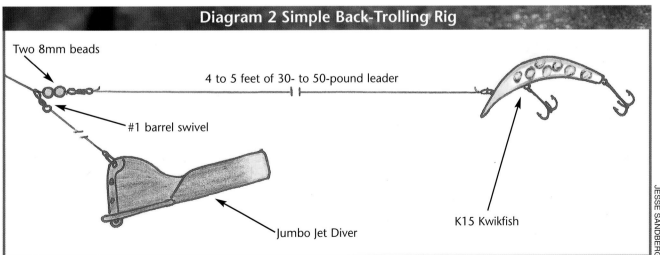

Two 8mm beads

4 to 5 feet of 30- to 50-pound leader

#1 barrel swivel

Jumbo Jet Diver

K15 Kwikfish

JESSE SANDBERG

Diagram 3 Wrapping a Kwikfish

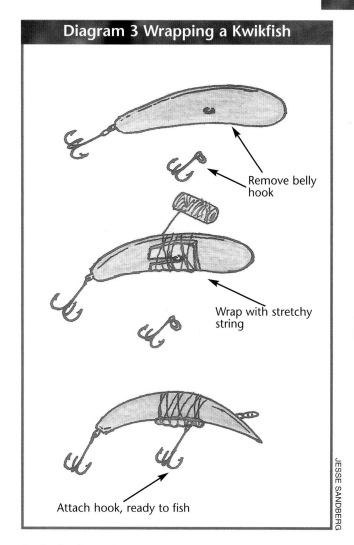

Remove belly hook

Wrap with stretchy string

Attach hook, ready to fish

JESSE SANDBERG

is critical that all of the anglers in a boat are using the same gear. Reels should all be the same make or at least the same size so that the running depth of the plugs remains consistent. The size and type of line should be the same as well so that the divers plane at the same rate. Rods should be similar in length so that all the rigs are being presented at the same angle, this way, when a fish is caught at six passes, all the anglers in a boat can run their rigs out that distance and be fairly confident that they are all fishing at the magic depth for the conditions at hand. Also, it can be advantageous to start the day by staggering the depth of several rigs to determine the depth at which the fish are biting. The side rods—or rods nearest the bow—should be fished shallower than the stern rods in order to avoid tangles. Then, when a fish is caught, all the rods can be accurately fished at the proper depth to realize the best success.

Diagram 3 Salmon fishermen learned long ago that the enticing action of a wobbling plug like a Kwikfish could be further enhanced by affixing a small bait wrap to the underside of the plug. Pictured here is the proper way to wrap a Kwikfish. Most anglers use sardine for this because it is an oily bait that puts a lot of scent in the water and retains its smell longer than other baits. To wrap a plug, most fishermen will remove the belly hook to make the procedure safer and easier. Cut a small piece of sardine and leave the skin on. Place the skin side against the plug and secure the bait with elastic or nylon thread. The combined action of the lure and scent of the bait will drive spring chinook bonkers. Because wrapping several plugs on the water consumes valuable fishing time, most fishermen wrap their plugs before heading out on the water and store them in a small cooler to keep them fresh. Also, don't make your baits so large that they interfere with the action of the plug. Luhr Jensen recommends a bait strip measuring 3/4" by 2 1/4" for a K14 Kwikfish, 1" x 2 3/4" for the K 15, and 1 1/8" x 3" for the K16.

Diagram 4 This rig is used to probe the bottom of deeper holes, chutes and troughs on small to mid-size rivers where it is necessary to get the plug on or near the bottom in a hurry. Back-bouncing a plug lets an angler cover every inch of suitable water when springers are sulking near the bottom for security. This technique makes it easy to fish around structure like rock ledges and the break at the head of a hole where a diver may not work so well. Many fishermen prefer to rig this set-up on a slider as shown, instead of on a three-way swivel or spreader. That way, when a springer grabs the plug the line slips through the slider and the fish doesn't immediately feel the weight of the sinker and let go of the lure before it is hooked. Flatfish and Kwikfish are the two plugs most commonly used for this method.

Jumbo Jet Diver that works great for getting a plug down to depth. The color scheme shown here is new for 2005, and several other custom colors will be available soon in tackle stores. The Jumbo Jet Diver is designed to dive up to fifty feet with 100 feet of 17-pound line out, but because most anglers use much heavier line than 17-pound for springers, this is just a general guideline. Current speed also plays a role in how steeply the diver will plane, so there are several variables that determine how deep the plugs are running at any given time, and because springers will hold at different depths from day to day or even hour to hour, it is important to accurately know how deep a fish is caught so that all of the rigs in the boat may be returned to that depth after a salmon is landed.

Most anglers establish depth by counting the number of passes the level-wind mechanism makes across the spool on a reel when letting line out. And because different makes of reels have different-sized spools, a pass on one reel may pay out an entirely different amount of line than another, making it next to impossible for anglers to accurately determine where a fish was caught, let alone fish all of the rigs at that depth. That is why it

Yet another technique that presents a plug to springers is casting and retrieving. This method receives little attention from anglers but can be deadly under the right conditions, like when fish are staging off the mouths of tributaries waiting for rivers to rise enough to facilitate their upstream migration. Just such a fishery exists downstream from the mouth of the Wind River in Washington State, where each year dozens of springers are caught by bank anglers casting plugs from a point of land. These fish can often be found in fairly shallow water—often twenty feet or less—and sometimes it isn't necessary to fish right on the bottom. Aggressive salmon will rise up to take a slowly retrieved plug. And springers often suspend off the bottom so a fairly shallow-running plug may be right in the strike zone. Plugs are not exactly aerodynamic and don't cast particularly well, so choose a plug that has ample weight. Storm Mag Warts are an old favorite for casting, and Worden's new Flatfish M-2SP, at 3/4 of an ounce, promises to be easy-casting as well. The M-2SP should prove to be effective in deeper water, too, as Worden's claims this plug will dive to over twenty feet deep on 10-pound-test line. That's fairly light line to use for springers, but even on heavier tests this plug should dive deeper than others.

Flat-lining plugs, that is, back-trolling plugs with no added weight or diver, has been a deadly technique for catching spring chinook from Northwest rivers for decades. One of the pioneers of this technique, and perhaps the most advanced plug fisherman around, is professional guide Bob Toman. Bob started guiding in Oregon in 1968 and has been hard at it since. He

Jeremy and Becky Toman hold up a pair of springers for Dad. These fish were caught on the Clackamas River in 1982 on #30 Cop Car Hot Shots.

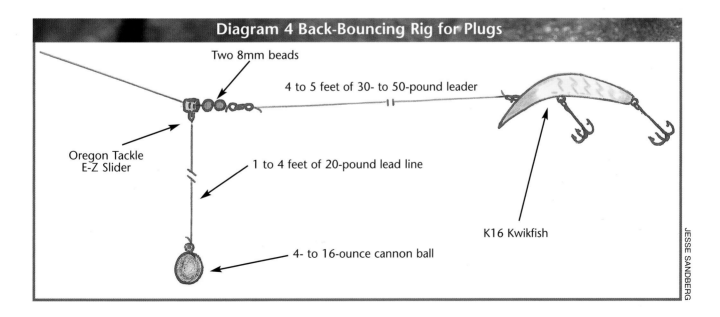

Diagram 4 Back-Bouncing Rig for Plugs

Two 8mm beads

4 to 5 feet of 30- to 50-pound leader

Oregon Tackle E-Z Slider

1 to 4 feet of 20-pound lead line

K16 Kwikfish

4- to 16-ounce cannon ball

Plugs for Flat-Lining

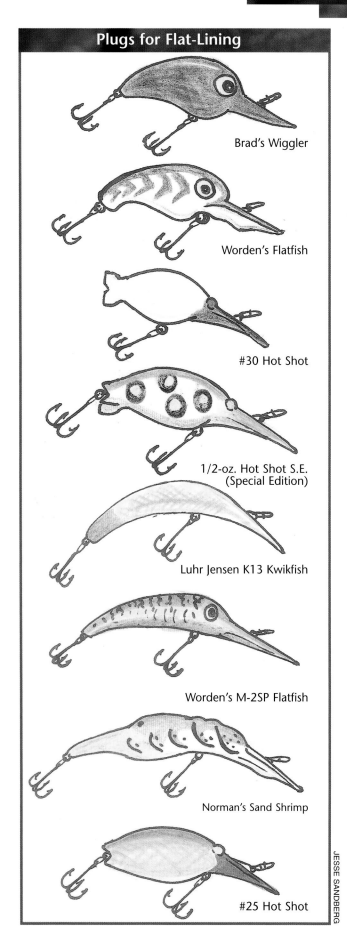

Brad's Wiggler

Worden's Flatfish

#30 Hot Shot

1/2-oz. Hot Shot S.E.
(Special Edition)

Luhr Jensen K13 Kwikfish

Worden's M-2SP Flatfish

Norman's Sand Shrimp

#25 Hot Shot

JESSE SANDBERG

fishes an average of 250 days a year, once fished 96 days straight, and his best streak was 596 consecutive trips landing at least one fish! How does Bob accurately keep track of such numbers? "I keep a detailed log," he explains. "It's a tedious task, but something I feel a serious angler should do. The value of a detailed angling log as an instrument of learning is incredible. I record facts on thirty-plus factors for EACH fish that is landed, and have this information on file for over 4,000 individual fish." By comparing data, Bob can determine which bait or technique produces better for his clients under a vast array of water and weather conditions. Considering Bob's extensive experience catching spring chinook while backtrolling plugs, I asked if he would share some of what he has learned over the years. Lucky for us, he graciously accepted.

"One of the first things I learned is that on the lower portion of the Clackamas River, spring chinook respond better to smaller plugs like Wiggle Warts and Hot Shots. Higher in the system they will hit the big stuff, like K15's and K16's, but down low they like the small plugs. If I had to rate them, I would say my number-one producer of all time would be the #25 Hot Shot in Green Pirate, followed by the original Storm Wiggle Wart in various colors, and number three would be a #30 Hot Shot. An interesting side note is that in 1978 I took Don Holm, former outdoor writer for the *Oregonian*, and some members of the Pittsburg Pirates out fishing for springers on the Clackamas. We caught a bunch of springers that day on #30 Hot Shots in my preferred color, and that day Don dubbed that color the Green Pirate.

"Another thing that I've determined is that springers aren't always on the bottom where most anglers believe them to be. Sure, that's where they are some of the time, especially when there's heavy boat traffic, but not always. I first began to suspect this when back-bouncing deep holes on the Clackamas. We would bounce bottom and not get bit, but when we reeled up a crank or two—fish on! Then, in the 1970s, Charlie White brought his underwater camera to the Clackamas to fish with me. What we saw when we lowered the camera down into the deeper holes was that many of the fish were suspended well off the bottom. Nobody knows for sure why they do this, but I theorize that it has to do with current and oxygen content. The water near the surface usually has the fastest current and plenty of oxygen. The water near the bottom, conversely, may have very slight current and little oxygen, and springers need plenty of oxygen. In lakes, this layer of the water column is called the hypolimnion and is often referred to as "the dead zone" because at certain times of the year it holds little oxygen and therefore little life. I think that in some of the deeper holes in the river it may be like that. But in between the bottom and surface is a mixing zone with medium current and good oxygen content,

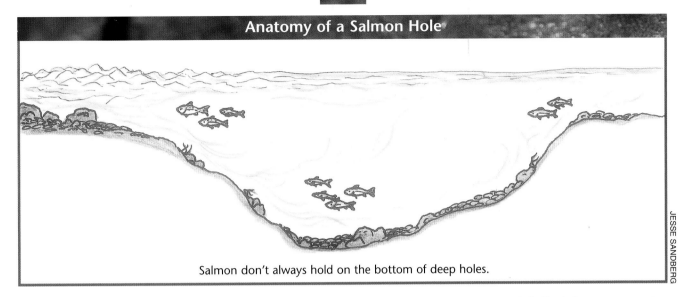

Anatomy of a Salmon Hole

Salmon don't always hold on the bottom of deep holes.

JESSE SANDBERG

and here you will often find the fish. It goes a long way in explaining why you caught a fish in fifteen feet of water on a plug that only dives to six feet.

"Another thing I learned on the Clackamas is that every year is different and the fish seem to change their preference of plug type and color. One year they may prefer a metallic blue Wiggle Wart, another year it may be the Green Pirate Hot Shot, so it pays to mix things up. I often fish several different colors to see what the fish want, then change all of my rods over to the preferred color once a pattern is established. Early and late in the day I like opaque colors like the cop car (black and white) Hot Shot. Later on when the sun hits the water, the metallics seem to work best. In murky water I like a darker color that silhouettes well, or fluorescent orange because it's highly visible. In water with color I may also switch to a larger plug that fish see better. I prefer to fish my plugs on an 8 1/2' rod that has a parabolic action. When a fish grabs the plug, this rod really gives, and I think the fish hold on longer resulting in a better hook rate. I feel that too stiff a rod lets the fish feel the rod more and it may spit the plug, resulting in less hookups. It's for this same reason that I still use monofilament line instead of braided line for pulling plugs; it has more stretch and I believe I hook more fish with it.

"Another aspect of plug fishing that I take very seriously is keeping the lures properly tuned. I can't really describe the action I'm looking for when tuning a plug, I just know it when I see it. I pull the plug through the water to see how it tracks in good current. If it runs to one side or rolls out, it's not right. A plug should track well even in heavy current, and if it's acting erratic or `flipping out' it won't catch fish like it should. Before moving the eye on the bill of the plug, check the screw eyes on the hooks to make sure they're straight. Many fishermen don't check these and never get the plug to run right no matter how

much they fool around with the bill. (Look for more on tuning plugs from Bob in a future issue.)

"I am also very serious about keeping my plugs clean," Bob continues. "I'm constantly washing my hands with Lemon Joy and try to handle the plugs as little as possible. Salmon have a very acute sense of smell, and foreign odors can be a big turnoff to them. Plugs that have sat around in a tackle box often get a real nasty smell to them, and if they smell bad to me, imagine how the fish react to them! I've been known to cleanse my plugs in the dishwasher, but now I mostly clean them with Crest toothpaste and a toothbrush. I use only Original Flavor because it contains silica which provides grit in order to scrub away rust and dirt. It also has mouthwash in it to kill the germs that cause bad odors, brighteners to make my lures shine, and a mint flavor they don't seem to mind!"

After hearing this I was sure that Bob was just pulling my leg, entertaining himself at my expense, perhaps. But Bob assured me he was not, and when a guy like Mr. Toman tips his hand just enough that you can see one card, you should bite. I now have a tube of Crest Original Flavor in my drift boat, do you?

Bob Toman fishes his home river, the Clackamas, for winter steelhead and spring chinook. During June and July he heads to Alaska where he runs his own king camp on the fabled Nushagak River. In August and September he is back in Oregon, fishing the legendary Deschutes for summer steelhead. And in October and November he's back chasing big kings on Tillamook Bay. To book a trip with Bob, call (503) 658-6493. And keep an eye out at the tackle shop for Bob's upcoming video with plenty of underwater footage of big kings, crabbing and more.

Author's note: A special thanks to Mr. Toman for contributing to this article.)

Hardware Rigs For Spring Chinook

Mike Scheehean hoists a big Willamette River springer.

pring chinook anglers learned long ago that as water temperatures warm with the advancing spring season the traditional baits for springer fishing start to lose their effectiveness. As rivers rise past the fifty-degree mark, spring chinook are less likely to hit herring, prawns, shrimp or roe. When rivers begin to drop and warm after spring runoff, many fishermen turn to an assortment of metal lures—or hardware—to target spring chinook that turn their noses at the smell of bait. This past winter has seen many areas of the Pacific Northwest receiving far less snowfall than usual, and as a result, our rivers should drop and warm much sooner than normal. While these conditions may not provide for very good bait fishing, they should prove to be excellent for fishing hardware for spring chinook in 2005.

"Hardware" is a term, as it applies to sport fishing, that refers to any of a vast array of metal lures used to fish for salmon, trout and steelhead. The two most common types are spinners and wobblers. Each of these two types of lures are available in a variety of sizes, shapes and colors, and choosing an effective fish-catcher for a particular fishery may be somewhat daunting for a beginner, so I will list some of the more serious players.

Good wobblers for trolling or anchor fishing include the Alvin, Clancy, Corn Wobbler, the Simon, K Lure, Luhr Jensen Manistee, Worden's F.S.T., William's Wabler, and the Buse Willamette Wobbler. Popular spinners for trolling or anchor fishing include Luhr Jensen's Clearwater Flash and Tee Spoon, Oregon Tackle's Rainbow Spinner and Prawn Spinner, Worden's Flash Glo and Bob Toman's Classic Spinner. Good spinners for casting include the Rattle Spin from Top Brass, Blue Fox Vibrax in #4-6, Mepps Aglia and See Best, Panther Martin, Stinger and Coho Bolo. Now that we're familiar with some great lures to try, let's look at some techniques for fishing hardware for spring chinook on Northwest rivers.

Anchor fishing from a boat is a great technique to use on larger Northwest rivers when spring chinook are on the move. By positioning a boat in the travel lanes that salmon use, anglers can present their lures to a ton of fish as they swim past or mill around. Once the boat is safely on anchor, bounce the rig back until the sinker is holding bottom and not rising off it when the boat bobs or sways in the current. Do not cast the rig out as this usually results in tangles. When fishing hardware in this manner it is not necessary to immediately grab the rod and set the hook the instant a fish takes. Instead, let the fish turn on the lure and double over the rod, as this usually results in a solid hook-up.

Diagram 1 In slow to medium current, wobblers really shine when anchor fishing, and this illustration shows a simple way to rig a wobbler. By using a slider instead of a spreader, the fish may not necessarily feel the weight of the sinker when it first grabs on and therefore may hold onto the lure a split-second longer, allowing for a better chance of hooking it. Leader and lead dropper lengths are determined by depth and bottom structure. Generally, the deeper the water, the longer they will be. On big rivers like the Columbia and Willamette, it's common to run a 5' leader with a 5' lead line. In areas with large boulders or other bottom structure it is also advisable to use a longer lead line to keep the wobbler up where the fish are. Also, always use a lighter line rating for the dropper than your mainline, that way, you can break off the sinker should it become snagged while saving your expensive wobbler. Always check the action of the wobbler before lowering it into the depths by holding it in the current near the surface. If it is spinning or rolling wildly instead of wobbling from side to side, the water may be too fast to effectively fish a wobbler and you may want to try a spinner instead.

Diagram 2 Here is a basic spinner rig to use while anchor fishing in water too fast for a wobbler. The Hildebrandt blade pictured here is a quality blade that is very popular with anglers who build their own spinners. Combinations of copper or brass blades, coupled with flame or chartreuse beads, are standard fare on Northwest rivers. If building your own spinners, don't buy cheap hooks, for these are your most important connection to the fish. Use hooks that are ultra strong and ultra sharp.

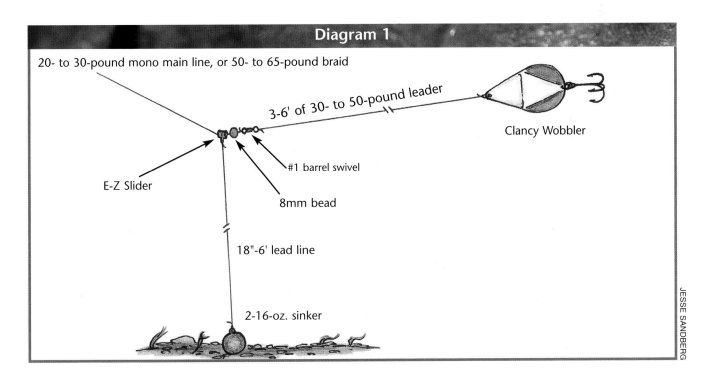

Diagram 1

20- to 30-pound mono main line, or 50- to 65-pound braid

3-6' of 30- to 50-pound leader

Clancy Wobbler

#1 barrel swivel

E-Z Slider

8mm bead

18"-6' lead line

2-16-oz. sinker

JESSE SANDBERG

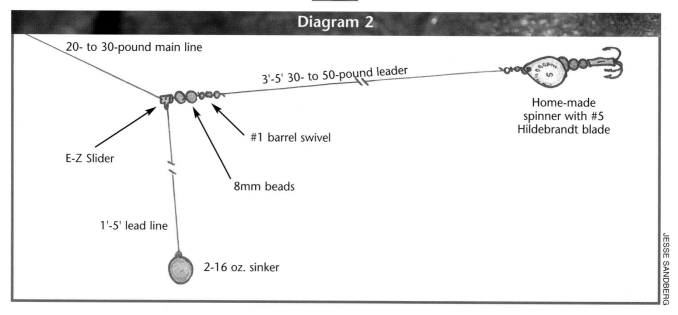

Diagram 2

20- to 30-pound main line

3'-5' 30- to 50-pound leader

#1 barrel swivel

E-Z Slider

8mm beads

1'-5' lead line

2-16 oz. sinker

Home-made
spinner with #5
Hildebrandt blade

JESSE SANDBERG

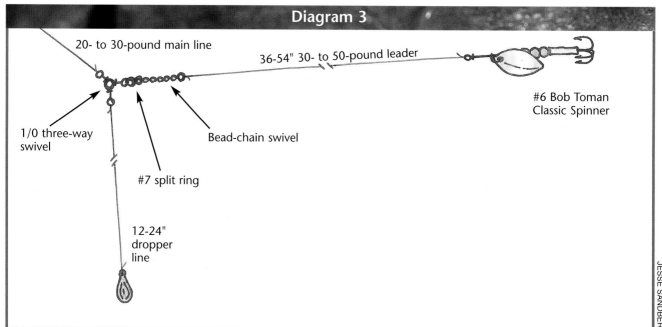

Diagram 3

20- to 30-pound main line

36-54" 30- to 50-pound leader

1/0 three-way
swivel

Bead-chain swivel

#7 split ring

12-24"
dropper
line

#6 Bob Toman
Classic Spinner

JESSE SANDBERG

Trolling hardware for spring chinook is another deadly tactic. Anglers will forward or back-troll spinners and wobblers in areas that lack sufficient current to provide good anchor fishing. Trolling is also the preferred method when fishing the tidal reaches of rivers on an incoming or slack tide. In shallow water, say twenty feet deep or less, it may be necessary to fish your rigs on or near the bottom, as this is where the fish will be most of the time. In water deeper than this, the fish often suspend off the bottom as they hold or push up river, so better success may be realized if the rigs are trolled shallower. In murky water colored by runoff, it may be surprising just how shallow the fish run, and savvy anglers on the Willamette River discovered that fish are often caught under these conditions, as shallow as six feet!

Diagram 3 Here is an effective set-up used to troll spinners for spring chinook. When using this technique it is advisable to hold onto the rod rather than putting it in a rod holder, as chinook will often stop a spinner and then let go of it quickly, and there may only be a brief moment to deliver a hook-set. Anglers who have a tough time sitting on their hands to watch a herring bite play out should love trolling spinners, because if you're not setting the hook at the slightest change in the lure's action, you're missing fish. Much of the time when trolling spinners the fish hit in what is called a slack-line bite and this can be hard to detect for the inexperienced. Basically what will happen when this occurs is that the vibration on the rod tip will stop and the line will go slack. What has happened is that a salmon has

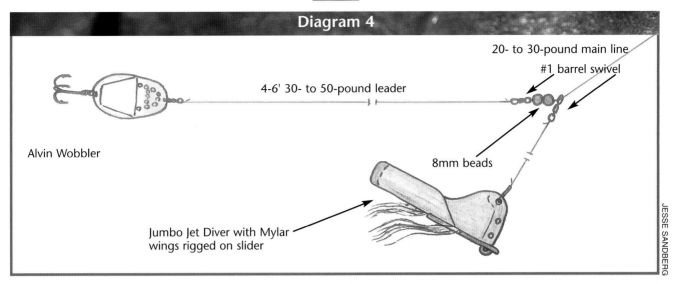

Diagram 4

4-6' 30- to 50-pound leader

20- to 30-pound main line

#1 barrel swivel

8mm beads

Alvin Wobbler

Jumbo Jet Diver with Mylar wings rigged on slider

JESSE SANDBERG

accelerated toward the spinner, bitten it, and its momentum has carried it toward the boat, thus removing the tension from the line. In this scenario it is necessary to reel down quickly and set the hook, otherwise the fish will sense something is wrong and quickly spit the blade. Due to the common occurrence of a slack-line bite, a rod with a sensitive tip that constantly telegraphs that the spinner is working properly is a must. The HSR 982C GL3 from G. Loomis is perhaps the finest rod available for trolling spinners for salmon, if a single blade of aquatic grass hits your spinner you will feel it.

Diagram 4 Pictured here is a set-up used to back-troll a wobbler on big water like the Columbia when covering large areas in order to find fish. The Luhr Jensen Jumbo Jet Diver works great for getting a wobbler, such as an Alvin down to depth, and can be trolled just off the bottom in order to reduce hang-ups. Because it is relatively snag-free, this rig is great for fishing large expanses of water while maximizing "wet time."

Diagram 5 Here is a trick double set-up used to troll wobblers in two different layers of the water column. This rig was shown to me by Mike Scheehean, a long-time salmon fisherman on the Willamette River near Oregon City. "Years ago we would use this rig to troll for springers on the Willamette above the old bridge, near the locks and the area around the catwalk," says Mike. "It worked great because you're fishing two lures at once which really adds to the attraction. In moderate current we slowly trolled upstream and in a stronger flow either held the boat or slowly slipped downstream in a back-troll. In this deeper water we wouldn't fish them very deep because the fish were usually suspended. In fact, when you stood up in the boat, lifted your rod and could see the first wobbler, you knew you were fishing the right depth. We would use this technique later in the season when the water had warmed some and the bait bite had fallen off. Wobblers like the Andy Reeker, William's, F.S.T., corn

Diagram 5

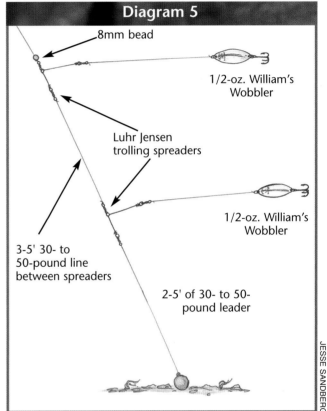

8mm bead

1/2-oz. William's Wobbler

Luhr Jensen trolling spreaders

1/2-oz. William's Wobbler

3-5' 30- to 50-pound line between spreaders

2-5' of 30- to 50-pound leader

JESSE SANDBERG

wobbler and old Herman wobbler worked great on the Willamette. The Herman wobbler was made by a well-known local angler named Herman Buse, and I recall that it was a particularly effective wobbler on the Willamette River at Oregon City. I think his son is still making them today. Regarding springer fishing on the Willamette, I remember Herman used to say to not bother going springer fishing until the dogwoods bloom."

Herman Wobblers are indeed still being made today by Herman's son, Kent, although they have been renamed the Buse Willamette Wobbler. "Dad started making the wobblers out back

Diagram 6 Casting and Drifting a Spinner for Springers

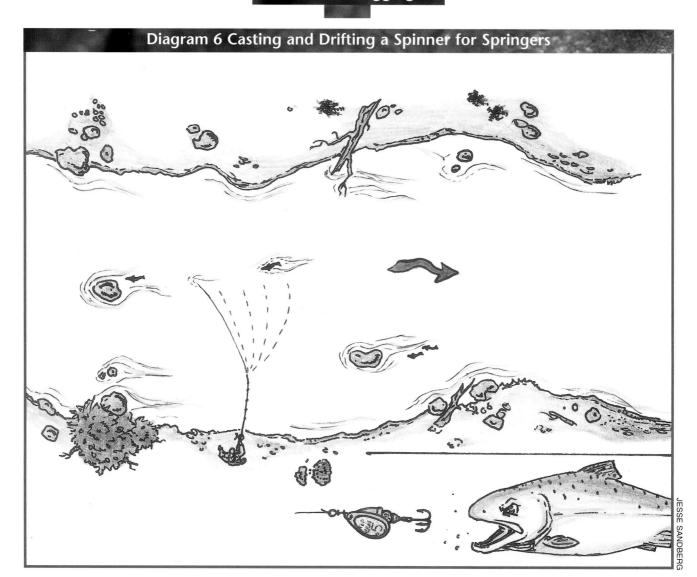

JESSE SANDBERG

Diagram 7 Weighted Rig for Casting Spinner

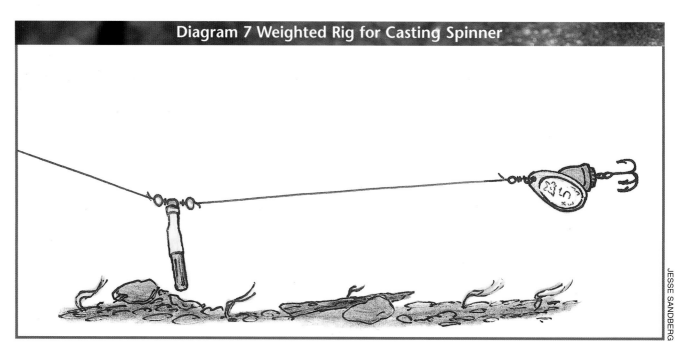

JESSE SANDBERG

Dave Neels, an accomplished angler and tackle guru, holds a gorgeous Sandy River springer that fell to a B.C. Steel Spoon.

in a shed sometime back in the 1930s as I remember." Kent told me. "He built the dies himself to stamp them out with, and did all of the fine shaping by hand. Dad's wobblers caught a lot of fish back then and are still catching them today. There is still somewhat of a demand for them and I'll make several hundred at a time between fishing trips to keep everyone happy. Because everyone likes to rig a wobbler their own certain way, I just make the blades and don't put any hooks or split rings on them. That way, a fisherman can rig the wobbler as he sees fit." To get your hands on a Buse Willamette Wobbler, call Kent at (503) 655-5317.

Another effective technique for catching springers on hardware is casting spinners. Springers can be caught by casting spinners virtually anywhere they swim as evidenced from the many areas where this technique is employed. From sprawling big rivers to small pocket water, spinners account for many springers each season. A casting spinner can be presented several different ways to the fish, but perhaps the most effective is by drifting it. This technique involves casting a spinner straight out or slightly upstream in order to let it sink before beginning the presentation. Then, before the spinner is hung on the bottom, the angler lifts

his/her rod in order to put tension on the line to get the blade spinning. At this point the blade is kept spinning by maintaining tension between the lure and the rod, not by reeling in; only reel when it is necessary to maintain tension—let the current work the blade. Then, the lure's progress downstream is followed by the rod tip to maintain tension and detect a bite. Sometimes a spring chinook will merely stop a spinner, other times they will hit so hard it's a wonder you can hold on! This presentation is a lot like drift-fishing because you are basically showing the spinner to the fish on a slow, downstream swing.

Diagram 6 This illustration shows the proper way to drift a spinner to holding springers. The spinner should be shown to the fish on the slowest swing possible in order to minimize the lift caused by the rotating blade. This will help keep the spinner down deep where the fish are. In shallower runs it is often unnecessary to use any additional weight to fish a spinner. In deeper holes and faster water, additional weight may be needed in order to keep the spinner down in the strike zone.

Diagram 7 Here is one way to weight a casting spinner in order to more effectively fish deep water.

Tidewater and Ocean Salmon Trolling Rigs

When fishing the outgoing tide at Tillamook Bay, where only a couple hundred yards of big swells separates you from the pounding breakers of the bar, it's comforting to have the Coast Guard watching over the sport fleet. When Tim Rooney landed this fall chinook, the boat had its limit of eight fish while fishing with exceptional guide David Johnson.

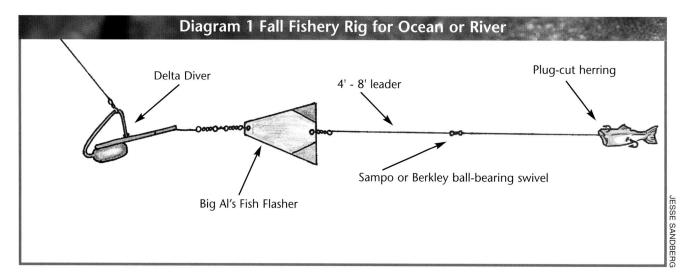

Diagram 1 Fall Fishery Rig for Ocean or River

Delta Diver

4' - 8' leader

Plug-cut herring

Big Al's Fish Flasher

Sampo or Berkley ball-bearing swivel

JESSE SANDBERG

Diagram 1 This set-up has quickly become one of the most effective used in the Astoria fall fishery. Whether used in the ocean or the river, this rig is deadly for both coho and chinook. The advent of the Big Al's Fish Flash a few years ago has been a boon to local salmon anglers. This attractor puts a lot of flash into the water without creating a huge amount of drag against your rod, allowing you to attract fish from farther off while still letting you detect a soft bite. Guide Tyler Courtney helped popularize the use of the Fish Flash, and he swears by them. "The Fish Flash has really increased my catch at Astoria the past few seasons. I run them at all times on all of my rods during this fishery. I guess it's to the point that I would feel naked without them." Tyler stresses that different colors seem to attract different species. "The coho are particularly attracted to the red, while chinook seem to like the chartreuse, green and lazer best."

Diagram 2 Classic Coho Ocean Rig

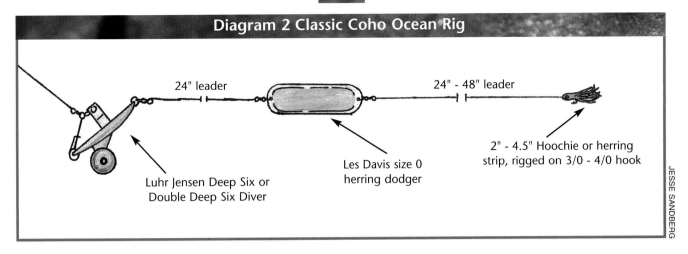

24" leader

24" - 48" leader

2" - 4.5" Hoochie or herring strip, rigged on 3/0 - 4/0 hook

Les Davis size 0 herring dodger

Luhr Jensen Deep Six or Double Deep Six Diver

JESSE SANDBERG

Diagram 2 This is a classic ocean rig responsible for the demise of thousands of coho over the years. It also takes chinook on a fairly consistent basis. The key to the success of this rig is the Les Davis Herring Dodger. The dodger puts an immense amount of flash into the water thus simulating an actively feeding salmon. This will attract other salmon from great distances. The erratic swimming action of the dodger is also responsible for activating the Hoochie in an enticing fashion. Because of this, do not use a leader any longer than four feet between the dodger and the Hoochie, as this will decrease the action of the lure. Standard leader length behind the dodger is 24-36". There is an archaic salmon fishermen's rule that states that the leader length behind the dodger should be 1.5 to 2 times the length of the dodger itself. Either way, keep the leader short for best results.

This set-up can also be rigged using lead instead of a diver, but because it is primarily used to target coho, I would stick with the diver. Coho respond very well to attractors that have a lot of flash and color, and divers such as the Luhr Jensen Deep Six pictured here help to "jazz-up" your rig. In fact, the chrome-colored Deep Six is one of my favorites at Astoria. It is a diver that delivers

incredible flash in the water. Also, the Deep Six doesn't seem to track as straight as other divers, instead, it pulses and squirrels from side to side as it reacts to currents and the tide, adding, in my opinion, a more seductive action to your bait. Just make sure when using a Deep Six with a dodger that the adjuster screw on the trip is tightened enough to keep the pull of the dodger from tripping the diver. Which brings us to the one disadvantage of the Deep Six—it must be reeled in and manually re-set after tripping. I find this a minor inconvenience considering the other fish-catching attributes of this diver.

Hoochies come in a variety of sizes and colors and they all catch fish, but combinations of green and chartreuse are most popular. Whichever you use, cut a small "sniffer" bait and attach it to the back hook of your Hoochie rig. Herring is most commonly used for this purpose, but don't hesitate to try sardine or squid, for being different often pays big dividends when salmon fishing. Make sure this bait is small and slim enough so that it doesn't affect the action of the Hoochie. Cut it in the shape of an acute triangle 2-3" long and rig it with the apex to the rear. The scent of this bait combined with the erratic action of the dodger-activated Hoochie drives coho crazy.

Diagram 3 Typical "Buoy Ten" Salmon Rig

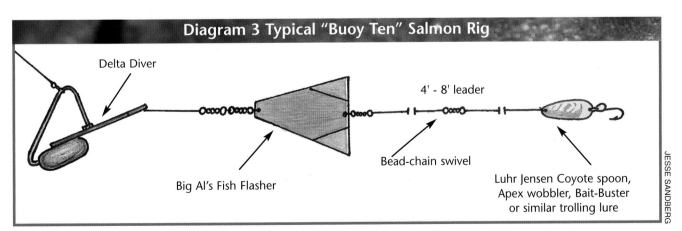

Delta Diver

4' - 8' leader

Big Al's Fish Flasher

Bead-chain swivel

Luhr Jensen Coyote spoon, Apex wobbler, Bait-Buster or similar trolling lure

JESSE SANDBERG

Diagram 3 The use of bait for salmon fishing is slimy, smelly, messy, and deadly-effective. But many anglers have discovered

that using hardware can be equally efficient at limiting a boat. This diagram shows a typical "Buoy Ten" rig with one very important difference, a light, high-action trolling lure is employed rather than bait. When salmon are still in the ocean and actively feeding, lures like the Luhr Jensen Coyote Spoon, Apex Wobbler and Bait-Buster can be deadly. During the kind of hot bite that has made Astoria salmon angling famous, the use of hardware versus bait can be of great advantage. Think about it. You hook a fish, fight it to the boat, then land it. The second that fish hits the deck you're back in the water, trying for number two—no time is wasted rigging a bait, testing it's action, tweaking it to get the right roll, etc. Another place to use hardware is when "holding the line" right at the Buoy Ten deadline on the incoming tide. This can be fast and furious fishing in a combat situation. Dozens if not hundreds of boats have converged on a relatively small area in anticipation of the next big tidal push of fresh ocean fish. The ocean has reversed the flow of the mighty Columbia and is pushing it back upstream at a dizzying speed. Meanwhile, your plug-cut herring has only been wet for a few minutes but is already shredded by the force of the current. Forget the herring, tie on a Coyote Spoon, and watch your rod bury! No need to skewer your thumb with a 6/0 hook while attempting to rig a herring while bouncing around on six-foot rollers.

John Posey of Lamiglas Rods displays a beautiful chinook caught on a Tom Mack Wobbler off the mouth of the Columbia River.

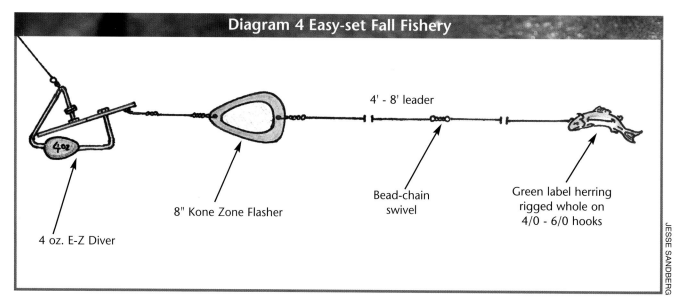

Diagram 4 Easy-set Fall Fishery

4' - 8' leader

8" Kone Zone Flasher

Bead-chain swivel

Green label herring rigged whole on 4/0 - 6/0 hooks

4 oz. E-Z Diver

JESSE SANDBERG

Diagram 4 Here is another set-up that promises to be a killer on fall fish at Astoria. The E-Z diver is a proven diver that's been in use for years. It doesn't plane quite as steeply as other divers, which can be an advantage when you feel the fish are being finicky and want to run your baits further back from the boat. Another advantage to this diver and the Delta Diver is that neither have to be retrieved in order to be re-set after tripping. Instead, just lower your rod and strip out a couple of pulls of line, and the divers will re-set. This will allow you a second chance at a fish that has tripped your diver but failed to continue its pursuit of your bait. The Kone Zone Flasher is new for

2003. It comes in several sizes and alluring colors and functions under the same theory as the Fish Flash: Lots of flash, little drag. Once again, don't neglect to use a high quality bead-chain or ball-bearing swivel to break-up your leader and avoid line twist.

Diagram 5 This is a typical herring rig used in the ocean when targeting coho or chinook that are running shallow while chasing bait. Leader lengths from the spreader to the bait vary a lot between anglers, but four to eight feet seems to be standard, with longer leaders of seven or eight feet increasing in popularity the past few seasons. When using these longer leaders,

The author landed this thirty-five-pound Buoy Ten chromer fishing with Tim Schoonover.

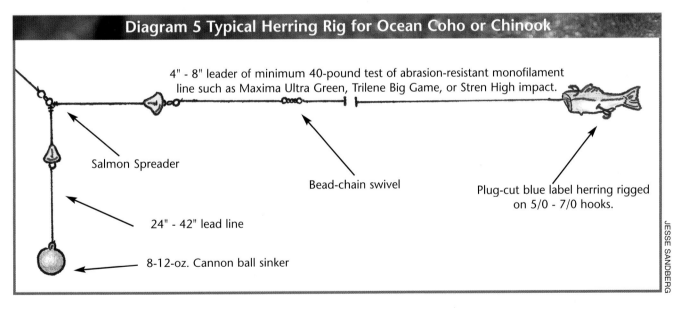

Diagram 5 Typical Herring Rig for Ocean Coho or Chinook

4" - 8" leader of minimum 40-pound test of abrasion-resistant monofilament line such as Maxima Ultra Green, Trilene Big Game, or Stren High impact.

Salmon Spreader

Bead-chain swivel

Plug-cut blue label herring rigged on 5/0 - 7/0 hooks.

24" - 42" lead line

8-12-oz. Cannon ball sinker

JESSE SANDBERG

remember to tie in either a bead-chain or ball-bearing swivel half way in order to avoid line twist, which can severely foul your rig, thus putting a damper on your success. Typical baits include herring, anchovies or even squid. Herring can be rigged either whole or plug-cut, but most favor plug-cut for both the consistency of the roll and the fact that it emits more scent into the water—always a good thing! Divers can be employed in this rig rather than lead, but when fishing shallow, say thirty feet deep or less, lead has an advantage over divers. Professional guide Terry Mulkey explains: "Chinook in the ocean are slow, lazy feeders. When a chinook first grabs your bait it may trip the diver, causing it to plane towards the surface, quickly taking your bait away from the fish. Only the most aggressive feeders will follow to hit it again. A lead rig keeps your bait in the strike zone, allowing a big chinook longer to chew on it so you have a better chance to get 'em!"

Some suggested guides: Mulkey's Guide Service: (503) 803-1896. T.C.'s Guide Service: (503) 780-4067.

Trolling Rigs for Buoy Ten and Ocean Salmon

Guide Terry Mulkey doing what he does best—and a 45-pound chinook is brought to the net.

The Buoy Ten/Astoria salmon fishery is regarded as one of the premier salmon destinations in the world, and for good reason: Astounding numbers of fish congregate here late in the summer, staging and milling until some strange cue in nature tempts them to once again dedicate themselves to fresh water. Both chinook and coho salmon amass at the mouth of the Mighty Columbia, riding the flood tides well up the river, following huge schools of baitfish and gorging themselves on the ocean's bounty until leaving the salt for good and heading to one of the Columbia's many spawning tributaries. In recent years, favorable ocean conditions have provided a pelagic buffet rife with entrees. Plentiful food has lead to plentiful salmon, and run sizes have been staggering for several years now. The 2004 season promises to be no different, with coho numbers predicted at somewhere around half a million fish and chinook numbers expected to be the third highest return since the 1950s.

Whether plying the tidal reach of the lower Columbia or angling in the ocean, this is primarily a troll fishery. Herring, either plug-cut or whole, is the bait of choice. Be sure to get the best-quality bait you can buy, for lousy bait makes for a lousy catch rate. Quality frozen herring will have no ice built up inside

the package. The bait's scales should be mostly intact and shiny and lustrous, not dull and faded. The same goes for the herring's eyes. Recently frozen herring will have fairly clear or only slightly clouded eyes, old bait will have eyes that are extremely opaque. Herring size is denoted by the color of the label on the package, and most anglers use either purple, blue or green label when fishing the ocean or the river.

In recent years, there has been a resurgence in the use of hardware in this fishery, especially late in the season when fewer fish are feeding and the bite has become more reactionary. Anglers have had great results trolling a variety of wobblers, spinners and plugs in both the ocean and the river.

The Columbia River Estuary is a huge area and can be somewhat daunting to the inexperienced. Knowledge of tides and how they affect fish movement is key to success in this fishery; with so much water to cover, being at the right place at the right time is vital. Longtime salmon and steelhead guide Terry Mulkey explains, "This is such a big area that you really need to understand how the fish move to realize the best success. Both chinook and coho will follow the bait balls as they get pushed upriver by an incoming tide, feeding as they go. That's why I like a strong incoming tide followed by a mellow outgoing. The strong push of ocean water forces a lot of fish up into the river, and the softer outgoing allows the salmon to mill around longer before dropping back with the tide.

"Ideally, I like a high that occurs early in the morning as I'm leaving my slip. I would begin fishing near the Astoria/Megler bridge on either the Washington or Oregon side (north or south channels), as fish tend to congregate in these areas at the top end of a high tide. Then, as the tide begins to recede, I troll with the outgoing tide to cover the most water and intercept the most fish. I'll continue to work the area from the bridge down along Desdemona Sands on the Washington side, or from the bridge down to Hammond on the Oregon side, as long as we're still catching fish. I'll troll down through an area where I feel the fish are, then fire up the big motor and run back up to make another pass. By trolling with the outgoing tide, you really cover a ton of water and present your baits to a bunch of fish.

"As the tide diminishes, the fish fall back and the area near the bridge slows down. During this part of the outgoing, the fish can be scattered anywhere between Buoy Ten and Chinook, Washington, so you may have to hunt for them. I generally continue to troll down toward Buoy Ten so I can be right at the line when the incoming tide begins to push in, bringing with it another slug of fresh fish. As the incoming begins to build, we point our boats into the current and 'hold the line,' picking off fish as they scream across the bar. This is the crowded scene for which the Astoria fishery is famous, or infamous. The fishing is fast and furious and the whole scene can get chaotic, and I love it!"

When trolling the lower Columbia or out on the ocean, anglers usually use a diver to keep their bait down in the strike zone. E-Z tackle's Delta Diver and Luhr Jensen's Deep Six and Double Deep Six are among the most popular. Divers plane consistently and don't hop as much as lead sinkers do when the boat is bouncing due to wind or wave. In the river, most anglers fish anywhere from 12 to 24 "pulls" of line out. A "pull" is the distance from the top of the reel to the first guide on the rod. On most salmon rods this is a distance of 18-22 inches. On any given day there may be a particular depth at which the salmon are running or feeding, so it's a good idea to stagger the baits at

different depths until a pattern is established. If a couple of fish are caught at 18 pulls, then by all means run all of the baits at that depth until something changes. Knowing the exact depth the fish are being caught is key, so make sure everyone in the boat is pulling line off their reels in the same manner, that is, in a straight line from reel to guide. That way, when a fish is caught, there will be no question as to how deep the bait was running.

When trolling in the ocean, the salmon can be found anywhere in the water column and fishing depth becomes more of a crapshoot. In general, though, salmon tend to hold closer to the surface early in the day or in overcast conditions. Salmon don't like bright-light conditions, and will go deeper as the day progresses, especially if it is bright and sunny. It's also widely accepted that coho run shallower than chinook, so keep this in mind when deciding what fish to target. There are exceptions to these rules, of course, and a huge ball of herring near the surface can be a big temptation for a gluttonous chinook even at noon on a sunny day. I've seen huge chinook caught on a bait trolled at six pulls and coho caught on a bait run at 32 pulls, so nothing here is set in stone, and it often pays to mix things up.

Diagram 1 This is the typical "plain Jane" Astoria trolling rig shown to me by guide David Johnson. The chartreuse Delta Diver attracts both coho and chinook. The bead-chain swivel breaks up the leader and eliminates line twist caused by the rotating herring. David prefers to use a heavy 50-pound leader so that he doesn't have to waste time re-tying a leader after a fish is caught, an important advantage during a hot bite. David uses a solid tie, double-hook mooching rig versus a sliding rig, because he believes it results in a more solid hook-up and fewer fish lost. Mr. Johnson uses 5/0 Gamakatsu hooks to rig his blue or green label herring, and trolls this rig on a G Loomis SAR 1084c salmon rod equip-ped with Shimano Calcutta reels spooled with 65-pound braided line.

Diagram 2 Typical plug-cut herring rig used in river or ocean. Hook placement is everything when trying to achieve the proper roll. Cross Section A shows the top hook pinned to the bait about halfway between the spine and lateral line of the herring. This results in the slow, lazy roll that chinook prefer. By moving

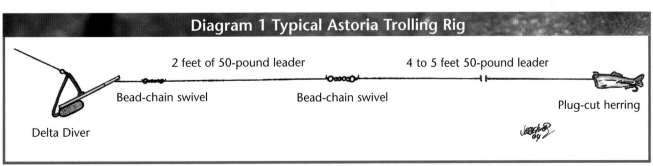

Diagram 1 Typical Astoria Trolling Rig

2 feet of 50-pound leader   4 to 5 feet 50-pound leader

Bead-chain swivel   Bead-chain swivel

Plug-cut herring

Delta Diver

JESSE SANDBERG

the hook only a quarter of this distance from the spine as shown in B, a much quicker roll is achieved which coho seem to prefer. The top hook is pinned through the high side of the bait, and the lower hook can be left to trail behind freely, or pinned in the side of the fish just forward of the tail with the hook point exposed. The trailing hook should always exit the body cavity on the opposite side of the bait from where the top hook is attached. Another tip from Terry Mulkey: "Cut the tail fin off the bait to provide yet another different action to your bait, and use sharp hooks!" Terry uses 4/0-7/0 Owner cutting point hooks depending on the size of bait being used.

Diagram 3 Another effective way to rig a herring is whole, that is with the head still attached. Herring rigged in this way provide a seductive roll and will stay on the hook and intact in the heavy currents and rips of the ocean and lower Columbia. Just make sure the top hook pierces both the upper and lower jawbone of the herring for the firmest attachment. Use a sliding mooching rig to put a bend in the bait to give it a good roll. The trailing hook must be pinned in the side of the fish to achieve

this. The Big Al's Fish Flash is a flasher that provides a lot of attraction with little pull on the line. Salmon will come from great distances to inspect the flasher, and when doing so, hopefully inhale your bait!

Diagram 4 Here is another way to rig for salmon on the troll. The Luhr Jensen Double Deep Six Diver works great when running baits deep to keep the baits down and to keep lines from tangling. The Les Davis Herring Dodger emits lots of flash to simulate slashing, feeding salmon, thus attracting more salmon to the perceived carnage. The Luhr Jensen Salmon Bungee was new on the scene in 2003, and many anglers boasted of increased hook-ups when using it. When a salmon stops your bait, the bungee stretches, allowing the salmon to hang on longer while chewing on the herring, resulting in a better chance for a fish on the line. Note the tail fin nearly completely removed from the bait.

Diagram 5 (See page 100) Most anglers who used the Salmon Bungee in the 2003 salmon season rigged the bungee behind the diver or flasher, with the leader to the herring attached to

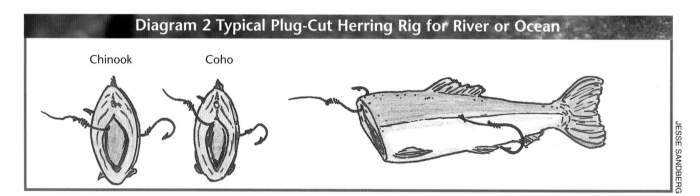

Diagram 2 Typical Plug-Cut Herring Rig for River or Ocean

Chinook   Coho

JESSE SANDBERG

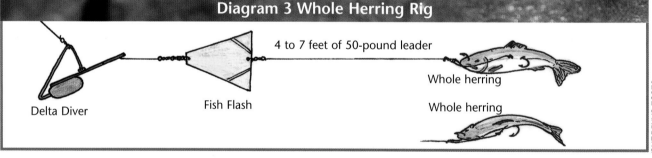

Diagram 3 Whole Herring Rig

4 to 7 feet of 50-pound leader

Whole herring

Delta Diver   Fish Flash

Whole herring

JESSE SANDBERG

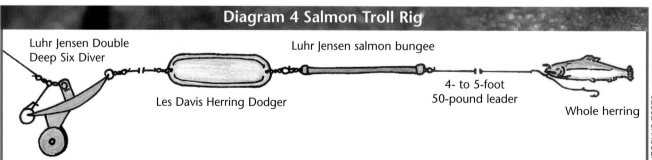

Diagram 4 Salmon Troll Rig

Luhr Jensen Double
Deep Six Diver

Luhr Jensen salmon bungee

Les Davis Herring Dodger

4- to 5-foot
50-pound leader

Whole herring

JESSE SANDBERG

Lee Darby and Arnold hefting a nice king.

the back of the bungee. But after experimenting, Terry Mulkey put the bungee between the diver and the Fish Flash, or "Twirley" as he calls it. "I felt that the elasticity of the bungee was affecting the action of my bait, but I still wanted to use the bungee, especially for coho in the ocean, because I was missing fewer fish with it. So I put it in between the diver and twirley and it worked great."

Diagram 6 There are many bait hoods and clips on the market, but those from Pro Troll have really increased in popularity at Astoria the past few seasons. The Roller Baiter is widely used both for the ease of rigging a bait that it provides and because the action it gives to the bait is a proven fish-getter. Merely pry open the clip, insert the herring or anchovy head first, and you're fishing. These clips also work great in heavy current because they hold onto the bait so well, a must-have when "holding the line" at Buoy Ten. New from Pro Troll is the Roto Chip, a herring clip that comes with an E-chip that emits an electronic signal similar to that of the nerve discharge of a wounded or frightened baitfish.

Diagram 7 As mentioned earlier, the use of hardware has seen a resurgence in recent years in both the ocean and the rivers. Anglers are realizing that bait is not the only method to employ to

hook a salmon. There are times when the flash and thump of wobbling steel will drive salmon bonkers. Wobblers like the Apex, Coyote Spoon, Luhr Jensen Tom Mack and the Silver Horde Lou Pack are all effective at luring salmon, and it's not just the coho that wallop these things; plenty of chinook are caught each season on wobblers, too. The Kone Zone Flasher pictured here was new in 2003 and provided good results at our coastal salmon fisheries. The Kone Zone has an action all its own and flashes very realistically like a feeding salmon. The Lou Pack Wobbler was originally used by commercial salmon trollers and was discovered by Mr. Mulkey several seasons ago. Since that time, it has been a mainstay in his salmon-trolling arsenal. Pink is his favorite color.

Diagram 8 I remember trolling rainbow spinners for salmon at Astoria when I was just a whelp, but it's a technique that seemed to lose favor among many anglers for some time. In the past few seasons, however, the method has experienced a revival. Pro guide Chris Vertopoulos explains, "Four or five years ago I had the pleasure of hosting Buzz Ramsey on a trip at Astoria. As to be expected, Buzz brought his own gear and had a rod rigged with a Tee Spoon Spinner behind a Dipsy Diver. I wasn't exactly overwhelmed with confidence when I saw the set-up, but I figured 'what the heck, it's Buzz Ramsey.' His rig was in the water no

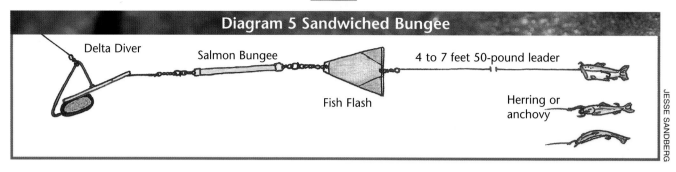

Diagram 5 Sandwiched Bungee

Delta Diver — Salmon Bungee — Fish Flash — 4 to 7 feet 50-pound leader — Herring or anchovy

JESSE SANDBERG

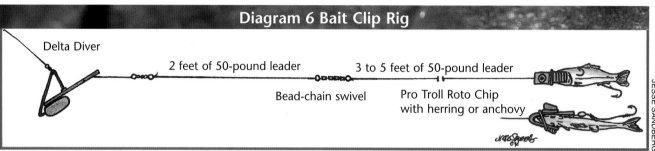

Diagram 6 Bait Clip Rig

Delta Diver — 2 feet of 50-pound leader — Bead-chain swivel — 3 to 5 feet of 50-pound leader — Pro Troll Roto Chip with herring or anchovy

JESSE SANDBERG

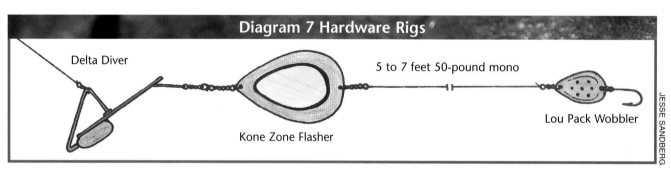

Diagram 7 Hardware Rigs

Delta Diver — Kone Zone Flasher — 5 to 7 feet 50-pound mono — Lou Pack Wobbler

JESSE SANDBERG

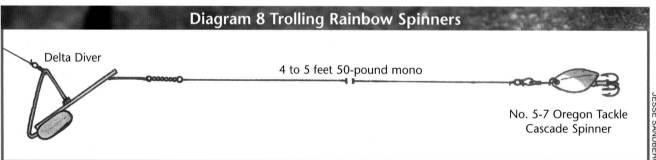

Diagram 8 Trolling Rainbow Spinners

Delta Diver — 4 to 5 feet 50-pound mono — No. 5-7 Oregon Tackle Cascade Spinner

JESSE SANDBERG

more than a couple of minutes when he got a nice coho. It was an enlightening occasion. A couple of years after that, guide Andy Betnar was experimenting with some Tillamook-type blades behind divers and doing quite well. Late that season, Andy invited myself and guides Bob Rees and Trevor Storley, as well as State Officer Trygvy Klepp on a fishing trip. We trolled with the tide and by 1:00 p.m. had thirteen chinook to the boat, and I don't remember us starting very early in the morning. Since then it has been a reliable tactic for me. We used to think that the red-and-white blade was the only way to go, but extensive experimentation has proved this untrue—just about any proven chinook color will work, and the coho will smack 'em as well.

"We troll them with the tide and run 4-5' of fifty-pound leader between the diver and the spinner. It's not like fishing spinners at Tillamook where you have to hold the rod and set the hook at any tick of the line. At Astoria, you put the rod in the holder and wait for it to fold over. It's a really relaxing, easy way to fish. Plus, there's no bait to mess with, and if a fish hits the spinner and doesn't stick, you just re-set the diver if it has tripped, leave the rig in the water, and let the fish have another rip at it!"

For more information call:

Terry Mulkey: (503) 803-1896;

Chris Vertopoulos: (503) 349-1377;

David Johnson: (503) 201-4292.

Kelly Fussell and the author care for the catch after a tough day at the Buoy Ten fishery. Only five fish were landed on this trip. That's right, folks, the salmon angling here can be so fantastic that a five-fish day is considered slow fishing!

Bay and Tidewater Salmon Rigs

"Get me a net, no, make that two nets!" Terry Mulkey and guests double down on Tillamook Bay salmon.

hicken Of The Sea. Most people will recall this as a brand of tuna fish that moms across America packed in so many brown bag lunches. But in my family, Chicken Of The Sea was me, and my siblings have never let me forget it. As a youth I was terrified of the ocean. Perhaps this was due to the many ill-timed runs we made across the Columbia River Bar in a 21-foot riveted Starcraft. Or maybe it was the sight of storm-powered waves pummeling Cape Kiwanda at Pacific City, Oregon, home of the dory fleet. Whatever the case, the ocean scared the living hell out of me. In spite of my fears, though, I still ventured out on the big briny with the rest of the family because that's where the fish were. In between pulling on fish and puking, I would secretly long for the days ahead when the salmon would enter the sheltered bays and tidewater reaches of coastal rivers, where fish would congregate and mill until rivers swelled to welcome them home; where a ten-year-old boy might keep his breakfast down!

The Pacific Northwest is blessed with abundant bays and coastal rivers that provide excellent angling for fall chinook and coho salmon. Nowadays, regulations vary from water to water as much as the various angling techniques, so it's always a good idea to double check the rules before venturing out. Salmon tend to congregate in and near the bays and tidewater reaches of rivers toward the end of summer, when biological changes within the fish cue them toward their spawning grounds. Some waters have decent numbers of fish present as early as the end of July, while others see the bulk return as late as October or November, thus extending our tidewater/bay fisheries over several months. It's a good idea to do some homework to determine when the best time is to fish the location you have in mind. Call a local tackle shop, hire a guide to learn new water or pick the brain of a buddy whose freezer is always full.

As is common with salmon fishing virtually everywhere else, bay and tidewater angling is dependent on water conditions and fish movement, with the latter often dictated by the various tides. Because of weather patterns and water conditions, some years offer better tidewater fishing than others. Dry autumns with little rain to raise rivers seem to be best, as the fish tend to stage longer in estuaries waiting for the rivers to rise sufficiently to draw them in. Conversely, a fall season with heavy rain and swollen rivers—the kind of weather avid back-bouncers hope for—usually provides less opportunity in bays and tidewater, as the fish tend to take advantage of higher flows to scream upstream to find good gravel. Not to say that good tidewater fishing is nonexistent during a high-water year, it just becomes more critical to have knowledge of how the salmon move according to the tides, that is, being at the right place at the right time to intercept migrating fish.

Salmon will ride a flood tide far up a bay and into the tidewater stretch of a river. As the tide reverses and begins to ebb, several scenarios may play out. If the river is high with runoff, the fish may just keep on finning upstream and commit to the river. If it is low, the salmon may simply turn around and ride the outgoing back down to the bay or even back out to the ocean. Ideally, though, some of the fish will hunker down in the deeper holes, ditches and channels and wait for another flood tide to push them farther toward their final destination. It is these holding fish that present excellent opportunity to the angler on the bottom end of the tide. Bays and tidewater stretches of rivers afford cover of many different sorts that appeal to salmon. Deep holes with relatively shallow water up and downstream are an obvious location for fish to stack up. Anywhere there exists a current seam between fast and slow water is another good place to target, especially if the seam is created by a back eddy or structure like a submerged log or root wad. It may take some exploration to locate ideal holding areas, and a crowded scene during the height of the season is not the best time to do this. Savvy anglers scout their fishing grounds just as a proficient hunter does his hunting grounds, taking advantage of low tides that expose potential holding water, then returning when fish are present to test their guesswork.

Generally, salmon are most active in tidewater around the tide changes. Something about the gradually changing current really fires them up. The hour or so on either side of a slack tide often sees the best bite, but keep in mind that salmon are curious, inexplicable creatures that will bite whenever they damn well feel like it. Once the current is moving again, the fish will move as well. This is where it pays to be familiar with the migration routes within a bay. Every bay has channels and ditches that the fish use to travel. Sometimes these routes remain constant for years, sometimes they change drastically from season to season due to storms, flooding or shifting sands. Once in the tidewater stretch of the river, salmon will progress very close to the shoreline, and that's where you need to present your bait to realize the best results on moving fish.

Diagram 1 Here is a simple but effective rig used to troll plug-cut herring in bays. The Oregon Tackle Salmon Spreader comes equipped with tee beads to help ward off the various grasses and weeds so common in our lower bays before fall rains flush them out. Breaking up the leader between the spreader and bait is a bead-chain swivel that helps reduce line twist which in turn keeps the whole set-up from getting fouled, thus extending fishing time. This particular swivel from Oregon Tackle features a weed guard that fishermen have dubbed the "swivel condom." The weed guard keeps aquatic vegetation from gobbing up on the swivel, therefore letting it do its job. Blue or purple label herring is most commonly used in our fall salmon fisheries, and most anglers plug-cut theirs to achieve the proper roll and emit a ton of scent into the water.

Diagram 2 The use of divers to troll herring is most often associated with open water that is somewhat deep, but some anglers employ divers in deeper bay waters, such as the jaws at Tillamook Bay. Divers are great for inexperienced anglers

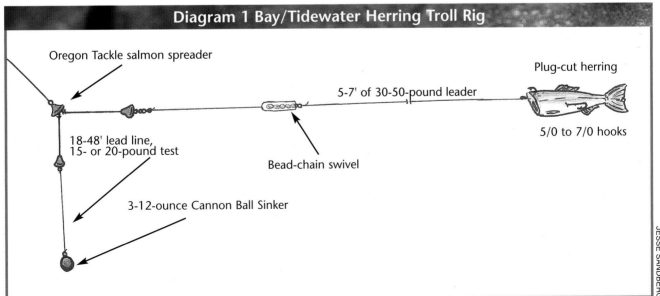

Diagram 1 Bay/Tidewater Herring Troll Rig

Oregon Tackle salmon spreader

Plug-cut herring

5-7' of 30-50-pound leader

18-48' lead line,
15- or 20-pound test

5/0 to 7/0 hooks

Bead-chain swivel

3-12-ounce Cannon Ball Sinker

JESSE SANDBERG

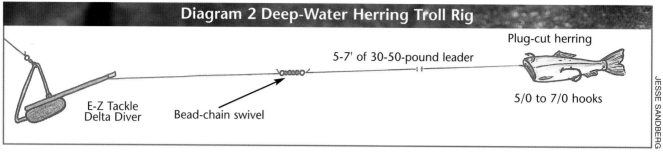

Diagram 2 Deep-Water Herring Troll Rig

5-7' of 30-50-pound leader

Plug-cut herring

E-Z Tackle
Delta Diver

Bead-chain swivel

5/0 to 7/0 hooks

JESSE SANDBERG

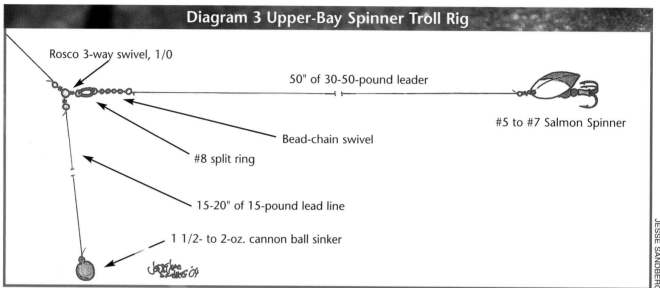

Diagram 3 Upper-Bay Spinner Troll Rig

Rosco 3-way swivel, 1/0

50" of 30-50-pound leader

#5 to #7 Salmon Spinner

Bead-chain swivel

#8 split ring

15-20" of 15-pound lead line

1 1/2- to 2-oz. cannon ball sinker

JESSE SANDBERG

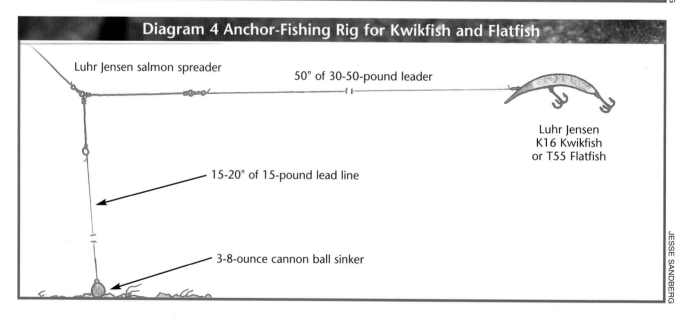

Diagram 4 Anchor-Fishing Rig for Kwikfish and Flatfish

Luhr Jensen salmon spreader

50" of 30-50-pound leader

Luhr Jensen
K16 Kwikfish
or T55 Flatfish

15-20" of 15-pound lead line

3-8-ounce cannon ball sinker

JESSE SANDBERG

because they help keep lines from becoming tangled and are easy to use. When trolling herring for salmon it is important not to set the hook the second a fish begins working a bait. Instead, let it chew on the bait until the rod is really throbbing, then firmly—not maniacally—lift the rod to set the hook. A viciously wild hook-set often results in broken tackle or a lost fish when trolling herring.

Diagram 3 As salmon make their way to the shallower upper bays, trolling spinners becomes the preferred method of anglers. Fishermen troll both with and against the tide, depending on current speed, and once again, the time around a tide change is usually best. The last two hours of an outgoing tide can often provide very good fishing as the fish will keg up in deeper water for cover as the tide retreats. "Deeper" water in these areas may only be four or five feet in depth, and hooking a big chinook in such an environment can make for an explosive battle. Salmon hooked in this skinny water will come unglued, testing an angler and his gear to the maximum. When trolling spinners in shallow water, it is advisable to hold onto the rod instead of putting it in a rod holder, as the fish will sometimes inhale your spinner in what is called a slack-line bite. This occurs when a fish moves up quickly to the spinner and grabs it while its momentum carries it toward the boat. The result is the loss of tension on the line and the disappearance of the telltale thump of the blade that tells you that the spinner is working properly. In this instance it is important to set the hook quickly and sharply because the fish will not hold onto the spinner for very long, and if the rod is in a holder you may never see the bite and rarely will the hook-set come in time.

When trolling spinners, begin by lowering the set-up into the water and letting out line until the sinker taps bottom. Then reel up a crank so that the sinker is gliding just above the bottom so it doesn't get snagged up as often. An experienced captain will watch the depthfinder for changes in bottom structure and will periodically call out the depth so that everyone in the boat can reel in or let out more line to suit the changing terrain. By doing this, the spinners dredge through the deeper slots and channels where the fish hold, and rise in the water column to avoid snagging bottom.

When trolling spinners, the fish may absolutely slam the lure or may just make your line go slack. Either way, a quick hook-set is necessary before the fish drops the spinner. Just remember that when fishing this way there isn't much line out behind the boat, so a powerful overhead hook-set may cause your entire set-up to fly out of the water toward your head! A sweeping hook-set to the side is safer and often more effective at driving the hooks home.

Diagram 4 Plunking a Kwikfish while anchored is a technique that works great when fish are on the move. Position the boat in a known travel lane, throw out the pick and take a nap. The inside bend of a tidewater river or channel with a cut bank is often a good place to start. This is leisurely fishing that can result in some thunderous take-downs. Just be sure that you don't anchor in an established trolling lane or you will become unpopular in a hurry.

Diagrams 5 and 6 When salmon reach the tight quarters of tidewater rivers, bobber fishing or "corking" becomes the most popular method. Properly executed, corking allows a bait to be presented at current speed in a natural manner. Bobbers come in

Chris Vertopoulos and a happy client show off a 43-pound Tillamook Bay chinook.

Diagram 5 Low-Water Float Set-up

Diagram 6 Heavy, Deep-Water Bobber Rig

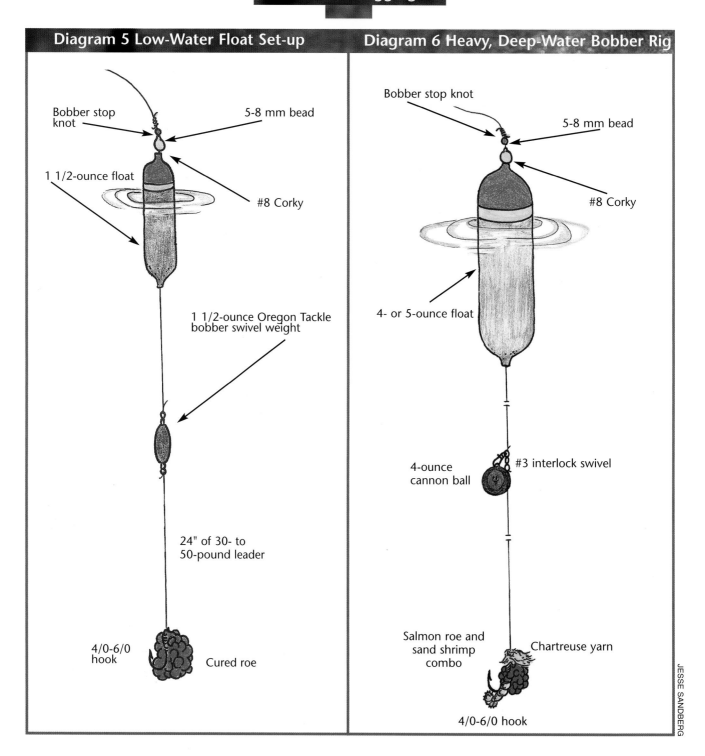

Diagram 5 labels:
Bobber stop knot
5-8 mm bead
1 1/2-ounce float
#8 Corky
1 1/2-ounce Oregon Tackle bobber swivel weight
24" of 30- to 50-pound leader
4/0-6/0 hook
Cured roe

Diagram 6 labels:
Bobber stop knot
5-8 mm bead
#8 Corky
4- or 5-ounce float
4-ounce cannon ball
#3 interlock swivel
Salmon roe and sand shrimp combo
Chartreuse yarn
4/0-6/0 hook

JESSE SANDBERG

many shapes and sizes, from the round cork-type my father is so fond of to the cylindrical foam "beer cans" used in deep water with heavy sinkers. Perhaps the most widely used in recent years are the cigar-shaped floats sometimes referred to as stick bobbers. These foam bobbers float well, signal the sometimes subtle take of the fish and offer little resistance when they go under water, prompting a salmon to hold onto the bait longer. When bobber fishing it is important to match the rig to the water conditions at hand. In deeper, heavier flows it becomes neces-

sary to hold the bait at the proper depth by using a heavier sinker, and therefore a larger float. In lighter currents and shallower holes, it may be necessary to downsize the rig in order to achieve the proper presentation, that is, at or near current speed.

Bobber stops can be purchased at tackle shops or be made by simply tying a UNI-knot made with Dacron to the mainline. Cortland Micron is a tightly braided fly-line backing that works great for bobber stops. Be sure to use a 5mm bead between the

CHRIS VERTOPOULOS

A successful day on Tillamook Bay fishing with guides David Johnson and Chris Vertopoulos.

float and bobber stop so that the stop doesn't get pulled into the float. Sinkers can be affixed in numerous ways, but the bobber swivel weights from Oregon Tackle are excellent for their ease of rigging.

Be sure to use quality hooks that are extremely sharp in sizes 4/0-6/0. Owner, Gamakatsu and Mustad Ultra Points are all excellent choices. Don't be shy when it comes to leader strength—fifty-pound test is not overdoing it. A big chinook hooked in tight quarters full of woody debris will soon part ways with a light leader. The bait of choice for corking is cured salmon roe. A wet cure that allows the eggs to milk in the water is preferable, for the more scent released, the better.

There are many excellent egg cures on the market today, but for some productive custom cures, check out the book *Egg Cures* by Scott Haugen (Frank Amato Publications). Every serious corker should own this book. When fishing crowded water or when the salmon are off the bite, try experimenting with different baits or combinations of baits in order to stir things up or to stand out in the crowd. Sand shrimp or a small chunk of sardine or herring can sometimes make the day.

Begin by casting the rig upstream along a current seam or cut bank with sufficient depth to hold fish. Allow the rig to drift naturally through the hole while keeping a fairly straight line to the float to facilitate a quick hook-set. Conflicting currents may cause the line to move downstream faster than the rig, forming a belly that can lead to drag that will pull the set-up downstream in an unnatural manner. This can be corrected by flipping the line back upstream with the rod tip, or mending as it is called, to eliminate the offending belly and maintain a natural drift. Tidewater salmon often suspend at varying depths in any given location, so some experimentation may be necessary to realize success, but most fish taken in tidewater are caught with the bobber stop set somewhere between six and nine feet. Salmon don't always pull the float under water when they bite, in fact, quite often the float will merely vibrate or twitch as the fish mouths the bait. When this happens, reel down to the fish and set up on him. Another type of bite occurs when the float just flips over on its side. This is the corker's equivalent of the spinner fisherman's slack-line bite. A fish has taken the bait and risen above the sinker, thus removing all the weight off the float and causing it to tip over. This is another cue requiring a quick hook-set.

Our Northwest bays and tidewater river sections provide excellent sport on salmon for several months every season. The varied waters and techniques appeal to many different anglers who prefer to fish their favorite method. Whether trolling herring, pulling spinners or bobber fishing eggs, tidewater salmon angling offers something for every serious salmon fisherman.

Buoy Ten Hardware Trolling Rigs

CHRIS VERTOPOULOS

This pot-bellied Buoy Ten chinook fell to a pleased client of Chris Vertopoulos.

CHRIS VERTOPOULOS

Hardware is once again gaining in popularity.

Isn't the Pacific Northwest a great place to live? It seems just yesterday that we were putting away our spring chinook gear and here it is time for the most prolific fall chinook and coho fishery on the west coast: The legendary Buoy Ten. Each year, hundreds of thousands of salmon pass this area on their way to upriver spawning grounds, and thousands of anglers turn out to greet them. According to a report on recreational salmon fisheries released by the fish division of the Oregon Department of Fish and Wildlife in December of 2004, an estimated 497,000 upriver bright chinook returned to the Columbia in 2004. Tule fall chinook numbered around 294,000 fish, while coho numbers were estimated at 429,000. According to my calculator, that's a fall run comprised of 1,220,000 fish! Staggering numbers, to be sure.

Also from this report, 74,000 angler trips resulted in an estimated 17,400 chinook being harvested (4th highest on record), and 16,600 fin-clipped coho—all from the Buoy Ten fishery—these numbers don't include all the fish caught from the remainder of the lower Columbia up to Bonneville Dam. (An additional 17,800 chinook and 1,300 fin-clipped coho.) While ODFW predicts the 2005 coho run to be "down from 2004," and the chinook run to be "strong but reduced," we should see yet another awesome season on the extreme lower Columbia.

The Buoy Ten fishery is primarily a bait/troll fishery and herring is the bait of choice. Anchovies are another popular bait, but the swift currents and violent rips of the lower Columbia often shred this soft bait before a fish can find it. In recent years, there has been a resurgence of anglers using hardware at or near Buoy Ten. This trend began with guides who turned to a variety of spinners and wobblers to induce some action when the bait

bite died as it sometimes does. No matter how good the herring bite can be—and it's often fantastic here—there always seems to be some point during the time and tide that there is a lull in the action. Maybe it's at high slack when gluttonous fish have "fed up the tide" and are now gorged and lazily milling around above the Astoria-Megler Bridge. Or maybe this lull occurs from the middle to bottom part of an ebb tide out in front of Hammond, where fish that pushed up to Astoria on the flood tide are now dropping back with the receding water. These are just two examples of where I've seen the bait bite die at this fishery, but it can happen any time, any place. Savvy anglers have learned that at times like these it pays to be different. How many trolled herring do you think the fish see on a typical day at this fishery? Conversely, how many spinners? When salmon fall off the bite at Buoy Ten, hardware provides a different kind of flash and vibration that will likely trigger a reactionary bite from a fish that has turned its nose from bait.

An Anecdote

During the 2004 Buoy Ten season I was fortunate to get to fish with part-time guide and full-time friend, Mike Scheehean. Along with us were two of Mike's clients and Kelly Fussell, a manager at the Oregon City Fisherman's Marine and Outdoor. We began the day at the Buoy Ten deadline in anticipation of the incoming tide. We fished through the first few hours of the incoming "holding the line" and caught a couple of fish on herring.

When the bite fell off at the buoy, we just continued trolling with the tide hoping to pick up a fish or two, a sound tactic for this area. We trolled up to Buoy 20 and held into the tide, back-trolling our baits. Mike was busy on the motor while I was busy cutting bait and keeping all the rods fishing. We were marking plenty of fish on the fish finder, but not getting bit. After an hour, this routine hadn't produced a take-down, and Kelly stood up and said, "This bites, where's that Wobbler?"

I had brought along some Silver Horde Lou Pack Wobblers in custom colors that Fisherman's Marine was experimenting with before ordering into production. Pro guide Terry Mulkey had turned me onto this lure several years prior and I had decent

success with it, but mostly on the ocean. Kelly tied on the only one I had in chartreuse. He rigged it on about five feet of forty-pound test behind a Delta Diver without a flasher and lowered it down. Within minutes he landed a seventeen-pound upriver bright chinook. Moments later he had a wild coho, then another chinook, which he passed off to one of Mike's other clients. (Party fishing rules apply at Buoy Ten.) Kelly hooked several more fish while the herring rods went ignored. I tied on a spinner, but Kelly had the lure they wanted on that day, and of course it was the only one on the boat.

After an hour or so of watching Kelly hook fish the bite died off and we decided to motor up to Hammond to see if we could intercept some more fish moving with the tide. We dropped in off Hammond and Kelly's Wobbler nailed two more chinook in quick succession. We didn't quite limit the boat that day, but we did have a respectable catch. None of us could exactly recall just how many fish Kelly had hooked on the Lou Pack but it was agreed by all that the Wobbler had saved the day, and that hardware rigs certainly have their time and place at Buoy Ten.

Diagram 1 Here is a common hardware rig used at Buoy Ten and on the ocean. The E-Z Tackle Delta Diver is a favorite at Buoy Ten because it planes true and doesn't yo-yo as much as

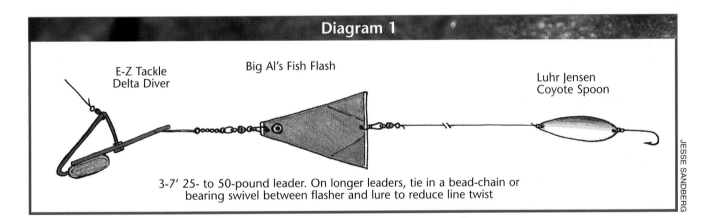

Diagram 1

E-Z Tackle Delta Diver

Big Al's Fish Flash

Luhr Jensen Coyote Spoon

3-7' 25- to 50-pound leader. On longer leaders, tie in a bead-chain or bearing swivel between flasher and lure to reduce line twist

JESSE SANDBERG

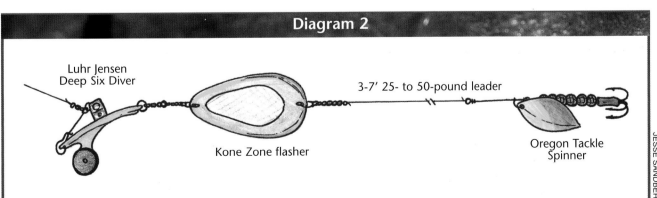

Diagram 2

Luhr Jensen Deep Six Diver

3-7' 25- to 50-pound leader

Kone Zone flasher

Oregon Tackle Spinner

JESSE SANDBERG

Diagram 3

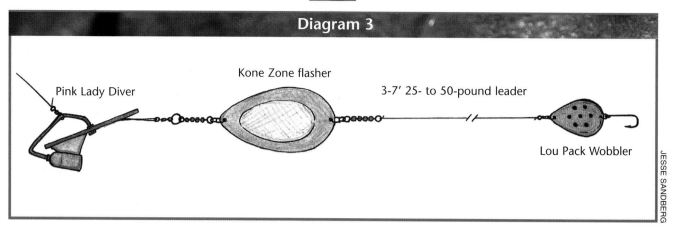

Pink Lady Diver

Kone Zone flasher

3-7' 25- to 50-pound leader

Lou Pack Wobbler

JESSE SANDBERG

Diagram 4

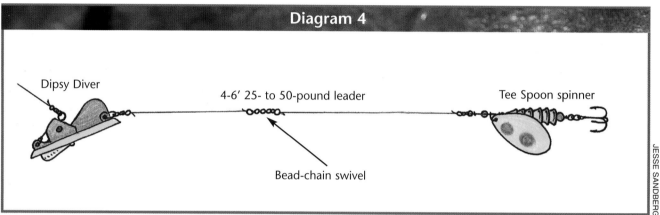

Dipsy Diver

4-6' 25- to 50-pound leader

Tee Spoon spinner

Bead-chain swivel

JESSE SANDBERG

Diagram 5

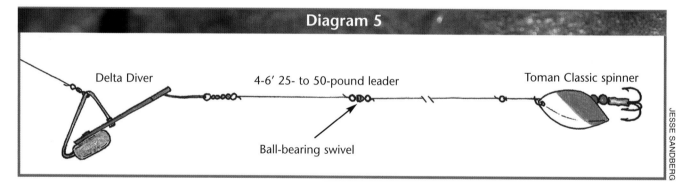

Delta Diver

4-6' 25- to 50-pound leader

Toman Classic spinner

Ball-bearing swivel

JESSE SANDBERG

lead rigs do when the boat bounces on chop or swell. The Big Al's Fish Flash provides color, flash and attraction without added drag against the rod. Red is generally accepted as the color of choice for diver and flasher when targeting silvers (coho), but you will catch chinook on it too. The Coyote Spoon from Luhr Jensen and Sons is a proven lure wherever salmon swim, not just at Buoy Ten.

Diagram 2 Luhr Jensen's Deep Six and Double Deep Six are also popular divers at Buoy Ten and they tend to move around a little more than Delta Divers which on some days may be a good thing. The Deep Six comes equipped with a positive trip mechanism that allows the angler to trip the diver in order to make it easier to reel in. The Kone Zone is another effective flasher that

will attract fish from great distances. Check out the new "crushed pearl glow" and "slick glow" colors that promise to be highly attractive as well. Oregon Tackle makes some great salmon spinners and the lemon-lime color pictured here is extremely effective. Chartreuse is one color of choice for anglers targeting chinook at Buoy Ten, but coho will fall for it, too.

I spoke with pro angler Buzz Ramsey regarding tackle trends at Buoy Ten and he agreed that hardware is once again gaining popularity. "Buoy Ten has been considered a herring troll fishery for so long that anglers forgot how effective hardware can be," said Buzz. "Now, spinners and Wobblers are being used again with great success. It has also been a trend to tie on as much gear as possible to increase the attraction of your rigging," continues Buzz. "Guys use a colored diver, add a flasher, sometimes even double up on the flasher, then tie in an orange or char-treuse Salmon Bungee to complete the show. All of this color and flash really attracts the salmon, and it now seems that the more gear you have on the line, the more you will catch."

Thanks, Buzz. If you're looking for a flashy rig for Buoy Ten, check out the new Comet Tail Delta Divers from Luhr Jensen Company.

Diagram 3 The Pink Lady Diver pictured here is an old school diver that doesn't plane as steeply as some other divers, making it a favorite of anglers targeting coho. Coho are generally found closer to the surface than chinook, and spend the majority of their lives in the ocean within the top thirty feet of the water column. There are exceptions to this rule, as silvers are ravenous feeders that will go where necessary to find forage. I've caught Alaskan silvers at two hundred feet deep while halibut fishing, and I've seen them caught at over one hundred feet deep off the Oregon Coast. But these are exceptions, of course, so if you're targeting coho at Buoy Ten, fish your rig out 6-16 pulls in the morning or under low-light (overcast) conditions, perhaps a little deeper later in the day if the sun is on the water when the fish tend to run deeper. A pull is the length of line from the top of your reel to the first guide on the rod.

Some fishermen run a stout monofilament bumper between the diver and flasher to extend the bait further from the diver, but this often results in frustrating tangles if the rig is not let out slowly. The flashers pictured here are all attached directly to the divers, and this helps reduce tangles and keep your rig fishing at all times. There's nothing more frustrating at Buoy Ten than reeling up your rig and finding that it hasn't been fishing. When using Wobblers with single siwash hooks you may increase your hook-up and landing rate by very carefully bending the hook point so that it is off-set from the shank approximately twenty degrees. This seems to hook fish better as the point is more exposed, and certainly holds better when a fifteen-pound coho is thrashing on the surface.

Diagram 4 The Luhr Jensen Dipsy Diver is a directional diver that can be made to angle away from the boat as it dives. This results in a better spread of the rigs and allows you to cover more water, and therefore, more fish. This also provides the added benefit of lines staying untangled. You can adjust how much and to which direction the diver will plane by rotating the base plate of the diver. The Tee Spoon spinner pictured here has been a favorite among salmon fishermen for a long time now, and for good reason. It is likely that this spinner is responsible for more salmon dinners than any other production spinner out there. While there

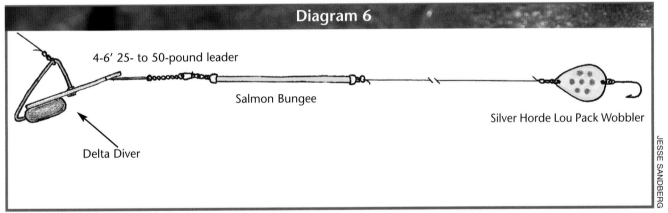

Diagram 6

4-6' 25- to 50-pound leader

Salmon Bungee

Silver Horde Lou Pack Wobbler

Delta Diver

JESSE SANDBERG

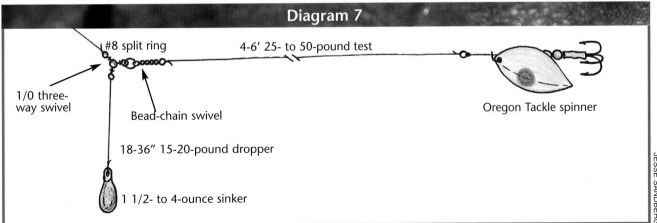

Diagram 7

#8 split ring

4-6' 25- to 50-pound test

1/0 three-way swivel

Bead-chain swivel

18-36" 15-20-pound dropper

1 1/2- to 4-ounce sinker

Oregon Tackle spinner

JESSE SANDBERG

More evidence that hardware has its place at the Buoy Ten fishery.

are other excellent spinners on the market today (Toman and Oregon Tackle, for instance), the flash and vibration of this particular blade has been a proven salmon killer for decades.

Diagrams 5, 6 and 7 As Buzz stated earlier, it seems that having a gaudy set-up is advisable most of the time at the Buoy Ten fishery. This is a big area and the more flash and color you put in the water, the better chance you have of attracting salmon from far off. There are times at Buoy Ten, however, when the salmon seem to favor a plainer rig. These final three illustrations show simple, tamer set-ups that are effective when the salmon are acting snooty. They also work great when the tide is really ripping, because with less gear on the line, there is less chance for tangles due to the swift current.

Diagram 5 shows a Bob Toman Classic spinner that has been dynamite at Buoy Ten the past several seasons. The red and white finish has been particularly effective, so effective in fact, that many fishermen don't bother using other colors. But guide Chris Vertopoulos advises against getting stuck on just one color. "Back when we first started using spinners at Astoria we caught a lot of fish on the red and white blades because that's all we were using," states Chris. "But since then I began experimenting with different colors and have found several other combinations that produce. Basically, any proven finish used in the Tillamook fishery seems to work at Buoy Ten. Another thing about fishing spinners on the lower Columbia is that I've noticed that I have better results when

all of the rods are rigged with them, rather than a couple with herring and a couple with spinners. I can't tell you why this is but I've spent time experimenting and have determined that my spinners get bit more when there's a whole gang of them versus just a couple."

Diagram 6 shows another simple hardware rig that incorporates a Luhr Jensen Salmon Bungee. The Salmon Bungee is the brainchild of pro guide Tim Juarez, a long-time and long-respected guide from Oregon. Tim arrived at the bungee as the result of frustration caused when short-biting silvers ran away with his bait while fishing the ocean. "I was fishing the ocean in early July for coho," says Tim, "and we were missing fish left and right and burning through a ridiculous amount of bait. I began to ponder what I could do to remedy this situation and recalled the bungees kokanee fishermen use to improve their hook and landing rate and thought, "why not for salmon?" So I purchased some 3/16" surgical tubing, attached bead chains to each end and went fishing. The results we had were amazing. In early July, you often have to cull through a lot of wild fish in order to get your hatchery keepers, and in two days of fishing we landed 83 out of 87 coho hooked! With such an improvement, I knew that I was onto something and took my idea to Buzz Ramsey at Luhr Jensen, who immediately liked the idea and wasted no time in putting the Salmon Bungee into production. By the end of August, nearly 100,000 of the bungees had been sold, which tells me that fishermen were having the same results using them that I was."

Dave Kilhefner with a hefty Buoy 10 king salmon. This up-river bright
was caught with a Delta Diver, Fish Flash and spinner.

Thanks, Tim. Salmon Bungees are available at finer tackle across the west and are even being used in the Great Lakes salmon fisheries. When you're at Buoy Ten this season and find the herring bite less than productive, tie on a spinner or Wobbler and watch what happens. You might be pleasantly surprised.

Fall Chinook River Fishing Rigs

Basic Backbouncing Rig

Backbouncing is an extremely effective technique used to catch chinook in our Northwest rivers. Here is a very simple set-up employed for this method.

Advanced Backbouncing Rig

Here is a more sophisticated backbouncing rig shown to me by Kelly Reichner, an avid chinook angler and tackle buyer for Fisherman's Marine and Outdoor. Instead of using a three-way swivel, Kelly likes to thread his mainline through an Oregon Tackle E-Z Slider and an eight millimeter bead before tying off to a six-bead chain swivel. "I like to use a sliding rig for a couple of reasons," Kelly explains. "First of all, I feel a sliding rig lets me detect a soft take better than a fixed rig because my lead dropper is independent of the mainline. Also, if a fish starts to move off with my bait before I detect it, I am more confident that he will hold onto it longer because he can't feel the weight of my sinker."

Make sure to attach a #52 or 53 Luhr Jensen duo lock snap onto the slider before tying on your leadline, or the mono will cut into the soft plastic of the slider. Also be certain to use the 8mm bead between the slider and swivel, as this both protects the knot and keeps the slider from getting fouled on the swivel. Another trick to this rig is to tie in an overhand knot halfway on your lead line, as this creates a weak spot that will break away more easily when snagged on the bottom. The bead-chain swivel

is far superior to a three-way for reducing line twist, and Kelly likes to use a double hook set-up rather than a single. "I just feel more confident with two hooks back there rather than one. I always put my bait on the first hook and let the rear hook trail, this results in a pretty solid hook-up." Kelly also recommends using one of the high-tech superbraided lines like Western Filament's Tuff Plus when backbouncing. These small diameter, low-stretch lines give you better contact with the bait and allow you to use lighter leads than monofilament.

Another tip on backbouncing: "Whenever possible, bounce your rod as gently as you can. I've found that I get bit more often when I use a softer, more fluid bounce. I think this is because the bait stays in the strike zone longer and isn't hopping around so much," says Kelly. "But when the bottom has a lot of structure and is really grabby, you will want to use a bigger 'hop' so that your sinker clears the obstructions and doesn't get snagged up."

Big-Water Backtrolling Rig

Backtrolling large wobbling plugs like the Luhr Jensen Kwikfish or Worden's Flatfish is another killer tactic for fall chinook. This diagram shows a typical "big water" rig used to search out chinook in large expanses of relatively undefined, deep water. The use of a #50 Luhr Jensen Jumbo Jet Diver in this rig allows for a lot of mobility when backtrolling, enabling anglers to cover large swaths of water. Professional guide Dan Ponciano regularly

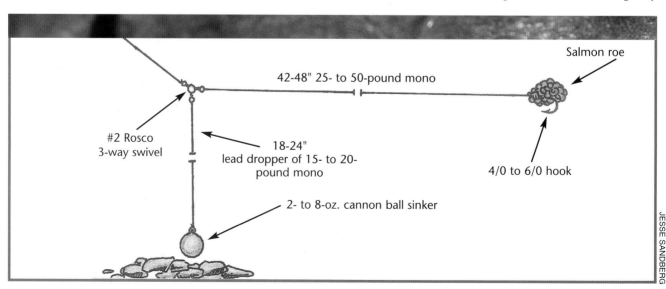

Salmon roe

42-48" 25- to 50-pound mono

#2 Rosco
3-way swivel

18-24"
lead dropper of 15- to 20-
pound mono

4/0 to 6/0 hook

2- to 8-oz. cannon ball sinker

JESSE SANDBERG

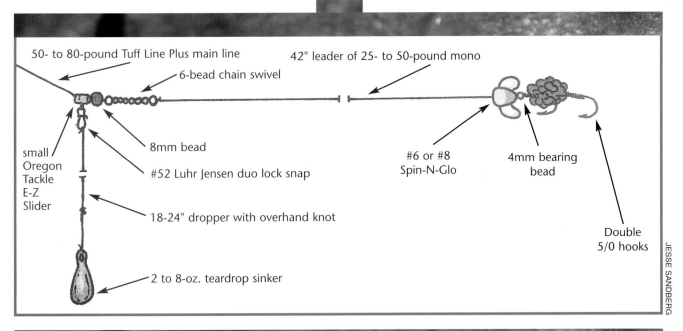

50- to 80-pound Tuff Line Plus main line

42" leader of 25- to 50-pound mono

6-bead chain swivel

8mm bead

small Oregon Tackle E-Z Slider

#52 Luhr Jensen duo lock snap

18-24" dropper with overhand knot

2 to 8-oz. teardrop sinker

#6 or #8 Spin-N-Glo

4mm bearing bead

Double 5/0 hooks

JESSE SANDBERG

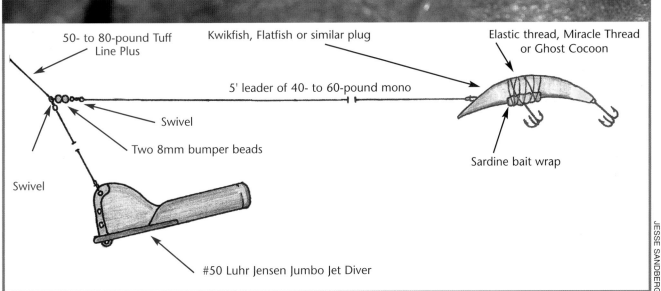

50- to 80-pound Tuff Line Plus

Kwikfish, Flatfish or similar plug

Elastic thread, Miracle Thread or Ghost Cocoon

5' leader of 40- to 60-pound mono

Swivel

Two 8mm bumper beads

Sardine bait wrap

Swivel

#50 Luhr Jensen Jumbo Jet Diver

JESSE SANDBERG

employs this set-up while fishing for upriver brights on the massive Columbia River. "This diver set-up really allows me to cover a lot of water, which is important on the Columbia, because the travel lanes the fish use are often very narrow and are always changing," reports Dan. "This rig is also very easy to use and hassle-free, which makes it nice for those clients who may have had little or no experience salmon fishing, and may have difficulty using another technique."

Dan stresses that leader length on this rig is very important. "A lot of the time we're letting out enough line that the diver is digging into the bottom, that's why I use a leader that's five feet long. When the diver is on the bottom, that length allows the buoyant lure to ride up in the water column to where the fish want it." Which brings us to the one question I hear most often

about this particular rig: How much line do I let out? As I understand it, the Jumbo Jet Diver is designed to dive to fifty feet when using one hundred feet of 17-pound test, but keep in mind that this is a very general guideline. There are a lot of variables to consider here. Line diameters between manufacturers vary greatly, and most of us use much heavier line than 17-pound test for fall chinook fishing. Also, current/trolling speed has an influence as well. The faster the flow, the more force against the diver and it planes more steeply. Because chinook are most often on or near the bottom, my solution to this dilemma is to let out enough line to find bottom then reel up a crank or two. You'll know when the diver is on the bottom when the repetitive vibration of the lure on the rod tip changes and becomes much more erratic.

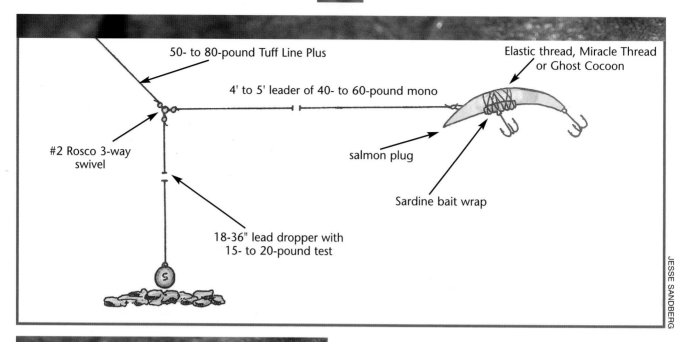

50- to 80-pound Tuff Line Plus

Elastic thread, Miracle Thread or Ghost Cocoon

4' to 5' leader of 40- to 60-pound mono

#2 Rosco 3-way swivel

salmon plug

Sardine bait wrap

18-36" lead dropper with 15- to 20-pound test

JESSE SANDBERG

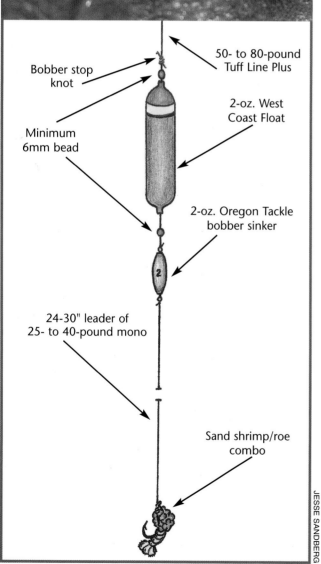

Bobber stop knot

50- to 80-pound Tuff Line Plus

2-oz. West Coast Float

Minimum 6mm bead

2-oz. Oregon Tackle bobber sinker

24-30" leader of 25- to 40-pound mono

Sand shrimp/roe combo

JESSE SANDBERG

Bouncing Rig For Plugs

This rig is used primarily on coastal streams and when fishing shallower areas like rock shelves and gravel bars on bigger rivers where big chinook are most likely to be hugging the bottom. Where the diver rig shines for its mobility, this setup does for its accuracy. The lead rig allows for pinpoint presentations in tight quarters, around structure, and in places where a diver does not work as well, such as at the head of holes where riffles break into deeper water—a place chinook often hang.

Once again, Kwikfish or Flatfish are the lures of choice for this tactic. Use Kwikfish in sizes K13-K16. Popular Flatfish sizes include the M2, T50 and T55. Both lures come in an assortment of appealing colors, with combinations of green and chartreuse being extremely popular. Luhr Jensen has even gone to the trouble of assigning nicknames to some of the more successful colors in order to help absent-minded fishermen like myself remember them. A non-angler may hear us utter these names and wonder what the hell we're talking about: Funky Chicken, The Slammer, Blue Magoo, Glad Clown, Fickle Pickle—at least they help us remember!

When using this tactic, be sure to cut a small chunk of sardine and wrap it to the underside of the plug with elastic thread, Atlas Miracle Thread, or Ghost Cocoon. This will put a ton of scent into the water and drastically increase your chances for a hookup. Just be sure to cut your bait wrap small enough that it doesn't negatively affect the action of the lure. And remember, your leader material should consist of a high quality, highly abrasion-resistant monofilament such as Maxima, Trilene Big Game or Stren High Impact.

NICK AMATO

Kris Olsen and John Koenig with a big fall chinook. This Washington State fish was hooked with a back-trolled K-16 Kwikfish.

Basic Bobber/Float Setup

Float fishing for chinook is another deadly tactic that works extremely well when the fish are suspended in deeper holes and runs. Anglers have many styles of floats to choose from, but the cigar-shaped ones are the most popular. Check out Oregon Tackle's bobber sinker, as this device doubles as both your weight and swivel, a nice convenience when tying up. For a bobber stop, tie a UNI-knot around your mainline with Cortland Micron fly line backing or some other soft line, or you can purchase them pre-made at area tackle shops. A good-quality hook is of utmost importance when bobber fishing in order to get a positive hook-set. Mustad ultra points, Gamakatsu octopus and the Owner SSW cutting points are each excellent choices. Some veteran float fishermen tie-in a small piece of chartreuse yarn above the hook and swear that this added attractant results in more hook-ups.

Most chinook anglers would probably agree that a bobber fisherman is only as good as his eggs. We've all seen this play out on the river, some of us more often than we would care to admit! There are a dozen guys fishing a hole chuck full of fresh chinook, but only a couple of them are catching all the fish. They have the right egg cure recipe for that day, and all the rest of us can do is watch as they get their limits. Egg cure recipes have traditionally been held as top secret, only begrudgingly being divulged through bribery or blackmail. But lucky for us, noted author and expert angler Scott Haugen has written the definitive work on the subject. The book is straight-forwardly titled *Egg Cures*, and if you want to catch more salmon and steelhead, check it out.

Author's note: To contact Dan Ponciano's Guide Service call (360) 573-7211.

*A Sandy River coho
destined for the barbeque.*

Miscellaneous Rigs

River Fishing Rigs for Coho

Left: An assortment of coho spinners by Dave Kaffke. Right: No, that's not a chinook that expert angler Jason Hambly is holding, rather, a large Marge hen coho caught from his "secret" river.

When autumn leaves begin to turn color and the first fall rains drop on parched earth in so many miniscule explosions of dust, Northwest anglers can soon count on the arrival of one of our gamiest fish to the rivers and streams of our great region. Coho, overshadowed in popularity by chinook, are often derided for their lack of size and fight. But these criticisms come mostly from anglers targeting chinook with gear that is exceedingly stout for fish that average 5-10 pounds. In some boats, coho have been relegated to second-class status. But hook a fresh coho in a small stream on a light spinning rod or eight-weight fly rod, and you will have a newfound appreciation for this fish. The return of coho, or silvers, usually coincides with rising rivers, shorter days and cooler nights. Coho will sneak into some river systems as early as August or September, but on most Northwest rivers, October and early November are prime time. Coho are prized by fishermen for their sometimes maniacal willingness to hit bait, fly or lure, and are appreciated for their even crazier antics once hooked.

Coho will writhe, twist, flip, run and jump with reckless abandon, sometimes it would seem, all at the same time. For the angler who pursued silvers on the ocean or at Buoy Ten only weeks prior while using hefty rods and heavy diver/flasher rigs, catching river coho on lighter gear can be an eye-opening experience. And, while river coho are quite often eager to bite and somewhat easy to catch, at other times they are cursed for their apparent moodiness and reluctance to participate in water sport. But if you show up at a river that's in prime shape and full of willing, hard-fighting silvers that are on the snap, it won't take long to be converted to a follower of our "second salmon."

Diagram 1 By far the most popular method for angling for river coho is drift fishing with roe. There are endless ways to rig for drift fishing, but for silvers I prefer to use a slinky rigged on a slider or snap swivel. Silvers will often take the bait very softly and I feel that the sliding system allows me to better feel the fish when it is subtly mouthing the eggs. When drift fishing, use the smallest amount of weight you can get away with while still maintaining contact with the bottom, as this allows for a more natural presentation. Ideally, you want your rig to drift downstream just slightly slower than current speed with your slinky or lead contacting bottom only occasionally. This presentation is more readily accepted by the fish than a presentation where the lead constantly drags along bottom. Also, by using the lightest weight possible, you won't snag up on the bottom nearly as much, meaning you can spend less time re-tying and more time fishing.

Because silvers sometimes take the bait very softly, it is imperative to use a high-quality, ultra-sensitive rod in order to detect the presence of a stealthy player. I have settled on the Bill Herzog rods from Lamiglas for the majority of my drift fishing. They have extremely sensitive tips and their ten-foot length helps keep the line up off the water to avoid drag and aids in casting long distances when necessary. It also helps that they were designed and built by expert Northwest fishermen and are a hell of a lot of fun to fight fish on. G. Loomis also builds extra-

*A pair of Sandy River silvers that succumbed
to a #4 Blue Fox spinner.*

the hook and the shank. This will allow for a reasonable gap between the bobber and hook point resulting in maximum hooking efficiency. Use #1-3/0 hooks for river coho. In some situations it may be advisable to forgo a drift bobber and fish the eggs "down and dirty," that is, so that they drift just off the bottom right on their noses. I've found this to work well on pressured or snooty fish that are pinned right to the bottom, as well as in shallow water when fish are also hugging the bottom.

When it comes to choosing a color there are so many variables to consider that it becomes downright dangerous for the writer to generalize. Water temperature, clarity, light penetration and color shift all come into play, so I will direct you to the definitive work on the topic: *What Fish See,* by Colin Kageyama and published by Frank Amato. I will say that I have caught river coho on red, orange, pink, purple, chartreuse, black, white, silver, blue and green, as well as combinations of these colors. It also seems to hold true that every year the fish seem to key in on a preferred color and this changes from season to season. I often fly-fish for silvers on Oregon's Sandy River and I have found that during one year the fish prefer a #6 orange Glo Bug to all else and the very next they'll hit nothing but a three-inch long black Bunny Leech and the next, nothing but a purple dredger. While this dilemma can be somewhat vexing, just remember to keep changing things up until success is realized. Like my old man says, "The best color to use is the one that they're biting on."

Diagram 2 Coho will sometimes take up residence in water that lacks sufficient current to effectively drift fish, and here is where float fishing comes into play. Silvers often hold in slow eddies, deep, froggy tailouts and deep, lazy pools with little current. By suspending the bait beneath a float, an angler can cover various depths while allowing it to drift freely with the current. Because coho are not always right on the bottom—especially in deeper holes—it is important to experiment with different settings of the bobber stop until fish are caught. You will see all shapes and sizes

sensitive rods that drift fish extremely well. Check out rods from their STR Series in the insanely telegraphic IMX graphite.

Drift bobbers come in many shapes, sizes and colors and everyone has their favorite, just remember to size them according to the hooks you are using. A drift bobber should not be so large as to obscure the hook point from the fish when it is biting. A good rule to follow when choosing a drift bobber is that it should fit, or nearly fit, into the opening between the point of

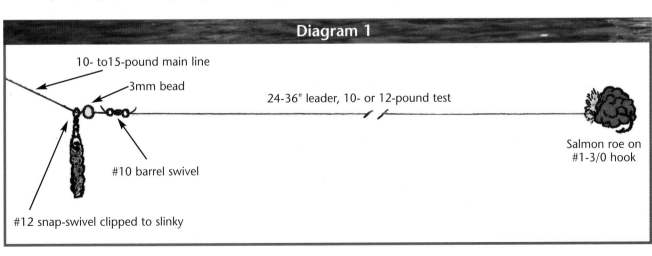

Diagram 1

10- to15-pound main line

3mm bead

24-36" leader, 10- or 12-pound test

Salmon roe on
#1-3/0 hook

#10 barrel swivel

#12 snap-swivel clipped to slinky

JESSE SANDBERG

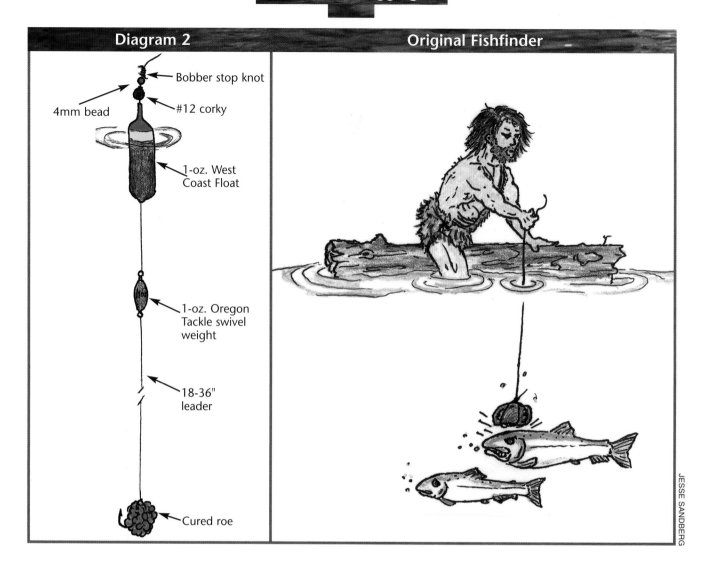

| Diagram 2 | Original Fishfinder |

Bobber stop knot

4mm bead

#12 corky

1-oz. West Coast Float

1-oz. Oregon Tackle swivel weight

18-36" leader

Cured roe

JESSE SANDBERG

of floats on Northwest rivers, but I favor the cigar-shaped floats like those from West Coast Floats because they slip under the surface with little resistance and don't automatically telegraph to the fish that something is amiss. The bobber swivel weight from Oregon Tackle makes in-line rigging of the weight a no-brainer and helps reduce tangles when casting. When float fishing, use extremely sharp hooks or you will miss your share of fish.

Hooking fish when float fishing with bait can be somewhat tricky, anyway, and for years I struggled to hook fish with the classic over-the-shoulder-into-the-bushes-frantic-rip-some-lips-fall-on-your-ass-hookset. But then Dave Eng of *STS,* a much better salmon fisherman than I, set me straight. Dave showed me how to improve my hook-up rate by reeling down until I felt the weight of the fish before lifting the rod. This method makes sense because it helps "point" the hook into the flesh before heavy pressure is applied, just the kind of pressure that can pull the hook straight out of the mouth if the hook point isn't already pricking something. Dave's advice has resulted in a much better landing percentage per bobber-downs, that is, when I remember to use it!

Catching silvers on hardware like spinners and wobblers can be a hoot as long as the fish are cooperating. Silvers will often follow a spinner several times before finally slamming it right at your feet. Other times they may merely stop the blade, and this calls for a quick hook-set by the angler. I asked "Spinner Dave" Kaffke, an Oregon native and expert spinner fisherman, to share some information on spinner fishing for river coho on Northwest rivers and in Alaska. Dave owned and operated Angler Specialties, a spinner component shop in Gladstone, Oregon, for five years. He also guided for Trophy King Lodge on the Kenai Peninsula, Alaska, for five years, and worked as a manager for Fisherman's Marine and Outdoor in Oregon City, Oregon. Dave is currently a sporting goods buyer for All Sports, a Clackamas, Oregon wholesaler. Dave honed his spinner-fishing skills on the small rivers and streams of the southern Kenai Peninsula, as well as the central Oregon Coast.

Dave begins, "I build my coho spinners primarily with French blades because they spin at slow speeds and emit a lot of flash. I use 1/4-, 1/3- or 1/2-ounce spinner bodies depending

Diagrams 3 and 4 Building a Coho Spinner

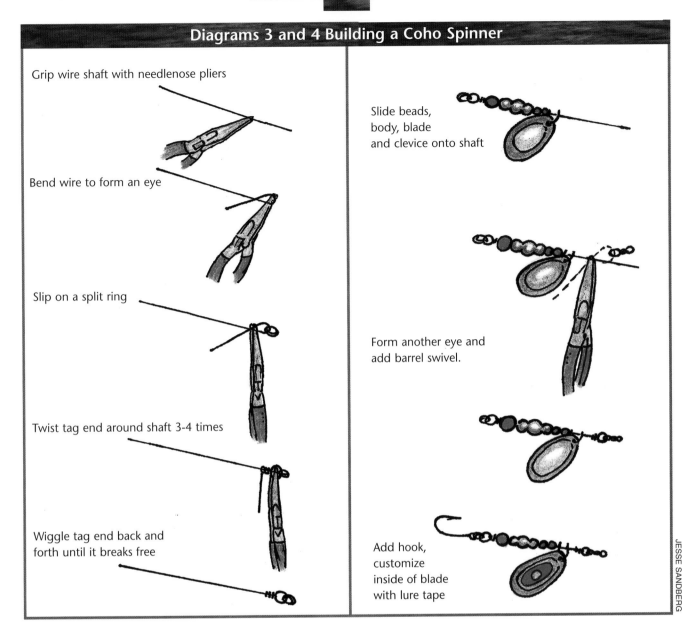

Grip wire shaft with needlenose pliers

Bend wire to form an eye

Slip on a split ring

Twist tag end around shaft 3-4 times

Wiggle tag end back and forth until it breaks free

Slide beads, body, blade and clevice onto shaft

Form another eye and add barrel swivel.

Add hook, customize inside of blade with lure tape

JESSE SANDBERG

on the water I intend to fish; heavier spinners in deep water or fast current where I need to get down to the fish, and smaller spinners in clear water for spooky or highly pressured fish. On cloudy days I like a spinner blade without flash, either black, white or glow, or combinations thereof. On a bright day I'll throw a nickel or 50/50 (nickel/brass) blade, and in stained water like you so often see in Alaska, a copper blade works great when there's sun on the water. My go-to blade when nothing else seems to be working is black. I'll often go through a hole throwing different color combinations and if I don't get hit I'll go back through with a black blade. Black also seems to work in a variety of water conditions including glacial or colored water.

Dave continues, "Much of the time silvers will be found in the slack and slower margins of a hole. In this type of water it is necessary to cast and retrieve while varying the speed in order to trigger a strike. Change colors often to determine what they want on any given day. Coho that are on the move can often be found in faster runs and pocket water, and here I'll either fish the spinner on a downstream swing, or pitch the blade upstream and retrieve with the current. When casting upstream, it's important to crank fast enough that the spinner doesn't settle and is presented near to the current speed. I can't stress enough the importance of having sharp hooks when fishing spinners for silvers. The moment a salmon feels the hook it immediately launches into a series of head shakes in an attempt to dislodge the offender, and if you don't have sharp hooks in this situation, you become a catch-and-release fisherman whether you like it or not."

I asked Dave if he had anything more to share on casting spinners to coho, and he flooded me with this: "Remember that silvers can be very moody. They will go on and off the bite all day long. If you aren't catching fish, keep changing things—speed of presentation, size, color—until you do. In my experience, silvers don't bite well when they are showing, that is, constantly jumping and rolling. Move, move, move. Cover water until you find cooperative participants. If a hole is crowded with anglers the fish may be put off or relocated. Try less obvious spots like tailouts, pocket water, the head of the hole, etc. Don't stand on the same rock all day long. Go small and go deep. Go fast and go slow. Silvers are neurotic fish and you need to treat them as such. Go through your spinner box from your most to least reliable blades, and always finish with black. And don't forget your crossover species. At any given time there may be chinook, chum or steelhead present in a particular river, so target their water-types when the silvers are off. And God forbid there should be pinks around—these guys can be nuisance or savior depending on how you look at it. I build my own spinners but that doesn't mean there aren't good production spinners available. The Blue Fox, Panther Martin, Mepps Aglia and Flying C, Rooster Tails, Rattle Spins, Sneaks and Bolos are all great blades for silvers. My favorite rod for casting spinners to silvers is the G. Loomis HSR 9000S. This rod has a light, sensitive tip but has plenty of butt strength for fighting fish. Finally, "you can't catch fish when your line is not in the water!" Thanks, Dave.

Diagram 5 Casting and retrieving plugs is another effective technique for coho in rivers.

Diagram 6 Hover-fishing is a technique developed in southwest Washington and is used to fish bait in deep holes where coho stack up while staging. In such water, silvers often suspend and are not always found right on the bottom. In this technique, the rig is lowered to the bottom and then reeled up to the level where the angler feels the fish are holding. For this reason, a good fish-finder that can accurately show what depth the fish are at is important. Once the baits are in the water, the boat operator either holds in the current or allows the boat to slowly slip downstream, covering the holding water that the salmon are known to frequent. Ideally, the baits will "hover" in and amongst the fish, providing a subtle presentation that even the moodiest of coho might be attracted to. When hover-fishing, the take is always a soft tick that can be hard to detect without a sensitive rod. Remember, the fish are not eating your eggs, they're killing them. Coho will suck in the bait, chomp them once or twice to crush them, then spit them out. If you're not on top of things you will burn through a lot of eggs when hover-fishing. Watch that rod tip and strike immediately at the slightest tap. Because of the light bite associated with this method, rig the sinker on a slider for better detection. The ultra-sensitive G. Loomis HSR 930C is the rod of choice for this technique.

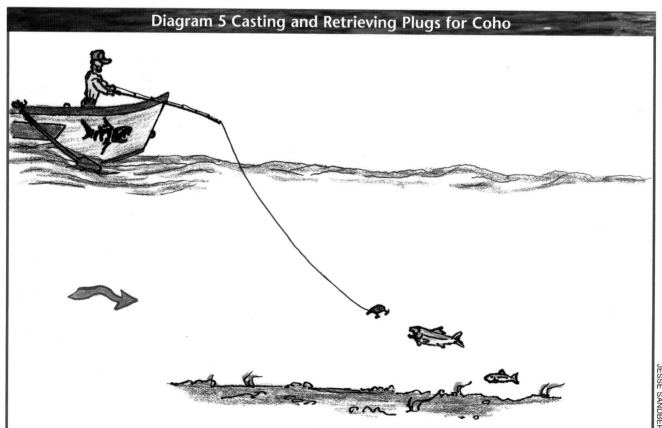

Diagram 5 Casting and Retrieving Plugs for Coho

JESSE SANDBERG

Diagram 6

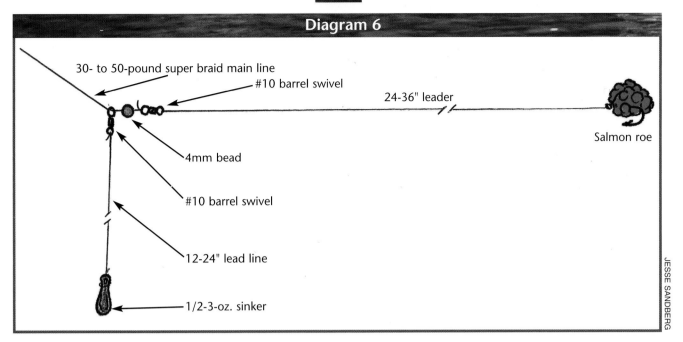

30- to 50-pound super braid main line

#10 barrel swivel

24-36" leader

Salmon roe

4mm bead

#10 barrel swivel

12-24" lead line

1/2-3-oz. sinker

JESSE SANDBERG

Diagram 7

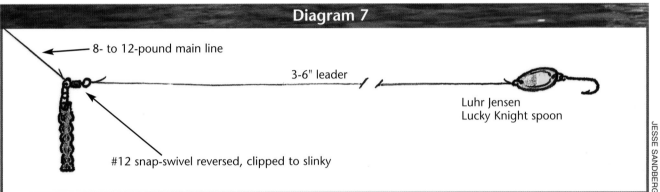

8- to 12-pound main line

3-6" leader

Luhr Jensen
Lucky Knight spoon

#12 snap-swivel reversed, clipped to slinky

JESSE SANDBERG

Diagram 7 Savvy Washington anglers also discovered that cranky coho could be made to bite by downsizing their gear and going ridiculously small. Tight-lipped coho can often be induced to striking a small lure such as the Luhr Jensen Lucky Knight spoon pictured here. Normally associated with trout, kokanee and shad fishing, this diminutive lure conveys a message of vulnerability that may trigger an instinctive predatory response from an otherwise uninterested silver. In good current, cast and let the rig swing through the best holding water. In slower holes, cast and retrieve slowly so the Lucky Knight flickers enticingly. Laying in the salmon fisherman's tackle box, the Luhr Jensen Lucky Knight looks pathetically small and misplaced, but serious coho fishermen will tell you that this lure is a ringer when nothing else works.

The aforementioned techniques are not the only methods used to catch river coho. Plenty of silvers are also caught backtrolling plugs, as is evidenced by the many fish taken from the Willamette River each fall by anglers fishing Wiggle Warts at or below the confluence with the Clackamas River.

Coho are also an excellent fly-rod fish and will absolutely smash a stripped fly or merely suck in a single-egg pattern. When fly-fishing for silvers, I usually employ a tight-line nymphing technique with a floating line. When silvers stack up in holes or runs, swinging flies on a sinking line usually results in hooking fish everywhere but in the mouth.

In recent years, anglers have found that bobber and jig fishing isn't just for steelhead and chinook. Whichever tactic you choose to employ, remember that native coho stocks are severely depressed in some watersheds. Check the regulations for your chosen water and gently release wild fish so they can continue on and do their thing. Harbor no reservations about bonking hatchery fish for the dinner table; that's what they are there for. This autumn, when the rain comes and the leaves begin to fall, check out a local river with a run of silvers and give 'em a go on light gear, heck, take the kids if you need a convenient excuse for targeting our "Second Salmon."

Salmon, Trout & Steelhead Fly-Fishing Techniques

Fly fishing for salmon, trout and steelhead has become wildly popular over the past decade. Once considered a difficult, cryptic art form by many, the angling masses are now figuring out that basic fly fishing skills are not that hard to attain. Never before in the history of this method has there existed such a wealth of skilled experts, excellent literature and informational video to help the neophyte jump headlong into the pastime. The transition from bait and hardware to fly-fishing need not be daunting. While some still believe that fly-fishing technique may handicap an angler when it comes to actually hooking fish, others are realizing that, in certain angling situations, fly-fishing provides the best method to facilitate a hook up. And while it's true that it may take years or even a lifetime for most of us to ascertain the highest levels of this sport, it remains that both the beginner and expert can equally appreciate the beauty of the perfectly executed 75-foot cast, the excitement of a steelhead smashing a swung fly, or the slurping rise of a five-pound brown trout. **Diagram 1** The dry-fly fished with a dead-drift presentation is an effective tactic to use for trout when insects are actively hatching and the fish are feeding on the surface. This is one of the most pleasurable fly-fishing techniques for trout because the angler gets the added satisfaction of actually seeing the fish take the fly. Mayflies, caddis, stoneflies and midges are the insects most likely to elicit a feeding spree on top. Terrestrial insects like grasshoppers, crickets, beetles and ants can be very good patterns to use during the heat of the summer months when these bugs are most active. Be sure to use a fly that mimics the size, form and color of the prevailing insect you wish to imitate, and be sure to use a quality floatant such as Dave's Bug Flote in order to keep the fly from sinking. A quality, high-floating fly line will make your day on the water that much more enjoyable, as it will both cast and mend better than an inferior line. Cortland, Scientific Anglers and Rio all make excellent fly lines.

The term "dead drift" describes a fly that is floating along as naturally as possible at current speed with very little drag. Drag is the unnatural affect the current plays on the line, leader, tippet and fly during the presentation. It is of the utmost importance to reduce drag as much as possible for best results, especially when fishing over wary, educated trout. Watch a natural insect as it floats down a stream, bobbing and whirling with every nuance of

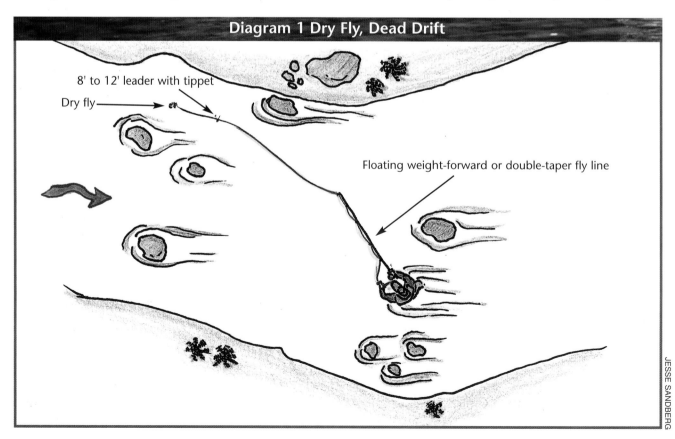

Diagram 1 Dry Fly, Dead Drift

8' to 12' leader with tippet

Dry fly

Floating weight-forward or double-taper fly line

JESSE SANDBERG

Diagram 2 Dry Fly, Waked or Skated on the Swing

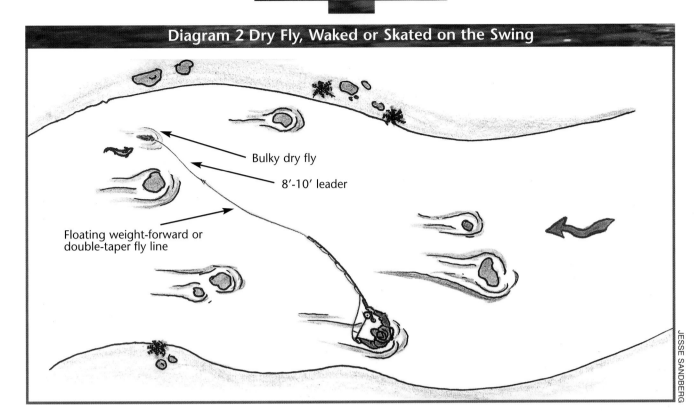

Bulky dry fly

8'-10' leader

Floating weight-forward or double-taper fly line

JESSE SANDBERG

the current. Because a fly is tethered to a tippet and leader, it loses much of the natural appearance of the actual free-floating insect. It is up to the angler to reduce drag and make the fly look as "untethered" as possible. This is best accomplished by having some slack line incorporated into the cast, either by an up or downstream wiggle cast, a reach cast, and/or proper mending. It also helps to use a lengthy leader and tippet to further reduce the current's hold on the fly.

Diagram 2 While most dry-fly anglers labor to reduce drag, there is a tactic used by steelhead and Atlantic salmon anglers which incorporates the deliberate use of drag to impart action to a floating fly as it slowly swings across a promising piece of water. Skating or waking flies are techniques that use the resistance of the current against the line, leader and fly to keep the fly either skating on top of the water, or pulling through the surface to cause a wake. These tactics are best used on active steelhead which are more likely to leave their lie in three to six feet of water to attack the fly on the surface. A good indication of steelhead activity is water temperature. The colder the water, the less likely a steelhead will be to move to a fly, especially one on the surface. Here in the Pacific Northwest, I don't feel confident using a dry fly for steelhead unless the water is at least forty-five degrees. If the water temperature is hovering right around fifty degrees, I feel even better. Flies used for this purpose are often bulky in form and tied with stiff materials like elk and moose hair, or calf tail, which help the fly ride up on the surface and remain afloat. Classic surface patterns for steelhead include the

Bomber, Waller Waker, Steelhead Bee, the Steelhead Muddler, and After Dinner Mint. Once again, a quality floating fly line is very important for fishing the dry fly. A ten-foot leader is a good place to start, and unless you are an expert caster, you may want to consider using a shorter, stouter tippet section in order to better turn over these bulky flies.

Begin the presentation by casting down and across, and mend to get the fly skating or waking as soon as possible. After the fly is activated, drop your arm and use the rod to lead the fly around in a long arc, thus covering the greatest expanse of water. The cool thing about this technique is that the fish may come to the fly anywhere throughout the presentation, and is therefore an excellent tool to locate fish in a broad piece of water. The take may be as subtle as a sipping trout, or more likely, violent in nature. For this reason, most steelhead rises to a dry fly, in my experience, do not result in a solid hook-up. But this is where the fun comes in! An adept steelhead-fly fisherman may get an active fish to rise to a fly several times, and by doing so, might eventually hook it. Or, maybe not. Either way, a bright ten-pound fish rolling on a swinging dry fly is certainly one of—if not the most—exciting moments in steelheading!

Diagram 3 The technique of swinging a wet fly near the surface was born on the Atlantic salmon rivers of Scotland. Traditionally called the greased-line method, I will avoid this term here as there are subtle differences between the classic greased-line method and how we most often swing flies stateside. Begin by casting across and somewhat downstream. How far downstream

Diagram 3 Wet Fly, Swung Near Surface

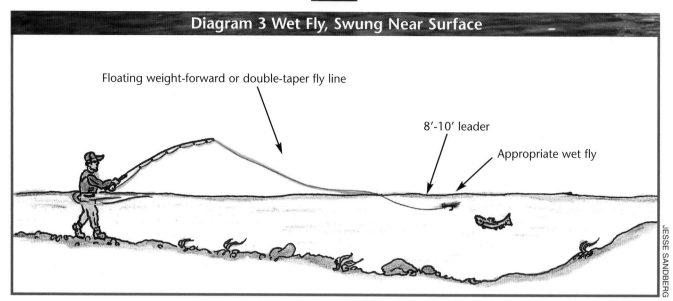

Floating weight-forward or double-taper fly line

8'-10' leader

Appropriate wet fly

JESSE SANDBERG

Diagram 4 Deeply-Swung Wet Fly

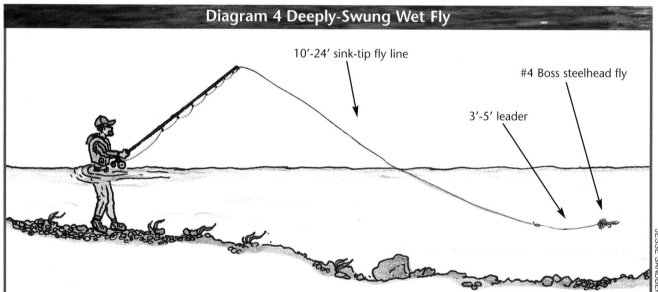

10'-24' sink-tip fly line

#4 Boss steelhead fly

3'-5' leader

JESSE SANDBERG

will depend on the current speed. Generally, the faster the flow the farther down you will need to cast so that the fly does not swing too quickly across the lie. It is usually necessary to immediately throw in an upstream mend to give the line and the fly the proper attitude, that is, pointing more or less upstream. Additional upstream mends may be necessary during the course of the swing to straighten out the fly line and slow the progress of the fly. The idea is to provide just enough tension on the line to activate the materials in the fly so that it looks alive. There is much debate on how to orient the rod tip when swinging a fly, but I let current speed determine this. On typical steelhead holding water—that flowing at the pace of a brisk walk—I slightly follow the progress of the fly with the rod tip to ensure proper tension on the fly. Towards the end of the swing where there might be softer water (as well as a resting steelhead), I may throw in a downstream mend to create a slight belly in the line,

thus preserving the tension on the fly. Then, I lead the fly with the rod tip in order to maintain proper tension. British anglers call this "pulling through," and it is a deadly tactic to entice a following steelhead into striking.

The take on a swinging fly most often occurs at the bottom end of the swing, when the fly is slowing down and becoming more vulnerable. Most often this is a vicious, jarring strike, as the fish is moving from its lie to intercept the fly. Do not set the hook at this moment, for most often you will pull the fly away from the fish before it is pricked. Instead, let the fish turn back toward its resting spot, thus hooking itself. This is why the majority of steelhead taken on the shallow swinging fly are hooked safely in the corner of the jaw; the hook is pulled there when the fish turns to go back in the direction from which it came.

Diagram 4 The deeply-swung fly is most often presented on a sink-tip or shooting-head line system, but can also be managed with a floating line, long leader and a weighted fly. When using the sinking lines, be sure to use a short leader of two to five feet in order to keep the fly down in the water column. Because the ability to effectively mend is somewhat diminished with a sinking line, the angle of the initial cast becomes even more pivotal. Also, a very strong upstream mend is needed to allow the line and the fly to sink to depth before the line becomes taut and begins the swing. A slow, controlled swing is what we're after here. This technique is most often used on lethargic winter fish that will not move very far to grab a fly, or for dour summer fish that are reluctant to move to the surface.

Diagram 5 A lightly-weighted nymph fished shallow is an often overlooked technique that can really shine when fishing over finicky trout during a hatch. During an insect hatch, the fish often key in on a particular phase of the insect, be it a deep nymph, emerging nymph, emerging nymph on the surface or the adult. For the best success, it's necessary to identify which stage of the insect the trout are feeding on and then make the proper presentation to mimic it. When trout are seen bulging near the surface but not actually taking adults, it's safe to assume that they are feeding on some form of emerger.

During the fall and early spring on Oregon's famed Deschutes River there is a somewhat reliable hatch of blue-winged olive mayflies. This hatch usually comes off some time during midday and is heaviest on cloudy days. Quite often the trout show an unwillingness to take the tiny adults, but can be seen feeding near the surface. This is when I tie on a leader ten feet in length with an additional two to four feet of tippet. I rarely use a strike indicator for this type of fishing because the fish will usually show themselves well enough to know that they

are onto the fly. Dead drifting the fly through actively feeding fish, it is a challenge to know when to set the hook as the take is rarely felt. This sight-fishing game of cat and mouse is some of my favorite trout fishing of the year.

Diagram 6 Nymph fishing with a strike indicator and deeply-sunk fly is a deadly tactic for salmon, trout and steelhead because it allows the fly to be presented at, or very near to, the current speed. This factor often makes the difference between multiple hook-ups and none. I recently took a novice nymph fisherman steelheading on a small Oregon river. The water was cold and clear and the fish were difficult at first. But Adam ended up hooking six steelhead—not bad for a dry-fly specialist from Montana! There were several good fishermen on the river that day, all of them drift fishing, but we didn't see another fish hooked. The difference in results, I believe, was that the fish wanted a natural presentation. The intended purpose of the strike indicator has always been to show the angler the subtle take of a fish before it spits the hook. But it also serves a second very important purpose, that of a fly delivery system.

To make the proper presentation with an indicator rig, quarter the cast upstream so that the fly has the chance to sink before reaching the intended target. Then let the fly and indicator drift unimpeded through a promising run. The presentation can   be further extended by feeding out additional line by stack mending. A key to this tactic is to mend aggressively, either upstream or down as the current dictates, in order to reduce drag and provide the most natural presentation. It is important to mend the line while upsetting the indicator as little as possible. Many

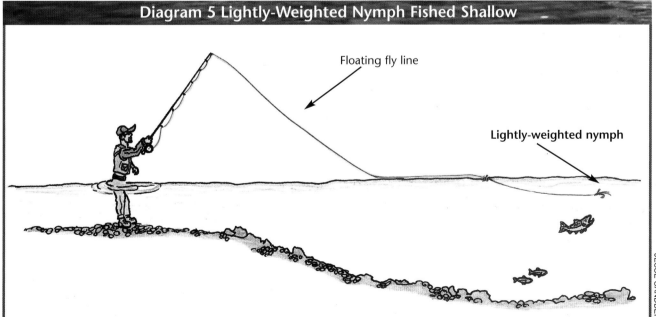

Diagram 5 Lightly-Weighted Nymph Fished Shallow

Floating fly line

Lightly-weighted nymph

JESSE SANDBERG

nymph fishermen have been taught that a nymph can only be fished on a short line with the rod tip held high to keep as much of the fly line off the water as possible. This works great when fishing tight to the bank, but at greater distances can actually add drag as the weight of the line draws the indicator toward the angler. I have found that it's possible to fish this set-up effectively with a lot of line on the water, as long as the line is mended aggressively to reduce drag.

There are as many ways to rig an indicator set-up as there are for drift fishing, but for easier casting and fewer tangles, I like to keep it simple. Set the indicator 1 1/2 to 2 times the depth of the water from the fly. Add just enough weight to gradually sink the fly; too much will unnaturally slow the drift of the rig. Use lead twist-on or split shot attached to the leader just above the tippet knot, or weight the fly itself with lead wire, bead heads or dumbbell eyes. Attach the fly of choice to the

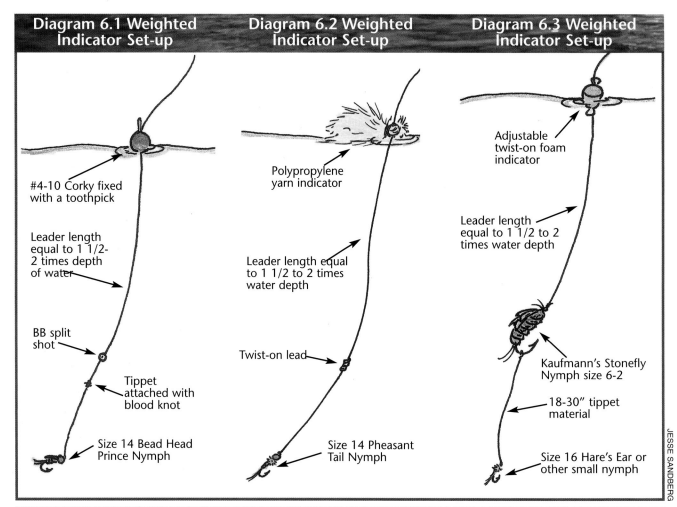

Diagram 6.1 Weighted Indicator Set-up

#4-10 Corky fixed with a toothpick

Leader length equal to 1 1/2-2 times depth of water

BB split shot

Tippet attached with blood knot

Size 14 Bead Head Prince Nymph

Diagram 6.2 Weighted Indicator Set-up

Polypropylene yarn indicator

Leader length equal to 1 1/2 to 2 times water depth

Twist-on lead

Size 14 Pheasant Tail Nymph

Diagram 6.3 Weighted Indicator Set-up

Adjustable twist-on foam indicator

Leader length equal to 1 1/2 to 2 times water depth

Kaufmann's Stonefly Nymph size 6-2

18-30" tippet material

Size 16 Hare's Ear or other small nymph

JESSE SANDBERG

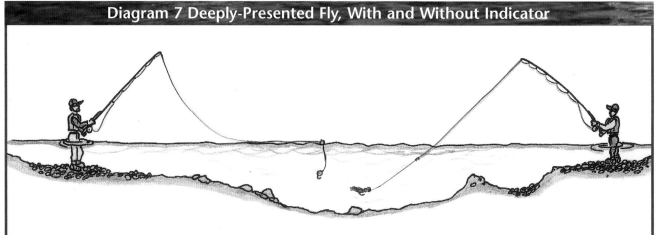

Diagram 7 Deeply-Presented Fly, With and Without Indicator

JESSE SANDBERG

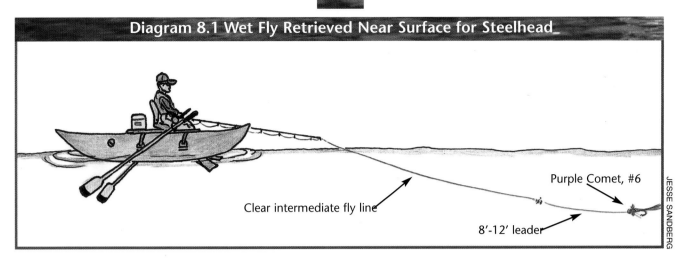

Diagram 8.1 Wet Fly Retrieved Near Surface for Steelhead

Purple Comet, #6

Clear intermediate fly line

8'-12' leader

JESSE SANDBERG

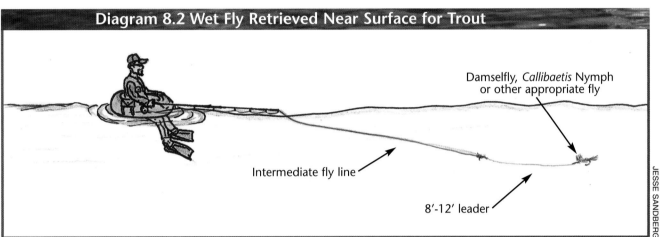

Diagram 8.2 Wet Fly Retrieved Near Surface for Trout

Damselfly, *Callibaetis* Nymph or other appropriate fly

Intermediate fly line

8'-12' leader

JESSE SANDBERG

tippet of appropriate strength for the targeted species, then let her rip! The moment the indicator dives, set the hook. It doesn't take long for a fish to spit a suspect fly.

Diagram 7 It is common to dead drift the deeply-presented fly both with and without an indicator. To do it without an indicator, use a floating line with a long leader and weighted fly. It is possible to dead drift a fly with a sinking line, but I like the floater for its mending capabilities. Again, begin by quartering a cast upstream so that the fly may sink. As the fly reaches depth, raise the rod to provide just enough tension to track the fly's progress, too much, and the fly will begin to swing. This is a great tactic to use around structure and in pocket water where there may not be room enough to employ another technique.

Diagram 8 The wet fly retrieved near the surface is a technique that can be used to catch trout, steelhead and even salmon. Stillwater trout fishermen often use a floating line with a long leader or a slow-sinking line to catch trout feeding shallow in lakes. I wouldn't dare venture to a trout lake without a clear intermediate fly line. These lines, produced by several manufacturers, have been a boon to stillwater trout fishermen everywhere. Because they are clear, they tend not to spook wary trout as

easily as traditional colored lines. Also, their slow sink rate allows for a retrieve on a horizontal plane, thus keeping the fly in the strike zone longer. This is a great technique to use in lakes in late spring and early summer when insects first start hatching and the trout first start looking up. Try a damsel or *Callibaetis* nymph, water boatman or scud pattern and hang on! Just be sure to study up on the particular insect or forage you intend to imitate, and make your retrieve match the movements of the natural.

Another place to use this tactic is on the Columbia River summer steelhead backwater fisheries, such as Herman Creek, the White Salmon River and Drano Lake. Summer steelhead pour into these cold-water refuges beginning in mid to late July in order to escape the rising temperatures of the Columbia. Here they will mill around in large numbers until the Columbia sufficiently cools to allow them to continue their upstream migration. At times these fish can be ultra-snobby, at others they will smash any fly with reckless abandon. Vary your retrieve to see what the fish prefer on any given day. Usually, a slow hand twist or six-inch strip meets with good results. For best results on the wet fly retrieved near the surface, fish early and late in the day. During the heat of the day with the sun high overhead, it's a better to fish deeper.

Stillwater Trout and Kokanee Techniques

The author cast and retrieved a Rebel Crawdad over a drop-off into deep water to tempt this giant rainbow from Lost Lake on Mt. Hood.

So you just spent a ton of money on a new boat earlier this spring, and now the spring chinook fisheries are either closed or winding down. You're worried how you're going to justify such an extravagant expenditure between now and the beginning of our ocean and bay salmon fisheries? Not to worry. The Pacific Northwest is blessed with a myriad of opportunities for the boat angler, and the excellent trout and kokanee fishing provided by our many lakes and reservoirs is almost limitless.

The world of lake fishing is often overlooked by those who have long since graduated to the ranks of serious salmon and steelhead anglers. I'm not sure why. Rainbow and brook trout caught from cold, clean water are some of the best tasting fish around. If you have never tasted a fresh kokanee fried in butter over a mellow campfire, you don't know what you're missing. I often hear anglers complain that trout and kokanee lack size and therefore fight. While this is true in some cases, the thinking angler who is prepared to do some research will find that opportunities for big trout are many. Check out Lake Chelan, Crescent or Odell for mackinaw in the 10-to 30-pound range. Head to Idaho's Pend Oreille for a chance at a twenty-pound Gerrard Rainbow. Visit beautiful Northeast Oregon and ply the waters of Wallowa Lake for kokanee that are measured in pounds instead of inches! And who will be the lucky angler to pull the first forty-pound brown trout from Paulina Lake? These are just a few examples of places where giants lurk—and there are many, many more.

For anglers who are less interested in trophy fish and just want to escape to the outdoors, there are even more opportunities, many of them close to home. There are a number of lakes within an hour or two drive from most of our major population centers. This makes an after-work outing or weekend camping excursion both convenient and affordable. These lakes and reservoirs often have the added attraction of being heavily stocked with fish by state wildlife agencies. These fish are raised for your enjoyment, so don't hesitate to keep a few for breakfast, lunch or dinner. When it comes to wild fish or those of unusually large proportions, I mostly choose to practice catch and release. What you decide to do is your own private dilemma, but it makes sense to me that a ten-pound rainbow is too valuable to be caught only once. Master angler Lee Wulff once said something to this effect regarding all game fish, and I tend to agree where large trout are concerned, but there are always exceptions. Are you going to make your ten-year-old release his or her first twenty-inch rainbow? I would have a difficult time doing so. Instead, use it as a learning experience. Teach the importance of catch and release where relevant, gently nudging your child down the evolutionary path that most anglers travel. Which brings us to another great facet of stillwater fishing for trout and kokanee: It can be as laid-back or as intense as you choose to make it. If you choose to make it the former, this creates a great environment to enjoy some comradery with friends or family. Some of my favorite fishing trips of the year are those spent goofing-off on a lake with my wife, companions and relatives. On

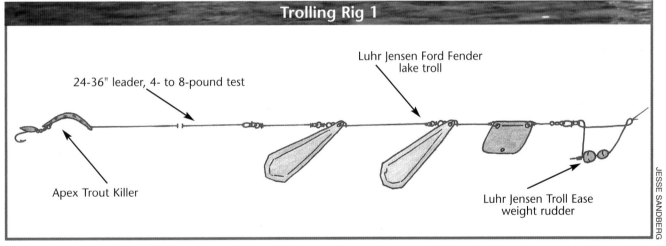

Trolling Rig 1

24-36" leader, 4- to 8-pound test

Luhr Jensen Ford Fender lake troll

Apex Trout Killer

Luhr Jensen Troll Ease weight rudder

JESSE SANDBERG

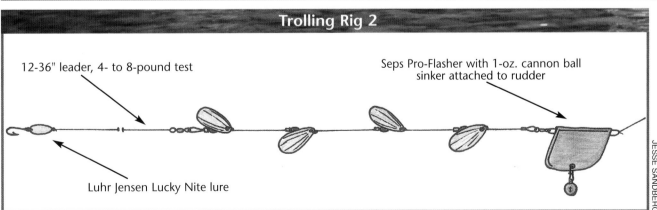

Trolling Rig 2

12-36" leader, 4- to 8-pound test

Seps Pro-Flasher with 1-oz. cannon ball sinker attached to rudder

Luhr Jensen Lucky Nite lure

JESSE SANDBERG

such trips the actual angling is often an afterthought, but this is always time well spent.

By far the most effective technique for fishing stillwaters for trout and kokanee is trolling, and unless you can walk on water, a boat is required for this method. Trolling involves slowly motoring or rowing around a lake while pulling behind the boat any of a vast array of lures, flies or bait. There are two elements of trolling that must be examined in order to realize the best success: Trolling speed and depth.

Trolling Speed Most of the time trout and kokanee prefer a lure or bait that is presented slowly. This is because, from a survival standpoint, it is pointless for an animal to expend more energy in the pursuit and capture of prey than it will actually gain by consuming it. There are exceptions to this rule, of course, and there are times that trout will react positively to a speedily-trolled lure, especially a baitfish imitation. But most of the time you will want to troll slowly, say .5-1.5 miles per hour. It is also advisable to vary your trolling speed over the course of the day because sometimes trout will respond to very subtle changes, and on any given day there is often a particular speed that the fish are attracted to. Another reason to observe a slow speed is that most trolling lures for trout and kokanee are designed to work best when trolled

Mike Kostel needs to invest in a bigger net for fishing the trout-rich lakes of eastern Washington.

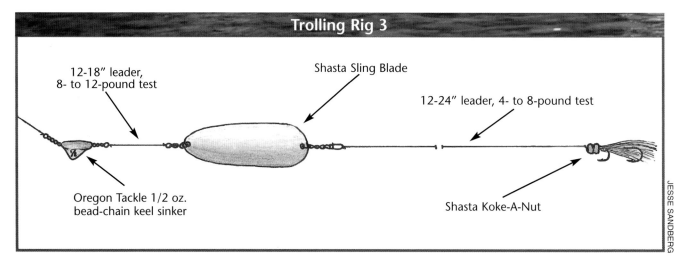

Trolling Rig 3

12-18" leader, 8- to 12-pound test

Shasta Sling Blade

12-24" leader, 4- to 8-pound test

Oregon Tackle 1/2 oz. bead-chain keel sinker

Shasta Koke-A-Nut

JESSE SANDBERG

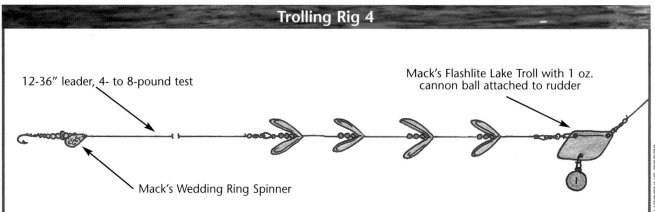

Trolling Rig 4

12-36" leader, 4- to 8-pound test

Mack's Flashlite Lake Troll with 1 oz. cannon ball attached to rudder

Mack's Wedding Ring Spinner

JESSE SANDBERG

Downrigger Trolling Rig

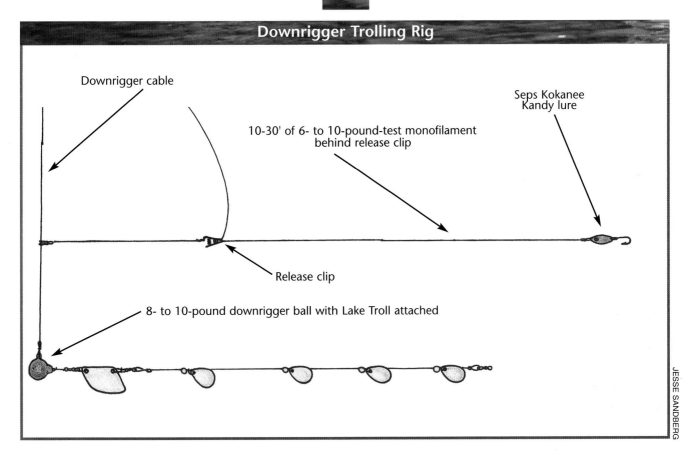

Downrigger cable

10-30' of 6- to 10-pound-test monofilament behind release clip

Seps Kokanee Kandy lure

Release clip

8- to 10-pound downrigger ball with Lake Troll attached

JESSE SANDBERG

slowly. Anyone who has ever reeled in a speed-trolled Ford Fender bird nest can attest to this. Trout and kokanee usually respond best to the lazy flutter, spin or wobble of a lure rather than one that is wildly spinning. A slow trolling speed is also necessary to attain depth when fish are located deep in the water column. The force of water against a line and gear creates lift that will cause a trolling rig to rise. The higher the speed, the more the lift increases, making it very difficult to keep the gear down where the fish are. Trolling speed can be maintained by purchasing a fish finder that has a speed feature, or by using a simple device offered by Luhr Jensen called the Luhr Speed that indicates your rate of progress. Many larger motors will not sufficiently "troll down" to an effective speed, so it may be necessary to drag sea anchors behind the boat or implement a trolling plate on your motor, a device that hangs down behind the prop in order to decrease thrust and therefore your speed.

Depth The depth at which you troll is often the difference between successful angling and watching others catch fish. Because lakes and reservoirs are usually stratified according to temperature and oxygen content, trout and kokanee will most often be found at the depth which provides the most comfort. Ideally, you want your gear to run just above where the fish are holding in order to see the best action. Early in the year when surface temperatures are still cool, trout and kokanee can be found near the top and are easily encountered. But as water

temperatures rise due to solar heat, the fish go deeper. This is when it becomes imperative to get your gear down to the fish. There are several ways to achieve this.

As long as the fish aren't too deep, lead sinkers can be used to take your gear down to the fish. If the fish are deeper than thirty or forty feet, however, a ridiculous amount of weight may be needed to reach them. It's no fun to fight a twelve-inch kokanee attached to a six-ounce cannon ball. Instead, try using lead-core line. It is very effective at taking gear down to the fish, and because it is color coded in ten-yard lengths, it allows the angler to return his or her gear to an exact depth after landing a fish. Be sure to use a long monofilament leader of 20-30 feet between the lead core and your terminal tackle, as the large diameter of the lead core is highly visible to the fish.

Downriggers are the high-tech answer to fishing deep, and have become extremely popular for lake trolling for several reasons. First of all, they are extremely efficient at reaching fish that are running very deep. Also, most downriggers are equipped with a counter that shows exactly how deep your gear is running. This allows you to consistently return to that depth after catching a fish. Perhaps the most appealing thing about downriggers is that they eliminate the need for lead, divers or planers, so once a fish has latched on and pulled the line from the release, there is no other gear between you and the fish. Scotty, Cannon and Penn are all reputable brands of downrigger equipment.

Trout and kokanee trolling lures.

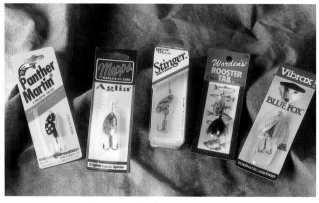

Kokanee jigging lures.

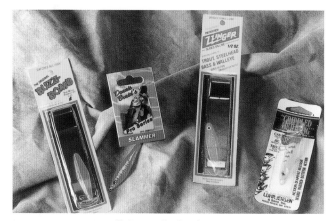

Trout and kokanee spinners.

Trout and kokanee casting spoons.

Where depth is concerned there are two areas that are often confusing. The first is knowing how deep your gear is when you're not using a downrigger. There are several ways to determine this. Using color-coded lead-core line is one way. Also, several reel manufacturers make reels with line counters on them, and while they may not tell you exact depth, they do indicate how much line is off the reel and in the water. Several companies also make line counters that clamp on to the rod just above the reel, allowing an angler to return to the same distance/depth after catching a fish. Perhaps the best way to determine what depth your gear is running at is to read Ray Rychnovsky's book, *The Troller's Handbook,* (Frank Amato Publications). The many graphs in this book that illustrate running depth as determined by trolling speed and gear used are invaluable. Every serious lake troller should check out this book.

The second issue with depth that causes confusion comes in determining how deep the fish are holding at any given time. As far as I know there are three ways to determine this if you exclude scuba diving or lowering down an underwater camera: Trial and error, other anglers, or electronics. Trial and error takes time and is fine if you have plenty to spare—most of us don't. Lodge owners, guides and fellow anglers can sometimes be helpful in finding out where the fish have been caught, but sometimes they can be as quiet as snow falling on water. A good electronic fish finder is the most reliable way to locate fish. Mark McCarthy is an expert on electronics who works at Fisherman's Marine and Outdoor in Oregon City, Oregon. I asked Mark what to look for in a fish finder for use on lakes and reservoirs.

"The first thing you need to decide," Mark replied, "is whether you want a unit that is fixed mounted or portable. A fixed mount is fine if it is to be used on one craft, and portables are great because they can be taken with you to use on any boat, for instance on a friend's or a rental. Fixed mounted units require a twelve-volt power source wired directly to the unit, and holes drilled in the lower transom of your boat in order to install the transducer. Portables usually will be powered by AA, C or D cell batteries, and the transducer is usually attached via a suction-cup mount. After you've decided which way to go, I suggest purchasing the highest-resolution screen (pixels) you can afford. A high pixel count will give you good definition of the bottom for structure like weed beds, drop-offs, logs, boulders, etc. For lakes and reservoirs I like a twenty- to sixty-degree cone-angle transducer. For shallow waters I'd go with a sixty-degree, and for deeper water, say fifty feet or more, I would go with the twenty-degree, that way you'll get the best definition in the deeper water. Good portable systems for shallow waters would be the Fishin Buddy 1200 or 2255. They side-find and give the depth along with

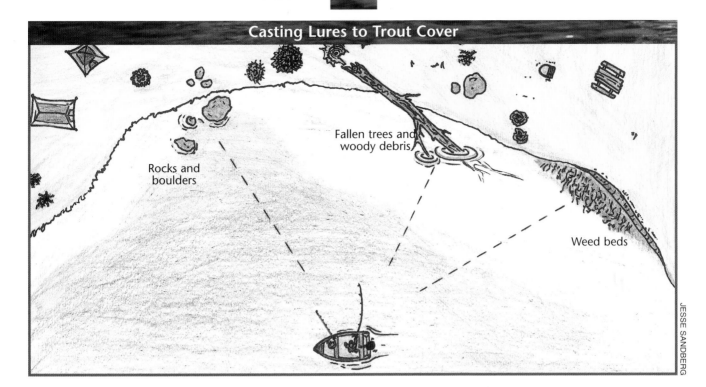

Casting Lures to Trout Cover

Rocks and boulders

Fallen trees and woody debris

Weed beds

JESSE SANDBERG

temperature. For a better deep water machine, try the Eagle FishMark 320, it's a great lake unit for under $200.00."

While trolling for trout and kokanee in lakes is the most popular method for boat anglers, there are plenty of other tactics that catch fish. Casting lures from an anchored or drifting boat can be very effective and is a diversion from the monotony of trolling. Because trout eat a variety of foods and these foods are often found in the shallower water near shore, anchoring in a shallow bay and casting lures to the kind of cover trout are attracted to can pay big dividends. Trout often lurk near fallen logs, weed beds and drop-offs waiting to nab unsuspecting prey like smaller fish, crawdads, and immature insects. Small spoons like the Thomas Buoyant, Acme Little Cleo and Luhr Jensen Krocodile are excellent lures to cast and retrieve to actively feeding fish. Experiment by changing the depth and speed of the retrieve until you figure out what the fish want. Spinners like Worden's Rooster Tail, Blue Fox Vibrax and Mepps Aglia are also deadly at times. Casting lures is a great method for kids as they get to dabble in independence while attempting to develop their own killer technique.

Kokanee are primarily plankton feeders and therefore are mostly found in the open water of a lake or reservoir. Kokanee use their gill rakers to strain tiny organisms from the lake water as they swim about. They are also purported to sometimes eat small fish, freshwater shrimp and immature aquatic insects. I have caught kokanee from Washington's Lake Merwin on a chironimid pupa fly pattern, so I can attest that they do sometimes eat insects. Kokanee are a lake-dwelling sockeye salmon and are

excellent table fare. It is a mystery why these fish, which normally feed on tiny creatures, will readily hit lures much greater in size than their normal prey. Just be glad that they do! Kokes often amass in great numbers where their food supply has become plentiful due to wind or water currents, and in the fall near tributaries when they are preparing to spawn. One of the most enjoyable ways to catch them when they are bunched up like this is by jigging. Kokanee in this situation will either smack a brightly colored jig or ignore it altogether. When they are on the snap, a brightly colored lure like the Buzz Bomb, Zzinger or Buck-Shot Spoon is just the ticket. Try them in Flame, Pink and Chartreuse, or combinations thereof. When a kokanee drills one of these things, they can't possibly think it's food; I believe it's more of an annoyance than anything. Kokanee have very soft mouth tissue, so you have to be careful when playing them. Use as light a rod as possible and don't horse them—a good-size koke is one of the toughest fish to successfully land. Another tip: kokanee love a lure tipped with Jolly Green Giant white shoepeg corn. Yellow corn works, too, but not like the shoepeg. This stuff can be hard to find, but a good tackle store should have it in season when available.

We are very lucky to live in an area so rich in angling diversity. Remember this when there is a lull in the salmon and steelhead fishing. Don't put away the boat and take out the lawn mower. Instead, round up the kids and head to the nearest lake. Their smiling faces and a smoker full of succulent kokanee will make it worth your while.

POWER NYMPHING:
Long-lining for Salmon, Trout and Steelhead

A big redside hooked on a No. 4 Kaufmann's Stonefly Nymph.

When considering the technique of nymphing for trout, most fly anglers think of the prevalent tight-line, high-sticking method used to keep as much line off the water as possible in order to avoid drag. When using this technique, the multitude of conflicting micro currents on the surface aren't allowed to play on the line and leader and negatively affect the natural drift of the fly. Basically, this is nymphing as we know it. But one of the drawbacks of this method is that it limits the amount of water the angler can effectively cover. Newcomers to the fantastically huge, powerful and brawling Deschutes River in my home state of Oregon are often advised to visually divide the river up into smaller rivers to better cover the water. While this is sound advice, it also leads ninety percent of the fishermen to the same section of the river, that is, the first twenty or thirty feet out from the shore.

Make no mistake, this part of the river with its shallows that support algae growth and the aquatic insects that feed on it, and overhanging brush that provides cover and a steady diet of terrestrial insects—supports a ton of trout. But over the course of a long season, these trout get an Ivy League education from some of the best anglers on the planet, leaving the rest of us scrambling for the leftovers. But there are plenty of other types of water the trout may frequent at any given time, much of it far from shore and difficult for the nymphing fisherman to reach

with traditional techniques. Over the years, I have also discovered that the largest Deschutes redsides are often caught far from the bank in powerful water not exactly suited to fly fishing. So how does one reach that twenty-incher that keeps rising midstream? Power nymphing.

My good friend and longtime fishing buddy Mike Kostel of White's Outdoor coined this phrase years ago after watching me struggle to reach fish that I had no business trying to make contact with. As if they were some lost tribe of the Amazon, I guess Mike figured it wrong of me to try to introduce the innocents to cold steel. I, however, felt differently about the matter. In power nymphing, the idea is to get as much line as possible onto the water and manipulate it as necessary to facilitate an extremely long, extended drift. As the term implies, there is nothing delicate or dainty about this method, as the angler must constantly work, work, work the line to mend, feed and stack it to minimize drag.

In a nutshell, power nymphing entails a long cast upstream and out to reach attractive water. Then, as the fly drifts downstream it is necessary to strip line in order to maintain contact with the set-up to allow a quick hook-set, should a fish climb on. By stripping line the angler also reduces the amount of slack that could drift downstream faster than the fly, form a belly, and cause unnatural drag. Some slack in the line is a good thing; a lot is not. As the fly reaches the angler's position and begins drifting downstream of he or she, now is the time to begin stacking the line on the water and feeding it into the cast in order to extend the drift. Sounds fairly simple, right? Let's break it down further.

The Set-up

For distance casting, improved mending capability and excellent roll casting, I prefer a long fly rod that possesses considerable power. Therefore, I have come to settle on the G. Loomis FR 1206 GLX as my nymphing rod of choice. This ten-foot for a six-weight is extremely light in weight but has considerable muscle to move a lot of line or cast a heavy rig. There are plenty of other excellent brands of rods to choose from, just make sure the one you choose has sufficient power to move a bunch of line. Reels should be the best quality you can afford, and, on a raging river like the Deschutes that hosts extremely strong trout, they should have a quality drag. I used to frequently use a Ross Colorado fly reel which has only a pawl-and-click mechanism to fish the Deschutes, but I got my butt kicked by so many big redsides that I now mostly use a Tibor Light with a silky-smooth drag.

The fly line you choose should be the highest floating you can find for a couple of reasons. First of all, a high-floating line will mend much more easily, especially if you are trying to lift and place a longer length, say fifty feet or more. Also, a high-floating line will interact less with the conflicting surface currents making it easier to achieve a drag-free drift. Once again, there are many excellent line manufacturers to choose from, so visit a fly shop or ask a buddy for input. The two brands that I employ most frequently are the Cortland 555 Dyna-tip and the Rio Wind-Cutter. Both of these lines float high, cast and mend well and are extremely durable to handle the rigors of this technique over time without breaking down.

When power nymphing I also like to employ the use of a large strike indicator for several different reasons. First of all, a big indicator is easy to see at a distance on a choppy or roily surface, and is buoyant enough to keep the tip of the fly line from being sucked under by currents that constantly pull at the line. Anyone who has had this happen when nymphing knows how annoying it can be. Secondly, a big indicator serves as an effective delivery system, allowing you to suspend a fly just off the bottom to cover tons of water without snagging up. A big indicator also serves as an anchor when mending. It takes a lot of energy from the rod to mend a length of fly line, and when this energy travels down the line and terminates at the indicator, it will cause a smaller float to jump from the water, thus moving the fly in an unnatural manner. A large indicator helps to reduce this problem. A good-size indicator also provides resistance when a fish takes your nymph and may aid in setting the hook, which is a big plus if you have a hundred feet of line on the water and your reaction time is diminished.

I usually use a tapered leader of 8-12 feet in length depending on the depth and speed of the water I am fishing. Size the tippet strength according to the size fly to be cast, average size and strength of the fish you are after, and overall weight of the complete rig you're attempting to cast.

I rarely use less than 3X when nymphing the Deschutes, and by using fluorocarbon tippet material you can "hide" larger-diameter lines from the fish. Where to place your indicator is a matter of experimentation, but 1 1/2 to 2 times the depth seems to work as a general guideline. In heavy water I use one BB-size split shot from 12-24" above the fly to help sink it to the

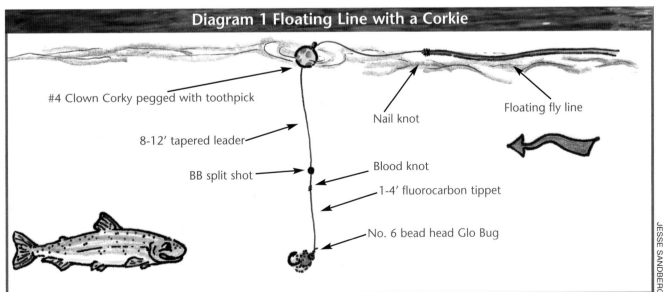

Diagram 1 Floating Line with a Corkie

#4 Clown Corky pegged with toothpick

8-12' tapered leader

BB split shot

Nail knot

Floating fly line

Blood knot

1-4' fluorocarbon tippet

No. 6 bead head Glo Bug

JESSE SANDBERG

Diagram 2 Frog Hair Large Indicator

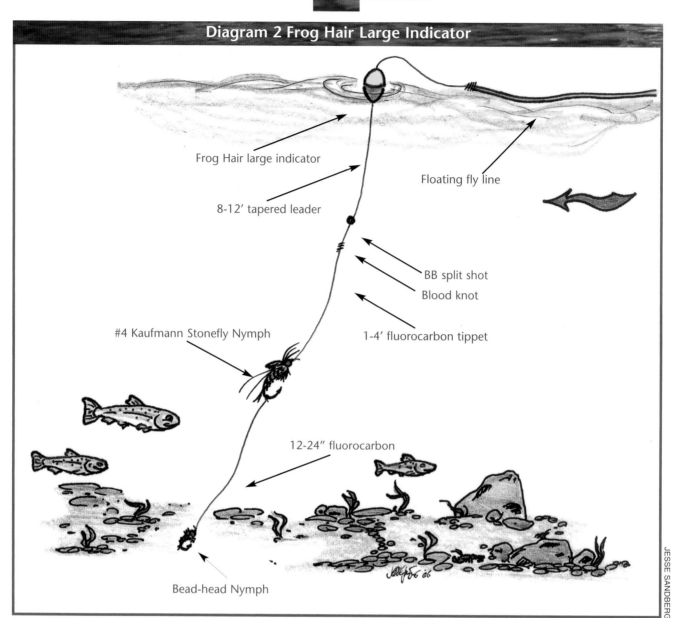

Frog Hair large indicator

Floating fly line

8-12' tapered leader

BB split shot

Blood knot

1-4' fluorocarbon tippet

#4 Kaufmann Stonefly Nymph

12-24" fluorocarbon

Bead-head Nymph

JESSE SANDBERG

Diagram 3 Large Bushy, Dry-Fly Indicator

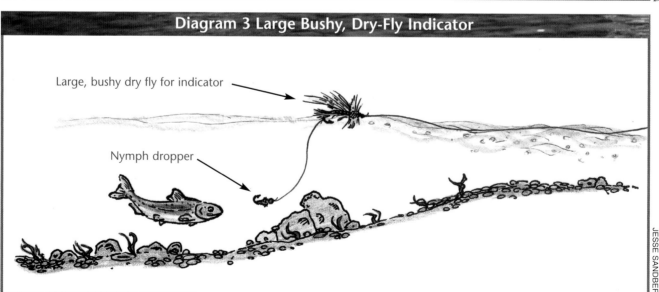

Large, bushy dry fly for indicator

Nymph dropper

JESSE SANDBERG

fish faster so that I'm covering more water. In softer water, a bead-head fly may be all the weight needed to sink to the fish. The idea is to quickly sink the fly down to where the fish are and have it glide along naturally in a dead-drift, much the same way a side-drifter presents a bait to a steelhead. If you use too much additional weight on the set-up, then the lead will tap, tap, tap along the bottom, increasing snags while decreasing hook-ups. (See Diagrams 1-4 for some simple but effective nymphing rigs).

The Cast

The better the caster you are, the better you will fare with this technique. I struggled for years to get to the point where I could effectively handle enough line to fish this way. If you are just starting out or you are a mediocre caster like myself, save yourself some grief and hire a good casting instructor like Rob Crandall of *STS*. The frustration this saves you is alone worth the price of admission. In power nymphing, there are several casts that will make life easier and learning when and where to employ them is half the battle. When fishing on open gravel bars with few obstructions behind the caster, use the straightforward overhead cast to reach far away water not normally covered by other anglers. Learn the reach cast so you can efficiently place your fly line upstream of the indicator, thus beginning your presentation with the equivalence of a mend. Wherever the bank is lined with brush it may be impossible to employ the overhead cast, so use a roll cast or lob cast to fire your line to the fish. On the Deschutes I often resort to a lob cast because it is easy to execute and will move a heavy indicator, fly and split shot with ease. (See Diagram 5). It is also possible to incorporate a reach into a lob cast to place the fly farther out in the river, but this takes some time to master. Roll casting is also important for feeding line into the presentation, or stack-mending. The wiggle cast

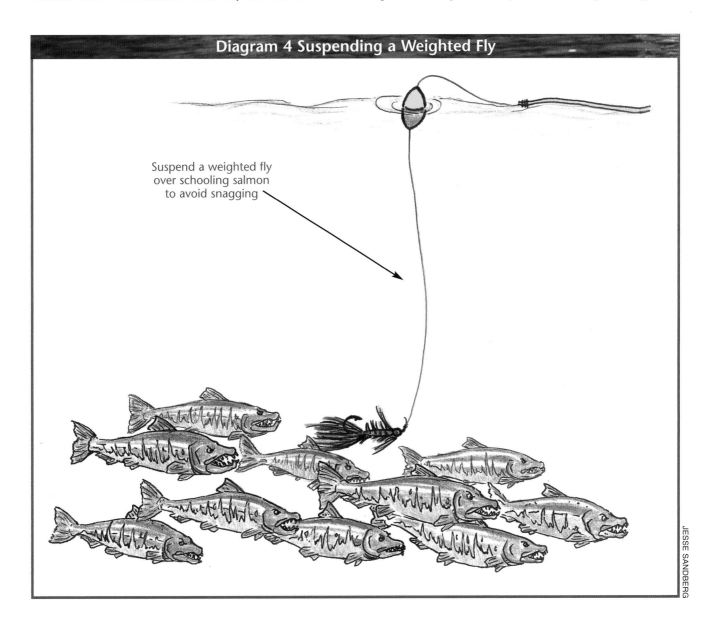

Diagram 4 Suspending a Weighted Fly

Suspend a weighted fly over schooling salmon to avoid snagging

JESSE SANDBERG

Diagram 5 The Lob Cast

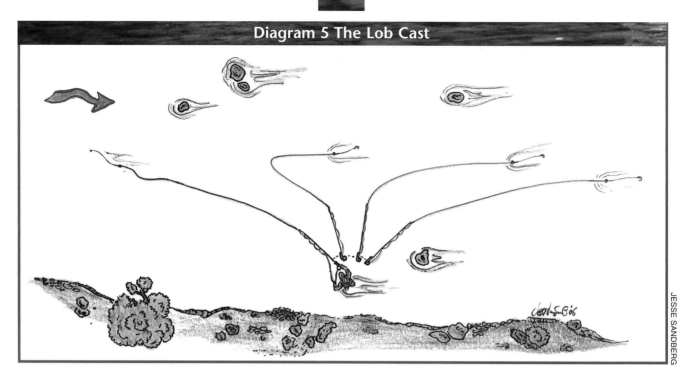

JESSE SANDBERG

is also good to know, as this will place gentle S's into the cast which will provide slack to reduce drag.

Mending

Mending the line is nothing more than manipulating it to reduce drag. Drag is any unnatural pull or push of the line that causes the fly to drift differently than it would if it was not tied to your leader. In long-line nymphing, drag usually occurs as a downstream belly in the floating fly line that causes the fly and indicator to be pulled downstream faster than they should. To fix this problem, use your rod to flip or reposition the line upstream of the indicator, affording you several more feet of drag-free presentation. (See Diagram 6). During a single presentation it may be necessary to mend several times, or mend one length of line upstream while mending another section downstream to avoid drag. Time spent on the water is the best way to learn how varying currents pull on the line and what you have to do to manipulate the line to get the best presentation. Bummer, eh?

Diagram 6 The Simple Flip Mend

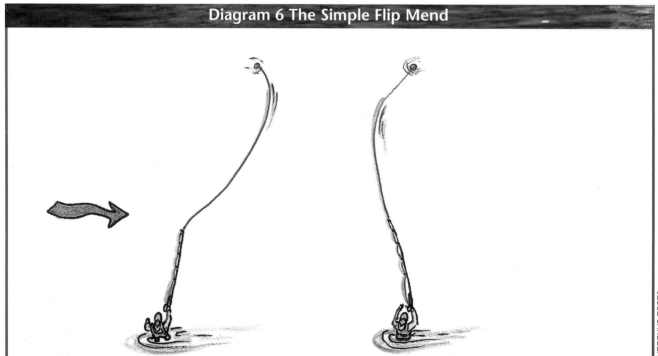

JESSE SANDBERG

Diagram 7 The Extended Drift

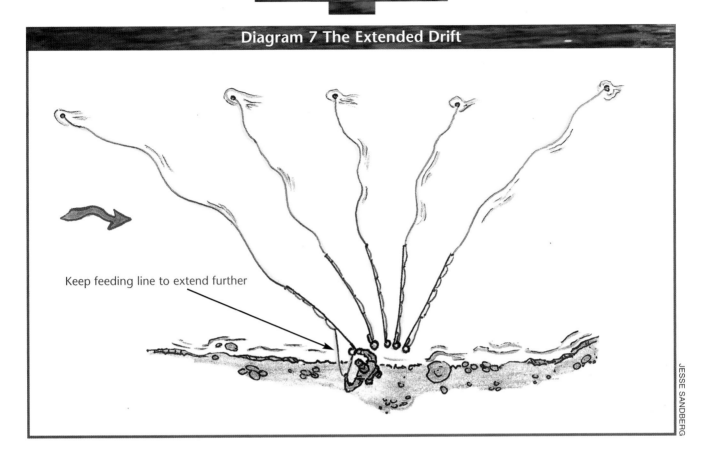

Keep feeding line to extend further

JESSE SANDBERG

Line Control

Proper line control is extremely important in realizing the full effectiveness of power nymphing and, once again, time spent on the water is the best way to learn it. As mentioned earlier, following the cast it is necessary to strip in line as the fly drifts downstream in order to maintain contact and be able to quickly set the hook. When doing this, most anglers allow the line to fall at their feet, which is fine if standing on clear ground where they land in loose, manageable coils. If standing in the river, however, this practice allows the slack line to drift with the current where it is free to hang up on any available obstruction, which it inevitably will. Because you will soon be stacking and feeding this same line you just stripped in, it makes sense to teach yourself how to gather it in neat, loose coils and hold it in your off hand until it is needed to extend the presentation. Trying to feed line that is tangled in a wad of alder roots is an exercise in frustration that defeats the whole purpose of leaving the house in the first place.

Feeding line into the cast is accomplished most easily in a two-part process. First, wiggle the rod tip from side to side to transfer the coiled line in your off hand onto the water where you can pick it up with a roll cast and position it in a stack behind your indicator. As your rig drifts downstream it will pull from this reserve of line and continue on a relatively drag-free drift. In this manner you can feed all of the line from the original cast, plus whatever remains on the reel. Under ideal conditions you may even be able to feed a bunch of backing into the presentation, covering even more water. Compared to high-stick nymphing where a good presentation may effectively cover a 30- or 40-foot swath of water, it's easy to see where power nymphing has its advantage. Using a fly line of 90 feet or more, a good caster and line handler can cover over 200 feet of water with one presentation! (See Diagram 7).

While nymphing is a technique usually employed to catch trout from rivers and streams, it can also be a highly effective technique for taking salmon and steelhead. Power nymphing can be used on rivers during low to medium flows to catch winter and summer steelhead, chinook, silvers, chum and even pink salmon. On the Deschutes, late in the season, summer steelhead will often pounce on a skillfully fished egg pattern or small nymph while ignoring all other offerings. During the winter when rivers are low and clear, winter fish will likewise gulp down a dead-drifted egg pattern when nothing else seems to work. When fishing over heavily stacked fish like coho, chum or pinks, a weighted fly may be rigged to suspend just above the fish in order to reduce foul-hooking fish while inciting them to riot. (See Diagram 4). In fact, this unobtrusive, natural presentation is often just the ticket to induce a strike from a heavily pressured or tight-lipped fish. Whether chasing salmon, trout or steelhead, power nymphing has a place in your fly-fishing arsenal.

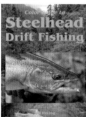